Communications
in Computer and Information Science   1188

Commenced Publication in 2007
Founding and Former Series Editors:
Phoebe Chen, Alfredo Cuzzocrea, Xiaoyong Du, Orhun Kara, Ting Liu,
Krishna M. Sivalingam, Dominik Ślęzak, Takashi Washio, Xiaokang Yang,
and Junsong Yuan

More information about this series at http://www.springer.com/series/7899

Salih Ofluoglu · Ozan Onder Ozener ·
Umit Isikdag (Eds.)

Advances in Building Information Modeling

First Eurasian BIM Forum, EBF 2019
Istanbul, Turkey, May 31, 2019
Revised Selected Papers

 Springer

Editors
Salih Ofluoglu
Mimar Sinan Fine Arts University
Istanbul, Turkey

Ozan Onder Ozener ⓘD
Istanbul Technical University
Istanbul, Turkey

Umit Isikdag ⓘD
Mimar Sinan Fine Arts University
Istanbul, Turkey

ISSN 1865-0929   ISSN 1865-0937   (electronic)
Communications in Computer and Information Science
ISBN 978-3-030-42851-8   ISBN 978-3-030-42852-5   (eBook)
https://doi.org/10.1007/978-3-030-42852-5

This Springer imprint is published by the registered company Springer Nature Switzerland AG
The registered company address is: Gewerbestrasse 11, 6330 Cham, Switzerland

Preface

-in memory of Mete Alp Ofluoğlu

Building Information Modeling (BIM) is becoming a more mature information management methodology and strategy that leads to a change of paradigm in the Architecture Engineering and Construction (AEC) industry.

The concept of BIM first emerged as a solution to overcome the interoperability barrier between different software applications. The implementation of the BIM concept in the industry accelerated when the AEC industry developed a standard information model schema, namely IFC, which depends on an earlier ISO 10303/STEP standard that was developed for facilitating information sharing and exchanges in production industries.

In the last 20 years, the AEC industry in many countries has aligned their business practices to adopt BIM in order to (i) enable efficiency in design through better collaboration and cooperation and (ii) utilize the model for simulating all construction process prior to the start of the actual construction which would, in turn, prevent errors during the construction phase for enabling a more agile, effective, and efficient construction process.

Although the main focus of BIM implementations is these two concepts, a new model-based information management strategy has also been utilized to help in the better management of facilities through providing detailed information with as-built BIMs and to help in the design/construction of more sustainable and energy-efficient buildings.

The core of the BIM concept is formed by an intelligent nD digital model of a building which is now evolving through another concept known as the Digital Twin. The concept of BIM is now supported with many standards and information exchange methodologies and formalizations (protocols), and BIM is becoming more integrated into business processes within the industry.

Furthermore, the owners of many large-scale projects (such as airports) are requiring formal definitions (i.e. BIM Execution Plans) explaining how BIM-based information and project management processes will be conducted. In addition, today, there are new formal job definitions in the industry which include BIM as a keyword, such as BIM Manager and BIM Coordinator.

The current advances include novel approaches for BIM varying from innovative modeling techniques, performance analysis, immersive visualization techniques, to new international standards. These developments create "a new BIM culture" which cultivates around a knowledge-based AEC economy. Since there are well-established conventions and business perceptions within the industry, the cultural transformation is challenging and necessitates mutual effort from the AEC community and academic initiatives.

From this viewpoint, this book covers a wide range of BIM-related subjects from academic and professional perspectives. The chapters bring together members of the academic community and industry professionals from different disciplines of the AEC industry and contribute to the discussions on BIM and its impact on research and practice. The topics include BIM adoption trends, BIM-centric business models and in-depth case studies, and BIM-based simulations.

The book focuses on providing a holistic view of BIM by concentrating on different aspects of the topic. It consists of four main parts. The chapters in the first part discuss issues and problems related to the adoption of BIM in public and private construction projects. This part is implementation oriented and is mainly focused on exploring the drivers and barriers to BIM implementation and adoption based on real life case studies and surveys. The second part of the book elaborates on the role of BIM in project management. It covers subjects such as how the management of projects can be facilitated using 4D/5D information from BIM as well as focuses on the role of BIM in health and safety management. The third part is about BIM and sustainable design, where issues related to the role of BIM in designing and building up more energy efficient and sustainable buildings are discussed. The fourth part of the book covers issues related to the role of BIM in urban contexts, in managing the buildings and facilities, and in infrastructure developments, and discusses how information about buildings extracted using remote sensing techniques can be utilized.

We hope that readers will find this book useful for exchanging academic and industrial knowledge as well as experience on the novel developments in BIM tools and technologies as well as BIM-based information and project management approaches. Finally, we would like to thank our family members for their support during the editing process and for the positive energy they have brought into our lives.

January 2020

Salih Ofluoglu
Ozan Onder Ozener
Umit Isikdag

Organization

Program Committee Chairs

Salih Ofluoglu	Mimar Sinan Fine Arts University, Turkey
Ozan Onder Ozener	Istanbul Technical University, Turkey
Umit Isikdag	Mimar Sinan Fine Arts University, Turkey

Program Committee

Cemil Akçay	Istanbul University, Turkey
Tahir Akkoyunlu	Medipol University, Turkey
Chimay Anumba	Pennsylvania State University, USA
Yusuf Arayıcı	Hasan Kalyoncu University, Turkey
Ken Arroyo Ohori	Delft University of Technology, The Netherlands
Levent Arıdağ	Gebze Technical University, Turkey
Maria B. Barison	USP-UEL, Brazil
Filip Biljecki	National University of Singapore, Singapore
Pawel Boguslawski	Wroclaw University of Science and Technology, Poland
Marzia Bolpagni	MACE, UK
Birgul Çolakoğlu	Istanbul Technical University, Turkey
Semra Çomu	Bogazici University, Turkey
Gülen Çağdaş	Istanbul Technical University, Turkey
H. Attila Dikbaş	Istanbul Medipol University, Turkey
Rani El Meouche	FIT, ESTP, Constructibility Research Institute, France
Esin Ergen	Istanbul Technical University, Turkey
Ömer Giran	Istanbul University, Turkey
Jack Goulding	UK
Eric Guilbert	Laval University, Canada
James Haliburton	Texas A&M University, USA
Alan Hore	Dublin Institute of Technology, Ireland
Zeynep Işık	Yildiz Technical University, Turkey
Umit Isikdag	Mimar Sinan Fine Arts University, Turkey
Mohsen Kalantari	The University of Melbourne, Australia
Alaattin Kanoglu	Istanbul Technical University, Turkey
İsmail Rakıp Karaş	Karabük University, Turkey
Tuba Kocatürk	Deakin University, Australia
Barry Mcauley	Dublin Institute of Technology, Ireland
Salih Ofluoglu	Mimar Sinan Fine Arts University, Turkey
Ozan Onder Ozener	Istanbul Technical University, Turkey
Derya Güleç Özer	Yildiz Technical University, Turkey
Şule Taşlı Pektaş	Baskent University, Turkey

Ehsan Saghatforoush	University of the Witwatersrand, South Africa
Rudi Stouffs	National University of Singapore, Singapore
Bilal Succar	ChangeAgents AEC, Australia
Joe Tah	Oxford Brookes University, UK
Ali Murat Tanyer	Middle East Technical University, Turkey
Regine Teulier	CNRS, École Polytechnique, Université Paris-Saclay, France
Belinda Torus	Bahcesehir University, Turkey
Bülent Onur Turan	Mimar Sinan Fine Arts University, Turkey
Emrah Türkyılmaz	Istanbul Kultur University, Turkey
Lucía Díaz Vilariño	Universidad de Vigo, Spain
Wei Yan	Texas A&M University, USA
Tuğrul Yazar	Istanbul Bilgi University, Turkey
Sisi Zlatanova	UNSW, Australia

Organizing Committee

Salih Ofluoglu	Mimar Sinan Fine Arts University, Turkey
Ozan Onder Ozener	Istanbul Technical University, Turkey
Umit Isikdag	Mimar Sinan Fine Arts University, Turkey
Kemal Şahin	Mimar Sinan Fine Arts University, Turkey
Sertaç Karsan Erbaş	Mimar Sinan Fine Arts University, Turkey
Bülent Onur Turan	Mimar Sinan Fine Arts University, Turkey
Salih Akkemik	Mimar Sinan Fine Arts University, Turkey
Burcu Esen Barutçu	AEC3 Deutschland, Germany
Sergen Cansız	Mimar Sinan Fine Arts University, Turkey

Contents

BIM Adoption and Implementation

Trends of Building Information Modeling Adoption in the Turkish AEC Industry

Ozan Onder Ozener[(⊠)], Ecem Tezel, Zehra Aybike Kilic,
and Merve Akdogan

Istanbul Technical University, 34367 Sisli Istanbul, Turkey
ozener@itu.edu.tr

Abstract. This paper presents the results from a comprehensive field study on BIM adoption and AEC integration targeting the Turkish AEC firms. The research objectives were to develop well-reasoned arguments supporting the role of BIM in the transformation of current business models in the Turkish AEC Industry as well as identifying the inclinations, challenges, and obstacles to BIM adoption. With in-depth interviews with industry representatives, the study returned valuable information that lead to context-dependent insights about the local AEC industry and influence of BIM adoption on all AEC operations. The findings from the study suggest that the existence of a rapidly growing interest in BIM-enabled processes and services due to local and global market dynamics and pressure. The influence of established business culture within the industry drastically affect perceptions towards the value propositions of BIM and IPD which are broadly known among the Turkish AEC firms which are different from the US and European counterparts. Results from this study motivate new discussions about BIM adoption and IPD from the perspective of the Turkish AEC Industry, and also provide arguments about the potential impacts of BIM deployment for the local and global construction projects which are undertaken by the Turkish AEC firms.

Keywords: Building Information Modeling (BIM) adoption · Architectural Engineering and Construction (AEC) industry · Turkish AEC industry

1 Introduction

The promise of integration and process automation in the Architecture, Engineering and Construction Industry (AEC) arising from the technology of Building Information Modeling (BIM) motivates in-depth studies on effective adoption models and implementation strategies. Recent articles on this subject emphasize the important relationship among technology, Integrated Project Delivery (IPD) methods, business cultures and domain-specific BIM adoption approaches [1–5]. With its growing operation scale, global project locations and established business cultures, the Turkish AEC Industry provide a unique case for research studies focusing on BIM adoption.

Being the World's 3rd largest construction/contracting industry with an annual operation volume of approximately $20 billion [6], the Turkish AEC Industry operates globally since 1972 amounting $366.5 billion. Including large scale projects in Russia,

© Springer Nature Switzerland AG 2020
S. Ofluoglu et al. (Eds.): EBF 2019, CCIS 1188, pp. 3–14, 2020.
https://doi.org/10.1007/978-3-030-42852-5_1

Eastern Europe, Central Asia, Gulf Region and North and South Africa, Turkish contracting companies undertook global projects valued at $14.6 billion in 2017 [7]. In recent years, the interest for BIM and IPD processes is growing within the Turkish AEC Firms in order to maintain the strong presence and competitiveness in the global markets, while construction volume is rapidly expanding within Turkey. As BIM becomes an industry-standard in North America and Europe, Turkish AEC firms are also influenced from this adoption trend. The interest is growing and there are ongoing large-scale projects in Turkey that utilize BIM methods and processes. There are also small or mid-size firms that are highly BIM-capable but still stay as boutique service providers. Despite these developments, the market penetration is at low levels and the technology adoption rate is relatively slow due to endemic factors and business perceptions in Turkey.

Although this interest is solid and evident, there are only a limited number of studies focusing on the levels of BIM adoption, business transformation for IPD and their potential benefits in the context of Turkish AEC Industry. In order to address this gap, this chapter presents the results from a comprehensive field study on BIM adoption and AEC integration targeting the Turkish AEC firms. The findings of the study provide evidence-based arguments for the current BIM adoption levels of Turkish AEC firms through focusing on their adoption process; from adoption decision to organizational and business transformations, as well as practical outputs of BIM implementation.

2 Background

The concept of BIM was introduced to the AEC industry both as a method and technology to enhance communication and coordination; reduce errors, omissions and rework; improve productivity and; reduce costs and durations at all phases of project lifecycle [8–13]. Because of the given emphasis on the operational benefits of BIM, operational implementations are largely being performed by a growing number of firms in the AEC. However, the review of previous BIM studies across countries revealed various implementation difficulties, fundamentally due to nations' development levels and cultural differences. This means that the characteristics of the local AEC business ecosystem can be considered as a key subject for understanding the processes of BIM adoption and its influence on the industry. For example, in developing countries such as China, inadequate knowledge and expertise stands as the primary risk factor against BIM adoption process [14]. Conversely, local AEC industries like in Australia and Sweden need to focus on attracting stakeholder interest in BIM and enhancing collaborative working environment [15, 16]. As numerous studies providing empirical evidence about the practical advantages of BIM, highly developed countries like the United States and the United Kingdom demonstrate the utmost progress. Since governmental initiatives encourage or mandate BIM use in the AEC, the pressure from the major clients—largely *public owners* can be given as the main catalyst of the transformation process [17, 18]. More examples can be given in this regard; however, the major argument is that each nation has different perspectives of BIM, its role and necessity from the industrywide efficiency point of view. Therefore, different adoption approaches and legal frameworks exist that influence the penetration levels of BIM within the local AEC industries. In order to increase the BIM use and achieve more robust AEC processes, every nation has a different take on the adoption issue and implementing new policies, generating broad standards and creating proactive strategies regarding their technological, economic and cultural characteristics.

As one of the leading contracting service providers in the World, Turkey has its unique case. Reaching the 30% share of the national economy, Turkish AEC firms also locate at the top places of ENR *(Engineering News-Record)* lists. To sustain high business volumes in the global construction market, some firms recognized the global transformation trend and started to experiment with BIM as a part of their business schemes. These firms can be identified as highly BIM-capable in terms of their business processes, technological infrastructure and knowledge capital. Arguably these exceptions do not accrue to the broader extent in the Turkish AEC Industry. Despite growing interest from the enthusiastic firms, BIM adoption within the local AEC industry remains at low levels compared to developed markets. The causes, obstacles and influencing factors are being discussed in the literature deliberately in the last five years. In addition to the studies claiming organizational culture and training needs of firms as the most common causes of lower BIM adoption in the local AEC industry [19, 20], two recent studies have been published focusing on the success factors for effective BIM adoption. The Ozorhon and Karaman [21] study focused more on the operational issues and claimed that the availability of qualified workforce, proactive leadership and relevant IT infrastructure are the crucial inputs for effective and pervasive BIM adoption, whereas Pekericli et al. [22] emphasized the absence of regulatory policies as one of the key negative factors which has to be overcome with the participation of industry stakeholders. Another relevant study by Ozener and Temiz [23] argued that Turkey is still in the transformation process to BIM and stressed that diverting from the well-established business practices in the local AEC industry as the greatest cultural challenge. To this extent, the study also underlined the limited BIM demand from the clients are causing local firms to implement BIM as a tool for supplementing internal tasks like quick documentation, parametric modeling or cost and performance analyses rather than a true collaborative IPD approach [23].

3 Research Methodology

In order to understand the current BIM adoption levels and current trends within the Turkish AEC industry, the study employed peer-interviewing as the primary research technique in a qualitative framework (see Fig. 1). Effectiveness of qualitative methods and research techniques like in-depth interviews or focus groups are widely validated in the BIM literature focusing on technology adoption. This particular study followed a similar research design in order to reveal different dynamics and industry-wide perceptions towards BIM.

As seen from the figure, the study followed a logic flowchart to ensure the trustworthiness of the collected data and the arguments based on the findings of the research

6   O. O. Ozener et al.

effort. Aligned with the study objectives, the employment of qualitative techniques provided a flexible research process where firm responses also contributed to the course and the content of the study.

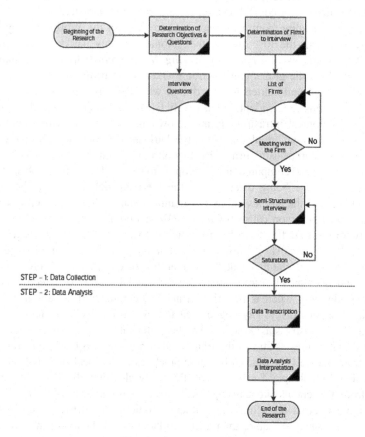

Fig. 1. Research flowchart

3.1 Literature Review and Interview Questions

An in-depth literature review was conducted for the identification of global BIM adoption trends, as well as common problems and potential benefits of BIM for AEC firms. Initial findings of the literature review process were used to formulate the interview question sets including primary and probe questions. These questions can be grouped under four categories as; (a) intrinsic business culture and BIM adoption decisions (b) organization-specific issues in BIM adoption process and (c) influence of BIM on the organization and performance and (d) local trends to adoption and strategies in the Turkish AEC Industry, respectively. The interview questions are given in Table 1 with domains, main questions, and follow-up/probe questions.

Table 1. Semi-structured interview questions

Domain	Main question	Follow-up/Probe questions
Firm characteristics	Can you tell us about your firm?	What services do you provide? How many years of experience does your firm have in the local AEC domain? How many people work in your firm? (including group as managers, office and site staff) What are their educational and professional background?
BIM adoption process	Can you tell us about the details of the BIM adoption process in your firm?	When did you decide to adopt BIM? What were the main drivers that led your firm to adopt BIM? How do you integrate BIM into your existing business processes? What kind of strategic and tactical methods do you use during BIM transformation? Do you receive BIM consultancy during the transformation process? Do you have a BIM-centric organizational structure? What kind of positions do you have on your organizational chart? How do you hire, employ and train your staff for BIM? How do you manage the adoption process with your stakeholders? What are their current BIM capabilities? Do you have internal BIM standards in your firm? How do you respond to BIM Execution Plan requests?
Challenges	What are the main barriers or obstacles you experienced during the BIM adoption process?	Can you elaborate more on the barriers and obstacles related to your firm, your stakeholders and the industry in general? What kind of strategies do you follow to encounter those barriers? (especially in terms of organizational culture) What are your suggestions in order to overcome those barriers?
Influences	Can you tell us about the effects of BIM adoption on your business tasks and operations?	What are the positive and negative effects of BIM adoption on your business routines? What are the effects of BIM on the quality of your projects? Do you have any internal benchmarking procedures? Do you observe time and/or cost efficiency increases in your projects?

(continued)

Table 1. (*continued*)

Domain	Main question	Follow-up/Probe questions
Turkish AEC Industry	How do you describe the current BIM perception and adoption levels in the Turkish AEC Industry?	How do you interpret the current pervasiveness of BIM in the Turkish AEC Industry under the influence of local business factors? What is the level of BIM capability of the local AEC firms? Do you have BIM-capable project partners and how do you add new partners to your business processes? What are your suggestions to start-ups about the digital transformation in the sector?
Foresights	What are your opinions about BIM adoption trends in Turkey?	No probes

3.2   Semi-structured Interviews

A series of semi-structured interviews were conducted with eleven professionals from six representative Turkish AEC firms. The interviewed firms were in different sub-fields including owners, contractors, and architecture, engineering, construction management as well as consultancy disciplines. The selection of the firms for the research study was made according to the BIM adoption strategies of the firms and their business volumes and stakeholder network in the local AEC domain in order to have a representative sample. Detailed information about the firms and interviewees were given in Table 2.

Table 2. Firm and interviewee details

Firm	Firm size	Field	Interviewee role in the firm
Firm 1	Middle	Multi-disciplinary	BIM Manager
Firm 2	Middle	Architecture	BIM Manager
Firm 3	Large	Multi-disciplinary	Associate, BIM Manager, Architect, Engineer
Firm 4	Large	CM & Consultancy	Project Manager, Lead Consultant
Firm 5	Large	Contractor	Executive Manager
Firm 6	Large	Owner	Senior Manager, Real Estate Director

The first interviewee was an experienced BIM manager from a multi-disciplinary firm, which was established in the early 2000's as a single consultancy office and still continuing its business operations with two offices in Ankara and Istanbul. Despite being a mid-size office, there are various project types in its portfolio, such as housing, urban transformation, hospitality, and shopping centers. The second interviewee was from a ten-year-old mid-size architectural design office. This office provides architectural design and architectural controller services in numerous urban transformation, residential, office, hotel, and administrative projects for the public and private sector with more than 80 employees. The four interviewees of the third firm were from the Turkey office of a UK-based large-size global engineering and consultancy company. This global firm provides various services from architectural design to engineering and consultancy for infrastructure projects to both public and private sector. The firm employs a large team of engineers, architects, consultants and technical specialists. The two interviewees of the fourth firm were from a large-size construction management and consultancy firm established in 1990's and provides wide-range CM and consultancy services for large scale infrastructure and capital projects. As the fifth firm of the list, a comprehensive interview was conducted with the executive manager from a large-size contractor firm with local and global operations particularly in the Gulf Region and Russia. Finally, the last two interviewees were from a large-size owner which currently constructs and operates large quantities of building space for its various operations in Turkey and abroad.

Each interview took approximately an hour and all responses were recorded with a voice recorder with the consent of each respondent. These interviews were later transcribed for content analysis for the identification of key concepts, trends, viewpoints and issues regarding BIM adoption and transformation of business models.

4 Findings

The concept analysis of the collected data helped to identify existing trends, business perceptions and common issues related to BIM adoption and utilization. Participant responses and analysis results were corroborated with existing industry reports from Turkey and also compared with similar studies from different AEC domains like North America and Europe. As a general evaluation, the research study revealed different findings in various levels from operational to strategic level as the participant firms provided both industry-wide viewpoints and organization-specific information regarding BIM adoption.

From the business culture perspective, there exist significant differences in terms of adoption trends, problems, obstacles, technological perceptions and potential benefits besides some common issues in comparison to the US and European counterparts. Considering widely accepted uncertainty levels in project processes in the local business culture, participant firms confirmed that Turkish AEC firms tend to control a state of flux for business viability and competitive advantage, which necessitates novel adoption approaches for BIM in this specific business domain. The influence of established business models, work culture, project cycles, and internal characteristics drastically affect perceptions towards the value propositions of BIM and IPD which are broadly known among the Turkish AEC firms. Findings also underline the existence of different social subgroups for BIM use and AEC integration according to their expertise areas, project types and operation scales. More specifically, the interview responses point out the existence of a knowledge divide between Turkish firms which are able to incorporate BIM into their all business tasks and the others without BIM capabilities. This also causes a dam-like situation where project-specific information cumulates on the

BIM-enabled side and limited information and know-how are transferred to the other stakeholders mainly due to the conversion from BIM model to conventional documents (Fig. 2). Here, the barrier is composed of technological capability and knowledge-enabled workforce as well as the restricted pervasiveness of BIM tools and methods.

Parallel to this problem, participant responses also indicate the absence of an IPD understanding largely caused by the existing contractual procedures. The domination of Public Procurement Law connected regulations and even fee structures create strict and inflexible local business schemes which are arguably incompatible with BIM approaches and the core values of IPD. Another organizational issue in the local AEC firms is reported as the perception of risk related to the sharp technological transformation which may have a significant impact on business schemes and organizational structure. In a tight and highly competitive market like Turkey, the profitability of the construction projects is the paramount concern. Under this pressure, firm owners and also professional managers are more likely to have a reluctance towards BIM in order to sustain existing project pipelines and business viability using conventional methods. Both initial expenses for the BIM infrastructure, BIM-ready workforce and internal project costs are seen as negative aspects of adoption.

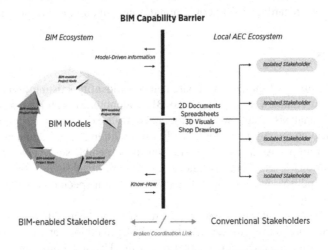

Fig. 2. The BIM Barrier in the local AEC Industry

Participant firms also confirmed the existence of similar barriers to their adoption processes. In order to overcome those barriers, each firm has its own strategy which are intrinsic to their internal project tasks and business model. One of the common obstacle is reported as the employee resistance to the complex BIM processes. As expected, experienced professionals more inclined to use established methods and processes for project development. In addition, simultaneous software training and utilization of BIM tools during ongoing projects make this particular group more concerned about the effectiveness and feasibility of BIM methods. Based on the anecdotal information from the interviews, it can be concluded that the existence of the well-known J-curve was clearly evident in initial adoption cases for the participating firms. Some firms solved this issue with just-in-time support and in-situ training of project team members. Couple participating firms reported sharp requirements from the employees, even making BIM literacy as a contractual obligation throughout the organization and also employ and train more open-minded professionals who are open for change.

Organization specific advantages and issues are related to utilization, information sharing and maintenance of consistence BIM information throughout project phases. Focusing on more operational levels, participant firms reported that unclear role of BIM manager within the firm as a common problem. Despite the clear job description of BIM manager's position and responsibilities, firms tend to assign them in different roles like a BIM coordinator, project architect/engineer or even as a BIM modeler according to the specific needs of the ongoing projects.

Although there are no established BIM standards in Turkey, participating firms indicated high levels of awareness about BIM standards, common file formats, interoperability and data integrity. Due to their experience with foreign project partners from UK, Gulf Region and Europe; these firms developed common data share environments, software use procedures, information exchange guidelines and BIM execution plans based on the British BS 1192 standard while considering internal rules and regulations in Turkey. Each finished project within this standardization effort created more know-how, firm-wide capabilities and reliable procedures which can be transferred or reutilized for new projects. However, these standardization efforts are also limiting the firms for finding capable firms which have BS 1192 compatible infrastructure and project development processes and experience with this particular technology standard. In the same regard, information share and coordination are reported as one of the current problems. Existing project processes based on the 2D file exchange are dominant and it is still hard to find BIM-enabled engineering and consulting services while staying in affordable project budgets. On the other hand, like one of the study participants, integrated firms—multidisciplinary project teams under one roof are more capable of realizing the benefits of BIM through online document management like Aconex, BIM 360 and various ERP software. Interoperability stays as a major concern which can be mitigated by contractual agreements and signing on a BIM execution plan based on existing BIM standards like BS-1192. As an extension to these issues, BIM-enabled firms reported sharp changes in coordination meetings as federated BIM models and reports extensively transformed how multiple project teams communicate, process project data comprehend project-specific problems, provide solutions. It is also stated that BIM processes expanded the scope of projects with up-to-date, reliable and consistent information simultaneously cycling between project stakeholders.

Another identified issue is the characteristics of the AEC business operations. Large Turkish AEC firms generally operate as main contractors or key subcontractors in the local and global projects. This can be interpreted as a conventional AEC business approach with extensive organizational effort for limited profit gains as opposed to knowledge-enabled EPC (engineering, procurement and construction) operations where design and know-how create more viable, competent and value-added businesses. The participating contractor firms reported that the transformation from conventional AEC to EPC requires such critical knowledge that may be catalyzed by fully-BIM enabled project experiences. Parallel to this point, it is reported that the BIM utilization in firms transformed both the profile of the employees and their responsibilities as BIM necessitates design, implementation and wide-range decision assessment skills at all levels. These capabilities inevitably invite new business methods and operations along with marketable know-how in terms of design and engineering which are consistent with a typical EPC organization. Considering the established culture in the local AEC industry in Turkey, the pace of this industry-wide transformation may be slow but the need is evident in terms of global competition and market pressure from the operation domains such as Gulf Region, Eastern Europe and large capital/infrastructure projects in Turkey. Derived from the firm feedbacks, we can expect that some firms will divert to BIM-enabled and digital-rich business models while discarding conventional local contracts for being more active in the profitable markets that demand hi-end technological expertise and BIM-enabled services.

As a subtopic of local culture within the industry, participants underlined the role of project owners as a significant driver of BIM adoption both in positive and negative directions. According to interview feedbacks, project owners have different attitudes to BIM utilization as it increases direct project costs due to expertise demands and organizational expertise. These costs include all AEC project services with BIM but also BIM capable CM firms which will act on behalf of the owner. This means an added dimension-the BIM capability and comprehension on the owner's side that includes BIM-based project management using BIM models and model-based data and document processing capacity. There is no doubt the services offered by these firms adds to the upstream project costs which repay in the long-term. Existing contractual and legal processes are based on conventional approaches and BIM-based projects not only changes the scope of services but all processes varying from design, engineering and consultancy to project management. It has been reported that there are few but highly sophisticated organizations that demand these hi-end design and engineering solutions for their spatial infrastructure despite the increased project costs. On the contrary, the cost-driven perceptions in the market still dominate the industry which underestimate the optimization of lifecycle costs and building performance with high-quality project investments. This may be assumed as the key obstacle for pervasive BIM adoption in the Turkish AEC domain.

5   Conclusions

Results from the study invite new discussions about BIM adoption and IPD from the perspective of the Turkish AEC sector, also provide well-reasoned arguments about the potential impacts of pervasive use of BIM on the local and global construction projects which are undertaken by the Turkish AEC Firms. The findings confirm that the Turkish AEC Industry has its own internal dynamics and endemic issues that have a major influence on BIM adoption which are significantly different than other markets like North America and Europe. Based on the findings, it is evident that the cultural aspects of the local business environments have a strong influence on the firms' perceptions towards BIM. Well-established approaches to BIM coupled with IPD methods may not be valid for the existing business processes since the local AEC culture prioritizes initial investment costs and short term benefits. In addition to this, highly possible fluctuations in the local AEC economy may prevent the majority of firms to transform their business models with BIM methods. The local contractual and legal frameworks are more likely to stay as sources for BIM incompatibility but project-specific solutions and mutual agreements between project stakeholders may help to mitigate these problems. It can be stated that such novel, adaptive and flexible business models are necessary for effective BIM adoption among the Turkish AEC firms. These models may base on the identification of low-risk tasks for BIM use and partial integration of several stakeholders for specific project phases around BIM models. The major need for BIM-enabled workforce adds another dimension to the existing issues since the dominance of current business cultures also drives young professionals to develop skills for conventional project delivery methods and techniques. In addition, such absence of local BIM standards should be discussed in the context of local business perceptions with its negative impacts but also unexpected advantages for technological adaptability. It can be also expected that Turkish AEC firms operating in the global markets will continue to adopt BIM for retaining their technological and business competency, however, their influence on the local AEC market may stay at limited levels.

References

1. Gu, N., London, K.: Understanding and facilitating BIM adoption in the AEC industry. Autom. Constr. **19**(8), 988–999 (2010)
2. Clayton, M.J., Johnson, R.E., Vanegas, J., Ozener, O.O., Nome, C.A., Culp, C.E.: Downstream of design: Lifespan costs and benefits of building information modeling. Technical report, CRS Center for Leadership and Management in the Design and Construction Industry, Texas A&M University, College Station (2008)
3. Smith, D.K., Tardif, M.: Building Information Modeling: A Strategic Implementation Guide for Architects, Engineers, Constructors and Real Estate Asset Managers. Wiley, Hoboken (2009)
4. Taylor, J., Bernstein, P.: Paradigm trajectories of building information modeling practice in project networks. J. Manag. Eng. **25**(2), 69–76 (2009)
5. Howard, R., Bjork, B.: Building information modelling – experts' views on standardization and industry deployment. Adv. Eng. Inf. **22**(2), 271–280 (2008)
6. McGraw-Hill Construction: The Top 225 International Contractors & The Top 225 Global Contractors 2011, McGraw-Hill Construction, ENR (2011)
7. INTES Construction Sector Report 2018. https://intes.org.tr/wp-content/uploads/2018/05/SEKTÖR-RAPORU.pdf. Accessed 07 Mar 2019
8. Ghaffarianhoseini, A., et al.: Building information modelling (BIM) uptake: clear benefits, understanding its implementation, risks and challenges. Renew. Sustain. Energy Rev. **75**, 1046–1053 (2017)
9. Zhou, Y., Ding, L., Rao, Y., Luo, H., Medjdoub, B., Zhong, H.: Formulating project-level building information modeling evaluation framework from the perspectives of organizations: a review. Autom. Constr. **81**, 44–55 (2017)
10. Bryde, D., Broquetas, M., Volm, J.M.: The project benefits of Building Information Modelling (BIM). Int. J. Proj. Manag. **31**, 971–980 (2013)
11. Love, P.E.D., Simpson, I., Hill, A., Standing, C.: From justification to evaluation: building information modeling for asset owners. Autom. Constr. **35**, 208–216 (2013)

12. Azhar, S.: Building information modeling (BIM): trends, benefits, risks, and challenges for the AEC Industry. Leadersh. Manag. Eng. **11**(3), 241–252 (2011)
13. Suermann, P.C., Issa, R.R.A.: Evaluating industry perceptions of building information modeling (BIM) impact on construction. ITcon J. Inf. Technol. Constr. (ITcon) **14**, 574–594 (2009)
14. Zhao, X., Wu, P., Wang, X.: Risk paths in BIM adoption: empirical study of China. Eng. Constr. Architectural Manag. **25**(9), 1170–1187 (2018)
15. Lindblad, H.: Black boxing BIM: the public client's strategy in BIM implementation. Constr. Manag. Econ. **37**(1), 1–12 (2019)
16. Hosseini, M.R., et al.: BIM adoption within Australian small and medium-sized enterprises (SMEs): an innovation diffusion model. Constr. Econ. Build. **16**(3), 71–86 (2016)
17. Lee, S., Yu, J.: Comparative study of BIM acceptance between Korea and the United States. J. Constr. Eng. Manag. **142**(3), 05015016 (2016)
18. Eadie, R., Browne, M., Odeyinka, H., Mckeown, C., Mcniff, S.: A survey of current status of and perceived changes required for BIM adoption in the UK. Built Environ. Proj. Asset Manag. **5**(1), 4–21 (2015)
19. Aladag, H., Demirdögen, G., Isik, Z.: Building information modeling (BIM) use in Turkish construction industry. Proc. Eng. **161**, 174–179 (2016)
20. Isikdag, U., Underwood, J., Kuruoglu, M., Goulding, J., Acikalin, U.: Construction informatics in Turkey: strategic role of ICT and future research directions. Inf. Technol. Constr. **14**, 412–428 (2009)
21. Ozorhon, B., Karahan, U.: Critical success factors of building information modeling implementation. J. Manag. Eng. **33**(3), 1–10 (2017)
22. Pekericli, M.K., Sari, R., Tanyer, A.M.: An investigation of building information modeling maturity in Turkish architecture and engineering firms. In: Gonenc Sorguc, A., Ozgenel, C.F., Krusa Yemiscioglu, M. (eds.) 11th Computational Design in Architecture National Symposium, MSTAS2017, pp. 214–227. METU Faculty of Architecture, Ankara (2017)
23. Ozener, O.O., Temiz, G.: Mimarlık ve inşaat sektöründe YBM odaklı dönüşüm [BIM-oriented architecture and construction industry]. Ege Mimarlık **93**(2), 34–37 (2016)

An In-Depth Inquiry on the Drawbacks of BIM Implementation

A Case of a Large Scale Public Construction Project in Turkey

Ece Kumkale Açıkgöz[✉] and Merve Çetin

Faculty of Fine Arts, Design, and Architecture, Department of Architecture,
Başkent University, Ankara, Turkey
ecekumkaleacikgoz@gmail.com

Abstract. This paper presents an in-depth enquiry for a case in the current condition of BIM implementation in Turkey. The research study is based on the specific collaborative experiences of an architectural design firm and a contractor firm on a large scale public construction project. It seeks to address the requirement for comprehending the idea of integrated project delivery provided with the collaboration opportunities of the BIM technology. It intends to demonstrate how the fields of policy and process interlock in the BIM activity of the selected case. It also aims to exemplify the handicaps of partial BIM implementation in a complex building production process. The research methodology is content-analysis of the in-depth interviews with the managers of the current production process from both architectural and contractor firms. Questions were designed to gather case-specific data in relation to the four fundamental features of the 3rd generation production process defined by Cooper [4]. The research findings indicate that although the production requirements fit the 3rd generation process, it is constrained by the public procurement law in force. It seems evident that there is a tension between the traditional workflow and the integrated process with increased productivity and quality that BIM enables and requires. This results in a noteworthy ratio of resource waste that the contractor has to compensate in this specific case. This study contributes to the ongoing research and discussion on the drawbacks of BIM implementation, by illustrating the requirement for the redefined and rearranged roles and processes of production with a precisely guaranteed resource economy and increased quality of work equally for all parties. It presents an example case for BIM implementation and process management to illustrate the current state of the public construction industry in Turkey.

Keywords: BIM implementation · Production process · Collaboration · Resource waste · Public procurement

1 Introduction

BIM implementation is one of the most important challenges that the construction industry has encountered. Its well-known benefits [2, 6, 8, 13] have resulted in irrevocable outcomes that have a changing effect on the roles of the building actors [15].

© Springer Nature Switzerland AG 2020
S. Ofluoglu et al. (Eds.): EBF 2019, CCIS 1188, pp. 15–27, 2020.
https://doi.org/10.1007/978-3-030-42852-5_2

Studies show that the building production processes under the influence of BIM implementation have to be redefined [7, 12]. It is commonly argued that effective BIM use requires new contractual relationships and reorganized collaborative processes [2, 7, 12, 14–16]. The requirement for understanding its effects on project management in design and construction is a part of this argument [3, 5]. This chapter intends to present a section from the current condition of BIM implementation in Turkey based on the specific experiences of an architectural design firm and a contractor firm working collaboratively on a large scale public construction project. It seeks to address the requirement for comprehending the idea of integrated project delivery (IPD), which Succar [17] explains as the goal state of BIM implementation. According to Succar [17], policy and process fields of the BIM activity have an interlocked structure together with the collaboration opportunities provided with the BIM technology and they shape the integration of the process. This study aims to exemplify the handicaps of partial BIM implementation where possibilities of collaboration are limited by the current policies through a complex building production process case.

The most common approach among the existing studies that focus on the processes of BIM implementation is detecting their most frequently experienced conditions and therefore collecting data from a sufficient number of BIM users to provide reliability [3, 7]. However, the findings of these studies are limited in content with the most frequent expressions of BIM implementation merits, like cost and time reduction, communication and coordination improvement [3, 18], which hardly provides an output that would lead us to exceed what Eastman et al. [6] have extensively paraded. On the other hand, each construction project has different parameters that are geography, location, scale, and context-dependent [11], and each case has its own content that can provide data beyond what is generalizable. For this reason, this study focuses on a single case with a deeper perspective for analyzing the content of a BIM influenced building production process.

The focus case is a public construction project with 422.000 m^2 built area procured according to the current Public Procurement Law (PPL) in Turkey. The case can be regarded as an example of incomplete BIM implementation. One reason for this incompleteness is the process requirements of the PPT. The design and construction project processes are structured separately and inflexibly (Fig. 2) in accordance with the law in force and related regulations. The architectural design firm completed the design process, completely independent of the contractor firm. The contractor firm is included in the process only after being commissioned with the construction procurement. In order to solve the revision problems of the construction project, the contractor firm has hired the same architectural design firm as their subcontractor architectural design consultant after being commissioned for the construction dues. At present, the construction process is conducted with the collaboration of these two firms. The contractor firm has completed its BIM implementation and before starting with the construction project, the construction project team has modeled the entire project with BIM from scratch in order to avoid any errors or drawbacks on the construction site. The firm is currently working on that BIM model, which also enables collaboration with some of the BIM user stakeholders like the mechanical subcontractor. However, the architectural design firm still works with CAD, which is one other reason why the process can be regarded as an example case for incomplete BIM implementation.

Regarding the example case of incomplete BIM implementation and the effect of PPT on the production process, the research questions of this study are:

1. What are the challenges of the current PPL that restricts the integration of all the stakeholders into the whole process from the early design stage to the operations stage?
2. What are the challenges of incomplete BIM implementation on the entire construction process?

2 Methodology

The production process of the selected case is studied with Cooper's [4] examination of the "evolutionary processes of production". He depicts that the first generation of the evolution; "phase review process" had only considered the technical risks but not the business risks. The second-generation "stage-gate process" has become stronger for considering business risks; however, with six deficiencies that Cooper [4] has listed (Table 1). Kagioglou et al. [11] explains how Cooper's proposition of a third-generation with four fundamental F's are compatible with the nature of the design and construction project processes. Today's BIM influenced architectural design and construction project processes are even a better fit with the four F's of what Cooper [4] has called "Tomorrow's Third Generation Process with overlapping, fluid stages and "fuzzy" and conditional Go decisions at gates" (Table 2). The Fallibility risk, on the other hand, can be eliminated by the ease-of-revision feature of BIM [1, 2, 6].

Table 1. The six deficiencies of the 2nd generation (stage-gate) process [4]

a.	Projects must wait at each gate until all tasks have been completed
b.	Overlapping of stages is all but impossible
c.	Projects must go through all gates and stages
d.	The system does not lead to project prioritization and focus
e.	Some new product processes are spelled out in far too much detail
f.	Some new product processes tend to be bureaucratic

Table 2. The F's of 3rd generation process [4] and the corresponding stage-gate deficiencies (Table 1)

Fluidity	No activity is fixed on a certain stage, overlapping fluid stages for greater speed	a, b, c, d, f, g
Fuzzy gates	Conditional decisions, situational dependency, Postponing finalization to not to interrupt the process	b, d, e, f, g
Focused	More than one projects at a time, Uses the entire portfolio as resource, Transferring the resources (labor, time, etc.) to the depicted priorities	a, c, d, f
Flexibility	No rigid stage-gate system, each project is unique	a, b, c, d, e, g
Fallibility	Increased risk of failure	

The research methodology is qualitative content analysis [9] of the in-depth interviews done separately with the managers of the current production process of the architectural design firm and the contractor firm. Each question designed for the architectural design firm is updated for gathering the corresponding information from the contractor firm (Table 3). The interview was designed to gather data on two distinct concerns addressing the study's two research questions. The first part of the interview focused on the process-based experiences of the firms in general, while the second part was on the case-specific questions for the large scale public construction project that they work on collaboratively. The case-specific questions were altered according to the existing process information and the labor division among the two firms.

Table 3. The in-depth interview questions

ADF	CF
General processes of the Architectural Design Firm (ADF) and Contactor Firm (CF)	
1 Does the process require waiting for the departments to complete their tasks before taking decisions?	Does the process require waiting for the departments to complete their tasks before taking decisions? Does BIM affect this condition?
2 Does collaboration with different departments bring drawbacks to the process?	Does collaboration with different departments bring drawbacks to the process? Does BIM affect this condition?
3 Can you continue with the process with adaptable solutions where there are uncertainties?	Can you continue with the process with adaptable solutions where there are uncertainties? Is BIM beneficial for this?
4 Do you think BIM implementation is a good reference in your portfolio?	Do you think BIM implementation is a good reference in your portfolio?
5 Do you think your process management would change after BIM implementation?	Did your project management customs change after BIM implementation? How would you describe the BIM benefits on process management?
6 Do you think that a certain task should necessarily belong to a certain stage based on your project management experiences?	Do you think that a certain task should necessarily belong to a certain stage based on your project management experiences? How does BIM affect that?
7 Can you collaborate simultaneously with other departments in your design team?	Can you collaborate simultaneously with other departments in your design team? How does BIM contribute to that?
8 Can two different processes run parallel?	Can two different processes run parallel? Does BIM allow that?
9 Does simultaneous collaboration have its risks?	Does simultaneous collaboration have its risks? How does BIM affect that?
10 How often and with what reasons are the reporting, paperwork, red tape, and meetings needed?	How often and with what reasons are the reporting, paperwork, red tape, and meetings needed? Does BIM have advantages to eliminate extra work?

(continued)

Table 3. (*continued*)

ADF	CF
11	Do you find the bureaucratic expectations of the procurements effective?	Do you find the bureaucratic expectations of the procurements effective? Is BIM enough to compensate them?
12	Do you know what will exactly happen in the process at which stage? Do you prefer every minor task be defined formerly?	Do you know what will exactly happen in the process at which stage? Do you prefer every minor task be defined formerly? How does BIM affect this concern?
13	Do you strictly obey the predefined tasks or do you flex them?	Do you strictly obey the predefined tasks or do you flex them? How does BIM affect that?
14	Does your project management allow momentary decisions as exceptions from your process plans?	Does your project management allow momentary decisions as exceptions from your process plans? Does BIM allow this?
15	Who takes responsibility for your momentary decisions?	Did the project manager's responsible dues change after BIM implementation?
16	Is the project manager also a team member?	Is the BIM manager also a team member?
17	Is it risky to flex the process? Who takes the risk? What is the precondition to flex the process?	Is it risky to flex the process? Who takes the risk? What is the precondition to flex the process? How does BIM respond?
Questions on the case-specific processes of ADF and CF		
18	How was your coordination with the demand side during the architectural design process?	What were the major stages of the construction project? How did BIM function for this?
19	What were the stages of work before and after the design project submission?	At which stages did you notice the malfunctioning parts of the project?
20	Which stakeholder was involved in the process at which stage?	What were the major revisions required to fix the malfunctioning parts?
21	Did you experience time loss and drawbacks after collecting feedback from different departments?	Did you experience time loss and drawbacks after collecting feedback from different departments?
22	Were the meetings with the demand side efficient?	How does the demand side contribute to your process?
23	Why do you think the project was subject to a major revision?	Why do you think the project was subject to a major revision?
24	What is your division of labor in your collaboration with the contractor firm?	What is your division of labor in your collaboration with the architectural design firm?
25	Does collaboration with the CF require extra revisions?	Does collaboration with the ADF require extra revisions?
26	Do you experience problems while collaborating with the CF?	Do you experience problems while collaborating with the ADF?

(*continued*)

Table 3. (*continued*)

ADF	CF
27	Do you think that, if the design and construction projects were prepared by the same firm would affect the project cost or duration? Why?	Do you think that, if the design and construction projects were prepared by the same firm would affect the project cost or duration? Why?
28	What differences do you think would minimize the drawbacks of the process?	What differences do you think would minimize the drawbacks of the process?
29	Do you think that the current PPL is correspondent to the actual project management requirements?	Do you think that the current PPL is correspondent to the actual project management requirements?

Both the general process questions and the questions seeking case-specific data were designed in relation to the fundamental features (4 + 1 F's) of the 3rd generation production process defined by Cooper [4]. Figure 1 displays the distribution of the 4 + 1 F's of Cooper's process definition on the questions by number. Because questions 4, 5, 16, and 28 are directly addressing the BIM implementation concerns, they have remained unrelated to the process features.

Question Number	1	2	3	4	5	6	7	8	9	10	11	12	13	14	15	16	17	18	19	20	21	22	23	24	25	26	27	28	29
Fluidity	•		•			•	•	•		•	•	•	•	•	•								•	•		•	•		•
Fuzzy gates		•	•					•	•	•	•	•	•	•	•			•		•									•
Focused		•					•		•	•	•												•	•					•
Flexibility	•					•				•	•	•	•		•		•	•	•		•					•			•
Fallibility							•									•					•			•		•	•		

Fig. 1. Distribution of the 4 + 1 F's of Cooper's process definition among the interview questions

3   Findings and Discussion

The content analysis provided subthemes of the 4 + 1 F's of the third generation process of production, as case-specific factors that prevent their operations (Table 4). The findings indicate that the fluidity of the entire production process was prevented by the rigid submission sub-stages that the current PPL requires. By its nature, the design process fits the feature of being focused [11]. However, in this case, it was activated with the unstable submission requirements of the demanding side, which has resulted in postponed revisions or stages. It is visible in the interview transcripts that; the primary source of process-related problems was reported as the revision works caused by changing requirements of the demand side. While BIM can overcome these problems without a significant resource waste with its ease of revision feature, the CAD users have frequently explicated about the resulting labor and time consumption that these revisions caused. The CAD users' process was paused with the shift of focus towards the solutions of the revisions caused by additional demands. The inflexibility of the submission deadlines have also been a source of economical resource waste for the offices while at the same time condemning them to a production quality of minimum requirement. On the other hand, when compared to CAD, BIM was expressed to reduce the risks of flexing the process into minimum with its scheduling feature. The project/BIM managers of both firms frequently expressed that the design and construction processes should not be kept separate starting from the early design stages. Also, the frequency of meetings with the demand side and red tapes that they required were expressed as causes of unnecessary consumptions of labor, time and economical resources. It was a common statement among both firms that the demand sides control on and intervention in the process should be kept limited.

Table 4. Expressions collected separately from the architectural design firm (ADF) and the contractor firm (CF) indicating the reasons that prevent the F's of the 3rd generation process

The 4 + 1 F's	Sub-themes	N. of Exp.		Sample expressions
		ADF	CF	
Fluidity	Revision frequency	4	5	"Frequent meetings with the demand side causes frequent revisions." ADF "The documentation format required by the demand side emerges CAD-BIM transition Problems." ADF "Situational decisions are often taken by our project manager." CF
	CAD-BIM transition problems	6	10	
	Increased Risks	7	5	
Fuzzy gates	Labor resource waste or red tapes	14	10	"the processes defined by the demand side cannot be skipped" ADF "repeated and frequent detailed documentation and presentation requirements and meetings slowed down the design process" ADF "If the contractor was included in the early design phase, the wastes would not be experienced." ADF "If design and construction phases were simultaneous, the HVAC revisions would not be of concern." CF
	Disintegrated process management	12	14	
	Additional economic and time resource waste	8	6	
	Increased number of Errors	8	3	
Focused	Additional economic and time resource waste	6	2	"Additional demands is a source of time waste." ADF "Additional demands can be handled by the BIM control." CF "Collaboration meetings are organized in clash detections." CF
	Focusing on the (unnecessary) demand completion	6	2	
Flexibility	Inflexible process	9	3	"The requirements of the demand side may even pause the entire process." ADF "Flexing the process can cause costly problems." CF
	Additional risks and economic resource wastes	6	4	
Fallibility	Increased number of Errors	8	4	"Errors that were invisible in CAD drawings became apparent in the BIM model." CF

Eastman et al. [6] have put forward the contractual challenge that BIM integration has brought. The traditional disintegration of the design and construction phases can neither meet the requirements of BIM integration nor collect its merits [6]. The process structure of current PPL has a traditional nature and is a better fit with the stage-gate than the 3rd generation, which is why observing it leads to a possible encounter with all six deficiencies given in Table 1. According to Sebastian [16], the effective use of BIM requires a new procurement approach that needs the architect to build a partnership with the contractor; not the client. This condition has been inevitable for the construction project phase of the studied case (Fig. 2). This corresponds to Eastman et al.'s [6] remark about how the business models that separated design and construction tasks have compelled some contractors to rebuild entirely new project models in a separate BIM environment. Also, a large extent of the architectural design firm's labor and time spent at the initial design project procurement phase was wasted because of the lack of feedback from the actual contractor (Fig. 2). In the current case, this consequence is brought by the 2D representational limitations of CAD used by the architectural design team in the first place. But it is also because of the separated, non-collaborative design and construction processes that the PPL required. As Sebastian states, at minimum all stakeholders are required to be responsible for the entire process, starting from the early design phases to the project handover [16].

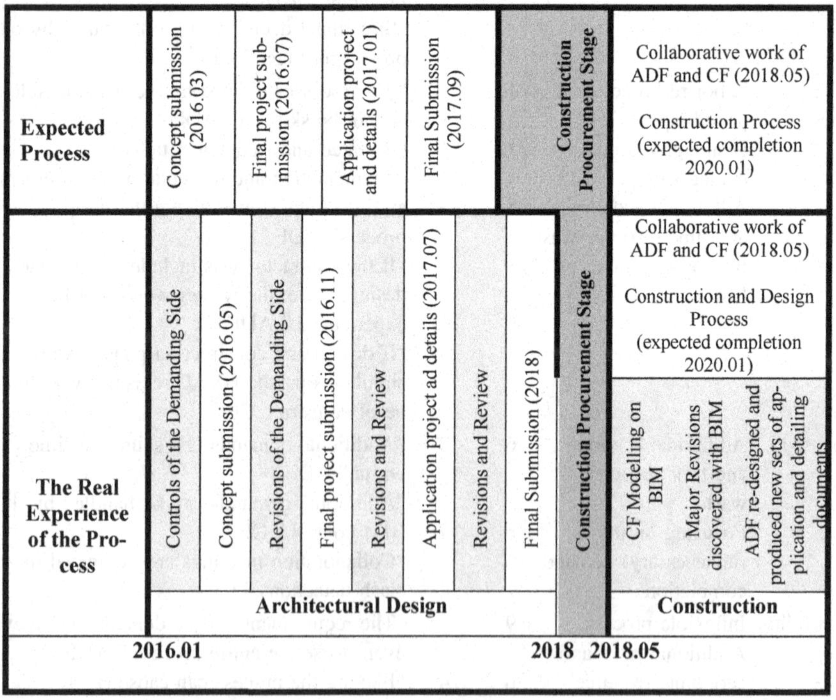

Expected Process	Concept submission (2016.03)		Final project submission (2016.07)		Application project and details (2017.01)		Final Submission (2017.09)		Construction Procurement Stage	Collaborative work of ADF and CF (2018.05) / Construction Process (expected completion 2020.01)		
The Real Experience of the Process	Controls of the Demanding Side	Concept submission (2016.05)	Revisions of the Demanding Side	Final project submission (2016.11)	Revisions and Review	Application project ad details (2017.07)	Revisions and Review	Final Submission (2018)	Construction Procurement Stage	Collaborative work of ADF and CF (2018.05) / Construction and Design Process (expected completion 2020.01)		
										CF Modelling on BIM	Major Revisions discovered with BIM	ADF re-designed and produced new sets of application and detailing documents
	Architectural Design									**Construction**		
2016.01								2018	2018.05			

Fig. 2. The expected and experienced production processes of the case

The data on the challenges of incomplete BIM implementation were gathered through the entire set of transcripts of the interviews with the firms. Table 5 displays the numbers of expressions regarding the six themes derived from the content analysis of the expressions that are related to the CAD-BIM comparison and/or integration.

The CAD-BIM integration of two collaborating firms caused time loss due to their inability to share a BIM model. This process has necessitated to manage the process through weekly meetings, revision processes and format translations that required extra time and labor from both firms. As expected, both the numbers of expressions and the content of the transcripts from both firms indicate that the contractor firm has provided more process-related information about the BIM implementation challenges regarding the case. The architectural design firm has stated about the error reduction potential of BIM, but not about how it reveals all the hidden information as the contractor firm has mentioned several times for answering different questions. Regarding the 5th question of the interview, the architectural design firm expressed the expected difficulty was the reason for their hesitation in implementing BIM into the firms' current process knowledge. However, the constructor firm's answer to the same question was that the CAD and BIM processes were quite similar.

On the other hand, it is understood that although the contractor firm has completed the firmwide BIM implementation and it has preferred to collaborate with BIM users except for the architectural design firm, it currently experiences problems with its subcontractors who do not have sufficient skills in BIM use, including its collaborators from other disciplines. Meanwhile, both firms indicate their presumptions that BIM implementation would become a requirement from the practitioners soon. This shared answer designates that for both of the firms question whether BIM implementation is optional is no more a matter of concern.

Table 6 displays the difference between the two firms regarding the content of their expressions on the BIM advantages over CAD in the design and construction processes. As the interviewed manager of the contactor firm has stated, the reduction in the construction expenses was worth the remodeling of the entire project with BIM from scratch, after being commissioned with the construction duty. Ilozor and Kelly [10] have mentioned about a deficiency within the literature that there had been no quantitative measures of pre and post BIM implementation productivity. This major decision of the construction firm, who is also experienced in and capable of managing the entire process with CAD, supports Ilozor and Kelly's argument that measuring the productivity rate differences could provide more prolific feedback about what is precisely modified with BIM implementation.

Table 5. Expressions collected separately from the architectural design firm (ADF) and the contractor firm (CF) indicating the concerns of CAD/BIM comparison and/or integration.

Themes	Number of expressions		Sample expressions
	ADF	CF	
BIM's superiority over CAD	11	41	"Revisions are made one by one manually" ADF "In 2d information is hidden, and may remain hidden until construction phase" CF "In BIM process error cannot remain hidden" CF
CAD BIM collaboration problems	7	12	"The required weekly data exchange ends up with time and data loss due to the necessary format conversion" ADF "Differences in the drafting techniques requires extra revisions of drawings" ADF "BIM model construction from scratch requires a great amount of time" CF
The existing BIM conception	2	13	"BIM implementation is postponed due to the lack of skilled labor" ADF "The concern is that the current process knowledge with CAD would not fit in implementing BIM" ADF "BIM users are considered as the BIM team that works parallel to the design process, this is a wrong conception." CF "If all firms' BIM application capacity was high, wastes could be minimized." CF
CAD-BIM collaboration process	3	10	"Revision solutions are produced by the ADF" ADF "The process flows in coordination through the weekly meetings." ADF "BIM project process quite resembles the CAD project process." CF
Current CAD system	5	0	"As all the disciplines work in the same space, face to face communication prevents possible drawbacks." ADF
Motives of BIM implementation	6	22	"Being a BIM office is regarded to be prestigious." ADF "BIM is regarded as advantageous for the error reduction that it enables." ADF "BIM prevents construction site problems before the construction starts." CF "With BIM sharing and instantly reaching the correct information became possible." CF

Table 6. Expressions collected separately from the architectural design firm (ADF) and the contractor firm (CF) indicating the superiority of BIM over CAD

ADF: CAD use compared to BIM			CF: BIM use compared to CAD		
Themes	N. of exp.	Sample expressions	Themes	N. of exp.	Sample expressions
Extra work	6	"The AD team controls the entire process of collaboration"	Error-free	11	"BIM is more advantageous than CAD for its clash detection feature"
Extra work and time loss	3	"Big revisions cause too much time and labor consumption"	Correct and fast	7	"BIM enables a shared and correct knowledge that is instantly reachable"
Error risk	2	"Problems are reported to the manager"	Error-free in the construction site	5	"BIM reduces construction expenses which is why we chose to re-model the entire project from scratch on BIM"
			No extra work	4	"Project management and control are easier with BIM"
			Fast	3	"BIM means not waiting for others to finish to start working"
			Unhidden errors	3	"BIM does not let errors to hide"
			Unhidden information	2	"BIM is the explication of what was hidden in CAD"
			Error-free economy	2	"BIM reduces the time consumption and costs"
			Correct and integrated	1	"BIM displays the design and interdisciplinary problems more clearly"
			Collaboration	1	"We can collaborate on the shared model"
			Integration	1	"BIM enables multitasking"

4   Conclusion

This study contributes to the ongoing research and discussion on the drawbacks of BIM implementation, by illustrating the requirement for redefining and rearranging the roles and processes of production with a precisely guaranteed resource economy and increased quality of work equally for all parties. It presents the state of the art of the public construction industry with a real case researched for BIM implementation and process management concerns in Turkey. This case exemplified how the interlocking structure of the policy and process fields in BIM activities [17] have a disrupting effect on the risk management of the production process when the policy field does not fit for the third generation production process [4]. It provides evidence for the urge for an overall update of the current PPL to afford a more integrated and risk-free production process that is compatible with the BIM requirements. This update is most likely to increase the productivity and quality levels of public construction projects.

Regarding the case-specific incomplete BIM implementation experiences of the two firms, it is understood that such experiences should be shared on a common ground for making necessary information on the actual advantages, case-specific problems and other related concerns available for all BIM enthusiastic firms. The survey results indicated that the knowledge of BIM implementation could not be transmitted from the contractor firm to the architectural design firm, although they have been working collaboratively on the same project. Related responses from both firms designate that the contractor firm knows how CAD users manage their processes by their pre-BIM experiences; however, the architectural design firm needs more detailed or procedural knowledge about how BIM affects the project management concerns. This case demonstrates that similar academic in-depth enquiries have vast potential to reveal the hidden obstacles of the BIM implementation process even further.

References

1. Arayici, Y., Coates, P., Koskela, L., Kagioglou, M., Usher, C., O'Reilly, K.J.S.S.: BIM adoption and implementation for architectural practices. Struct. Surv. **29**(1), 7–25 (2011)
2. Azhar, S.: Building information modeling (BIM): trends, benefits, risks, and challenges for the AEC industry. Leadersh. Manag. Eng. **11**(3), 241–252 (2011)
3. Bryde, D., Broquetas, M., Volm, J.M.: The project benefits of building information modelling (BIM). Int. J. Proj. Manag. **31**(7), 971–980 (2013)
4. Cooper, R.G.: Third-generation new product processes. J. Prod. Innov. Manag. Int. Publ. Prod. Devel. Manag. Assoc. **11**(1), 3–14 (1994)
5. Dossick, C.S., Neff, G.: Organizational divisions in BIM-enabled commercial construction. J. Constr. Eng. Manag. **136**(4), 459–467 (2009)
6. Eastman, C., Teicholz, P., Sacks, R., Liston, K.: BIM Handbook: A Guide to Building Information Modeling for Owners, Managers, Designers, Engineers and Contractors. Wiley, Hoboken (2011)
7. Elmualim, A., Gilder, J.: BIM: innovation in design management, influence and challenges of implementation. Architect. Eng. Des. Manag. **10**(3–4), 183–199 (2014)
8. Giel, B.K., Issa, R.R.: Return on investment analysis of using building information modeling in construction. J. Comput. Civil Eng. **27**(5), 511–521 (2011)
9. Hsieh, H.F., Shannon, S.E.: Three approaches to qualitative content analysis. Qual. Health Res. **15**(9), 1277–1288 (2005)
10. Ilozor, B.D., Kelly, D.J.: Building information modeling and integrated project delivery in the commercial construction industry: a conceptual study. J. Eng. Proj. Prod. Manag. **2**(1), 23–36 (2012)
11. Kagioglou, M., Cooper, R., Aouad, G., Sexton, M.: Rethinking construction: the generic design and construction process protocol. Eng. Constr. Architectural Manag. **7**(2), 141–153 (2000)

12. Love, P.E., Matthews, J., Simpson, I., Hill, A., Olatunji, O.A.: A benefits realization management building information modeling framework for asset owners. Autom. Constr. **37**, 1–10 (2014)
13. Miettinen, R., Paavola, S.: Beyond the BIM utopia: approaches to the development and implementation of building information modeling. Autom. Constr. **43**, 84–91 (2014)
14. Popov, V., Juocevicius, V., Migilinskas, D., Ustinovichius, L., Mikalauskas, S.: The use of a virtual building design and construction model for developing an effective project concept in 5D environment. Autom. Constr. **19**(3), 357–367 (2010)
15. Sebastian, R., Prins, M.: Collaborative architectural design management. In: Emmitt, S., Prins, M., den Otter, A. (eds.) Architectural Management: International Research and Practice, pp. 105–118. Willey-Blackwell, Oxford (2009)
16. Sebastian, R.: Changing roles of the clients, architects and contractors through BIM. Eng. Constr. Architectural Manag. **18**(2), 176–187 (2011)
17. Succar, B.: Building information modelling framework: a research and delivery foundation for industry stakeholders. Autom. Constr. **18**(3), 357–375 (2009)
18. Won, J., Lee, G., Dossick, C., Messner, J.: Where to focus for successful adoption of building information modeling within organization. J. Constr. Eng. Manag. **139**(11), 04013014-1-10 (2013)

Drivers of BIM Implementation in a High Rise Building Project

Beliz Özorhon[1] and Ahmet Karacigan[2(✉)]

[1] Civil Engineering Department, Boğaziçi University, Istanbul, Turkey
beliz.ozorhon@boun.edu.tr
[2] Civil Engineering Department, Turner International Project Management Inc.
and Boğaziçi University, Istanbul, Turkey
akaracigan@tcco.com, ahmetkaracigan@boun.edu.tr

Abstract. The Architectural, Engineering and Construction (AEC) industry is in a transition process that deeply affects the long-established ways of collaboration to complete a project. Building Information Modeling (BIM) is at the core of this process by enabling all the project data digitally available to all stakeholders. In recent years, AEC firms have spent great efforts and resources to implement BIM in their business tasks and they have both common and different reasons for the BIM-centered transformation. These reasons have to do with the pre-defined driving factors that initiate the utilization of BIM. In order to achieve a successful BIM implementation process, these driving factors need to be identified. The primary objective of this study is to systematically identify the drivers of the BIM implementation process using a high rise building project as a case study. In this respect, an extensive literature review was conducted to determine the driving factors that will be used for detailed analysis for a case study. A total of 42 papers were selected related to the BIM implementation process. An initial list of 44 drivers was identified and among these drivers, the frequency was calculated based on the total number of citations. This initial list was modified to obtain a more refined list by grouping/merging similar factors and deleting some irrelevant ones. Three levels of influences namely, industry-level, firm-level and project-level were defined to distinguish the perspectives of the industry, companies, and project teams. A high rise construction project was selected as a case study to analyze the identified drivers. Since high rise buildings consist of complex systems, BIM implementation is crucial for these types of projects. Interviews were conducted with five experts working at Turner International Turkey, which acts as the project management firm of this project. The interviewees were asked to specify the importance level of the listed driving factors on a 1–5 Likert scale. The average ratings for each driver were calculated. Additionally, interviewees were also asked to share their own experiences during the BIM implementation process for the selected project. A comparison of the literature and the case study reveals the key points that are discussed in the paper.

Keywords: BIM implementation · Construction management · Building Information Modeling (BIM) · Driving factors

© Springer Nature Switzerland AG 2020
S. Ofluoglu et al. (Eds.): EBF 2019, CCIS 1188, pp. 28–39, 2020.
https://doi.org/10.1007/978-3-030-42852-5_3

1 Introduction

The Architecture, Engineering and Construction (AEC) industry has unique product/process/group characteristics that necessitate effective management of information flow among project stakeholders. This need was formerly fulfilled by computer-aided design (CAD) applications. These applications are no longer sufficient as the projects have become more complex and the technology has developed further, and traditional design communication tools create ambiguities within project parties [1]. Recent construction projects also include a wide range of complex information that needs to be managed properly through effective coordination. The traditional methods of collaboration cause a lot of clarification demands, change orders and re-works that consequently result in a waste of time and resources. At this point, Building Information Modeling (BIM) enables AEC companies to manage all project information via a common model resulting in better communication and coordination among project parties.

NBIMS defined BIM as "a digital representation of physical and functional characteristics of a facility" [2]. Another BIM definition is "the information management process throughout the lifecycle of a building which mainly focuses on enabling and facilitating the integrated way of project flow and delivery, by the collaborative use of semantically rich 3D digital building models in all stages of the project and building lifecycle" [3]. Although the premises of BIM have been largely acknowledged, implementation of BIM for AEC processes is still a challenging task for the construction industry. Labor productivity of the AEC industry has been decreasing gradually since the early 1960s [4]. Certain initiatives addressed the low productivity of the construction industry by technological innovation [5]. Here, BIM is considered as a solution to facilitate continuous productivity improvement in the AEC industry [6]. The increase in the BIM adoption rates will likely help to achieve higher productivity rates.

The BIM implementation rate has been increasing in the AEC industry in the last decade but there exist significant issues that need to be addressed for ensuring efficiency and smoothness during this implementation [7]. Based on this argument, the motivation of this research is to facilitate the BIM implementation process while enhancing the recognition level of BIM among construction professionals. This study aims to investigate the drivers of BIM implementation process in a high rise building project case in order to achieve a successful BIM implementation. Within this study scope, a systematic literature analysis was conducted to identify the driving factors, and the identified driving factors were examined and also evaluated through the interviews held with industry experts. The selection rationale of the case study came from the fact that high rise buildings consist of various complex building systems and construction tasks. Thus, the use of BIM was found very appropriate in this context. The research findings are considered to reveal important driving factors for BIM utilization as the selected case study represent similar types of projects and contractor companies in a real context. The research findings hopefully provide useful insights about the BIM implementation process especially for industry organizations that are at the beginning stages of the BIM implementation for specific building projects.

2 Research Background

During the last decade, BIM has been an influential phenomenon for the construction industry for increased productivity and efficiency, and it has become a popular research domain for researchers and academicians. In BIM literature there are a number of publications that elaborated BIM adoption from different perspectives. Some of these studies also focused on the implementation process, productivity and performance gains as well as the change of service scopes.

The studies focusing on the implementation process generally discussed the risks and challenges and drivers of BIM. Dawood et al. [8] conducted a study to investigate the barriers and drivers of BIM. The study collected both qualitative and quantitative data through a Web-based questionnaire and found "time and cost", "resistance to change" and "lack of experience" as the main barriers for BIM implementation. The survey results also revealed that "integrated project delivery (IPD) systems" and "external and internal supports" are the main drivers for BIM adoption. The use of BIM was stated to be limited unless it incorporates the technology, end-users and process aspects. In another research effort, Eadie et al. [9] targeted the top 100 UK contractors with an extensive questionnaire. The study demonstrated that the significance of the driving factors of BIM implementation is highly correlated with the experience level of respondents. For example, non-BIM-users ranked the pressure (pressure of government, client or competition) as the most crucial driver; whereas, BIM-users ranked the clash detection and reduced rework as the top drivers for BIM implementation. On the other hand, research that focused on the results of BIM implementation generally aimed to define the benefits and impacts of BIM implementation. Ghaffarianhoseini et al. [10] discussed the reality of BIM by reviewing the literature. The research team grouped the current benefits of BIM into nine different components as technical, knowledge management, standardization, diversity management, integration, economic, planning/scheduling, building LCA and decision support. They expected BIM to have a transformational impact on the AEC industry. Furthermore, Stanley and Thurnell [11] designed a cross-sectional questionnaire to investigate the benefits of 5D BIM and stated that BIM offers advantages for quantity surveying by improving the efficiency and visualization together with earlier risk identification. A more recent study has revealed that there are 13 different positive returns of BIM. The primary benefits have been identified as "improving multiparty communication" and "3-D visualization" Jin et al. [12].

There are also other case studies that attempt to describe the best practices, performance measures and to identify the inputs and enablers for BIM implementation. Abbasnejad et al. [13] identified the key enablers for an effective BIM implementation. Based on an extensive literature review, they identified the enablers for different tasks that need to be achieved during the BIM implementation process and concluded that BIM can be assumed as organizational innovation, therefore the principles of organizational innovation are essential for consideration.

This study engaged to investigate drivers of the BIM implementation process in a high rise building project as a case study. For this purpose, 42 research papers were examined in detail and all the driving factors were noted. Factors were re-assessed, merged and grouped together according to their similarities. Each factor's level of influence has been determined as industry-level, firm-level and project-level. In order to determine the significance of the identified driving factors on a real construction project, interviews were held with industry experts working in a high rise building project.

3   Research Methodology

3.1   Determining the Driving Factors in the Literature

In order to identify the drivers of BIM implementation found in the literature, the driving factors were grouped as the primary and secondary factors that push a company to implement BIM. This study assumed that these drivers form the motivation for initiating the BIM implementation in AEC organizations.

An extensive literature review was conducted in order to determine the driving factors for further evaluation in the case study. A total of 42 papers were selected for the detailed analysis. An initial list of 44 drivers was identified based on this review. Among these drivers, frequencies were computed in order to depict the significance of each factor in the literature based on how many papers have referred to these factors. Then, this initial list was modified to obtain a more refined list of factors. Similar factors were grouped, merged or redefined under a comprehensive heading. Some irrelevant factors were deleted, and a more compact list of drivers was obtained. The final list contained 10 main drivers finalized as; "improving corporate performance", "improving project performance", "improving building's energy performance", "improving collaboration & coordination", "client requirement", "governmental push", "design improvement", "improving construction productivity", "improving HSE activities" and "reducing life cycle cost of the building". Three levels of influences, namely, industry-level, firm-level and project-level were identified. These influence levels are expected to help to distinguish the perspectives of the industry, companies, and project teams. The influence level of each identified driving factor was determined. These levels are expected to be logical and consistent with the literature review. Table 1 shows the final list of driving factors based on the literature review.

Table 1. Final table of the driving factors

No	Identified driving factor	Level of influence	Source
1	Improving corporate performance	Firm	[9, 10, 12, 17, 27, 30, 31, 35, 44–47]
2	Improving project performance	Project	[9–12, 15–17, 19, 22–25, 27, 28, 30, 32–50]
3	Improving building's energy performance	Project	[9, 12, 14, 15, 21–25, 27, 28, 31–33, 35–39, 41–43, 45, 46, 48, 50]
4	Improving collaboration & coordination	Project	[8–12, 15, 16, 22–31, 33, 34, 36–41, 43–50]
5	Client requirement	Project	[8, 9, 12, 17–19, 24, 25, 28, 30, 46]
6	Governmental push	Industry	[8–10, 12, 17, 18, 25, 32, 35, 40, 46, 47]
7	Design improvement	Project	[7, 9–12, 14–17, 20, 22–50]
8	Improving construction productivity	Project	[8, 9, 16, 20, 23–26, 28, 30, 31, 33, 35–46, 48–50]
9	Improving HSE activities	Project	[9, 23, 42, 48, 49]
10	Reducing life cycle cost of the building	Project	[10, 12, 15, 24, 27, 28, 33, 37, 38, 40, 42, 44–48, 50]

3.2 The Case Study

The case study project is a high rise building project consisting of two towers (40 and 45 stories) with a total construction area of 430.000 m². Since high rise building projects consist of complex MEP systems and include many specific architectural details, the project was selected as a case study to analyze the drivers of the BIM implementation process. The estimated duration of the project is 36 months. Due to the complexity of its systems and the required coordination, BIM implementation is vital for the project, and it can be assumed as a representative case for similar project types.

Turner International Turkey, the project management company for the selected case study, has been a part of this project since the design phase. Five interviewees from the Turner International Co. were selected to evaluate the driving factors. The interviewees were from the top management level to the project engineer level. The interviewees were asked to specify the importance level of driving factors for the use of BIM on a 1–5 Likert scale (1: very low, 5: very high) considering their experiences in the case study project. Based on the responses, the average values for each driver were calculated. Interviewees were also asked to share their own experiences during the BIM implementation process for the case study project (Table 2).

Table 2. Interviewers' profiles

No	Profession	Position	Industry Experience
I1	Civil Engineer, M.Sc., LEED AP	Country Director	20+ years
I2	Civil Engineer, M.Sc., LEED AP	Operations Manager	20+ years
I3	Civil Engineer, M.Sc., LEED GA	Design Manager	20 years
I4	Civil Engineer, LEED GA	PMCS Manager	16 years
I5	Civil Engineer, PMP, LEED GA	BIM Engineer	5 years

4 Findings and Discussion

Table 3 shows the driving factors as well as each factor's frequency in the literature. These factors were also assigned a level of influence in order to distinguish the driving forces for different levels. As explained a high rise building project was selected as a case study and the previously identified factors have been evaluated by the industry experts on a 1 to 5 Likert scale (1: Lowest, 5: Highest). Interviewees also shared their thoughts and experiences about the BIM implementation process. The case study is expected to reveal the significance of the driving factors for BIM implementation for the construction industry.

Table 3. Case study findings for the driving factors

No	Identified driving factor	Description	Literature frequency	Case study rating (Avg.)
1	Improving corporate performance	Company image, competitiveness, gain experience	12/42	4.4/5
2	Improving project performance	Efficiency, quality, speed, cost, risk reduction	34/42	4.6/5
3	Improving building energy performance	Sustainability, LEED, lean implementation	26/42	1.8/5
4	Improving collaboration & coordination	IPD, collaboration, coordination	33/42	4.8/5
5	Client requirement	Contractual obligation	11/42	2.6/5
6	Governmental push	Law enforcement	12/42	1.0/5
7	Design improvement	Clash detection, visualization, simple revision process	38/42	4.2/5
8	Improving construction productivity	Site logistics, optimized schedules, prefabrication	27/42	3.6/5
9	Improving HSE activities	Safety measurements, simulations	5/42	2.0/5
10	Reducing the life cycle cost of the building	Maintenance & usage costs	17/42	2.8/5

4.1   Improving Corporate Performance

The comparison of the literature and the case study results showed that "improving corporate performance" is one of the least mentioned driving factors even though it was evaluated as the second most important driver by the industry experts.

Based on the literature review, "improving corporate performance" was identified as a firm-level driver. It was generated by merging 4 initial driving factors namely; "social image of the company", "not to stay behind the industry (competitiveness)", "to gain experience (cross-project benefits)" and "marketing purposes". It was mentioned in 12 papers out of 42 in the literature with a low rate of frequency.

In contrast, industry experts evaluated the importance level of "improving corporate performance" as 4.4 out of 5. It is one of the most important drivers for the case project. The Country Manager of Turner International Turkey (I1) stated "Utilizing BIM gave Turner a competitive advantage in the market" and Operations Manager (I2) added, "It enabled us to act proactively". Having BIM experience reported as crucial for a company to take part in a high-rise building project.

Last but not the least, the only firm-level driver is "improving corporate performance" and it has a low frequency in the literature. Thus, more research is needed to address firm-level drivers.

4.2   Improving Project Performance

Based on 42 research papers, "improving project performance" was identified as a project-level driver. It comprises the driving factors such as "facility management", "risk reduction", "increase efficiency", "financial monitoring", "increase quality", "increase speed" and "decrease costs". It is one of the top drivers mentioned in the literature with a frequency of 34 out of 42.

The project performance was considered as an important criterion for high rise buildings and "improving project performance" was evaluated as the second most important driver by the industry experts with an average rate of 4.6/5. The Turner's Operations Manager (I2) stated, "It increases the speed on the site by minimizing mistakes and reworks as well as the cost". In high rise building constructions, coping with a tight schedule is crucial, and this can be achieved by good coordination among the disciplines.

4.3   Improving Building's Energy Performance

The comparison of the literature and case study findings showed that "improving building's energy performance" is a moderate level factor mentioned in the literature; however, the industry experts evaluated it as one of the least significant factors.

According to the literature review, "improving building's energy performance" was identified as a project-level driver. It consists of driving factors such as "sustainability", "green building purposes" and "reduce waste & lean purposes". The frequency of the driver is 26 out of 42. Thus, it has a medium level of frequency in the literature.

Although energy performance is very important for the high rise buildings, industry experts evaluated this driver as the second least important driver with an average rate of

1.8/5. The Turner's Design Manager (I3) stated, "Energy performance was not an important driver in our project; however, eliminating wastes and being lean is crucial. The lean purposes need to be examined as a separate driving factor".

4.4 Improving Collaboration and Coordination

According to the findings of this study, "improving collaboration & coordination" is one of the most important drivers that the industry and literature agreed together. Based on the research papers in the literature, "improving collaboration and coordination" has been identified as a project-level driver. 4 different factors have been merged under this driver. These are "improve collaboration and communication", "integrated project delivery (IPD)", "better document coordination" and "interdisciplinary data exchange". It has a high-frequency rate of 33 out of 42 in the literature.

Parallel to the literature frequency, the "improving collaboration & coordination" factor was also reported as the most important driver by Turner's industry experts. The average rate is 4.8 out of 5. In highly complex high rise building projects, coordination and collaboration play an important role throughout the construction and operation process. Turner's Operations Manager (I2) stated, "It is the most crucial factor that drives us to utilize BIM, and it naturally pushes for collaboration by all the project parties." and PMCS Manager (I4) added, "Collaboration and coordination is one of the most important functions of BIM for sure". In this particular high rise project, all RFIs were synchronized with a 3-D model to ensure the coordination among project parties.

4.5 Client Requirement

According to the literature analysis, "client requirement" was identified as one of the project-level drivers. It was also described as "contractual obligation" in the literature. This driver has a low-frequency rate of 11 out of 42.

Industry experts assessed its importance rate as 2.6/5. The Operations Manager (I2) indicated, "Some educated clients are asking us to utilize BIM in their project, but generally we need to inform and educate clients regarding BIM applications. The Client requirement will become a driver once the clients are aware of BIM benefits."

4.6 Governmental Push

Based on the literature analysis, the only industry-level driver was identified as "governmental push". It was also described as "law enforcement" in the literature. The literature frequency rate is 11 out of 42 which is quite low.

Due to the lack of law enforcement about BIM implementation in Turkey, this driver has an average rate of 1 out of 5. However, industry experts stated, "As BIM gains popularity, governments will provide incentives, and BIM utilization will become a precondition". As the only industry-level driver, "governmental push" needs to be prioritized with the government incentives.

4.7 Design Improvement

Based on 42 research papers, the most frequent driver in the literature was identified as "design improvement". It was also determined as a project-level driver and generated by merging 9 driving factors namely; "creativity", "solve design problems (clash detection)", "visualization", "code checking", "greater analysis capability", "putting information into objects", "simultaneous updates", "ease of use" and "parametrically linked drawings". The frequency rate is 38 out of 42 which is the highest frequency in the literature.

Accordingly, it was evaluated as one of the most important drivers by industry experts with an average rate of 4.2 out of 5. The Turner's BIM Engineer (I5) stated: "Clash detection is one of the most useful functions of the BIM. However, in order to have an effective usage of the tool, the level of clash detail you need to detect needs to be determined properly". BIM actively facilitated the design documentation process for such a high rise building project.

4.8 Improving Construction Productivity

According to the literature review, "improving construction productivity" was identified as one of the project-level drivers. It consists of 4 different driving factors namely; "site management (logistics)", "better scheduling (construction scenario)", "facilitating prefabrication" and "understanding constructability". It is one of the most mentioned drivers with a frequency rate of 27 out of 42.

Industry professionals have evaluated this driver with an average rate of 3.6/5. The Operations Manager (I2) stated, "You feel confident about sizing when it comes to pipes, trays and steel frame members, and this increases the productivity" and The Country Manager (I1) said, "BIM enables optimizing schedules with a well-organized construction scenario, and this is essential for construction productivity".

4.9 Improving HSE (Health and Safety Executive) Activities

"Improving HSE activities" was identified as the least mentioned driver according to the literature. It was also described as "safety simulations" in the literature. The frequency of the driver is 5 out of 42. Concordantly, industry experts have evaluated it with an average rate of 2.0/5 but they added, "Coordinating HSE discipline with BIM would be great to identify potential risks".

4.10 Reducing Life Cycle Cost of the Building

Based on the literature review, "reducing life cycle cost of the building" was identified as a project-level driver. It was also described as "reducing the maintenance and usage costs" in the literature and has a medium frequency rate as 17 out of 42 in the literature.

"Reducing life cycle cost of the building" was evaluated with an average rate of 2.8/5 by the industry experts. The Turner's Country Manager (I1) stated, "As-built drawings have always been a big deal in Turkey. Clients always ask for accurate as-built models in order to effectively manage their property. BIM is the key input for addressing this issue". For such a high rise building project, facility management should be planned at earlier stages to reduce operation costs. Thus, properly chosen MEP systems with accurate as-built drawings are the key factors for BIM utilization in these types of projects.

5 Conclusions

Although the BIM adoption rate has been increasing in the AEC industry, the pace of the adoption is relatively slow. Due to the lack of certain guidelines for BIM implementation, the majority of the AEC companies do not have any idea about what they will face during the implementation and organizational transformation process. The identification of key drivers for BIM through a substantial case study has the potential to reveal the real-world challenges and benefits for the construction companies that are at the beginning stages of BIM implementation.

Research findings revealed that 80% of the driving factors are project-level factors and companies have various expectations from BIM. This research showed that these expectations can be fulfilled with proper BIM implementation strategies and carefully devised transformation tasks. Industry professionals need to define what they are seeking and how they can benefit from this effort. Setting the targets and planning strategically at the beginning of the process is crucial. A well-organized BIM implementation is vital especially for complex building projects with multifaceted building systems.

This case study made it possible to evaluate the BIM implementation from the industry experts' perspective, and it is expected to offer both arguments and new perspectives for construction professionals in order to become aware of different dimensions of BIM use. Further studies may include the drivers proposed in this study for further evaluations in other case studies and assess the findings of this study.

References

1. Chelson, D.: The effects of building information modeling on construction productivity. Dissertation, University of Maryland (2010, Unpublished)
2. NBMIS: The National Building Information Modeling Standards (2007)
3. Underwood, J., Isikdag, U.: Emerging technologies for BIM 2.0. Constr. Innov. **11**(3), 252–258 (2011)
4. Hergunsel, M.: Benefits of building information modeling for construction managers and BIM based scheduling. Dissertation, Worcester Polytechnic Institute (2011, Unpublished)
5. Ozorhon, B., Oral, K.: Drivers of innovation in construction projects. J. Constr. Eng. Manag. **143**, 04016118 (2016)
6. Qian, A.: Benefits and ROI of BIM for multi-disciplinary project management. Dissertation, National University of Singapore (2012, Unpublished)
7. McGrawHill Construction: Smart Market Report the Business Value of BIM in North America: Multi-year Trend Analysis and User Ratings (2007–2012). McGraw Hill Construction, New York (2012)

8. Kassem, M., Brogden, T., Dawood, N.: BIM and 4D planning: a holistic study of the barriers and drivers to widespread adoption. KICEM J. Constr. Eng. Proj. Manag. **2**, 1–10 (2012)
9. Eadie, R., Odeyinka, H., Browne, M., McKeown, C., Yohanis, M.: An analysis of the drivers for adopting building information modelling. J. Inf. Technol. Constr. (ITcon) **18**, 338–352 (2013)
10. Ghaffarianhoseini, A., et al.: Building information modelling (BIM) uptake: clear benefits, understanding its implementation, risks and challenges. Renew. Sustain. Energy Rev. **75**(C), 1046–1053 (2017)
11. Stanley, R., Thurnell, D.: The benefits of and barriers to implementation of 5D BIM for quantity surveying in New Zealand. Australas. J. Constr. Econ. Build. **14**(1), 105–117 (2014)
12. Jin, R., Hancock, C., Tang, L., Wanatowski, D.: BIM investment, returns, and risks in China's AEC industries. J. Constr. Eng. Manage. **143**, 04017089 (2017)
13. Abbasnejad, B., Nepal, M., Drogemuller, R.: Key enablers for effective management of BIM implementation in construction firms (2016)
14. Yan, H., Damian, P.: Benefits and barriers of building information modeling. In: 12th International Conference on Computing in Civil Engineering (2008)
15. Sun, C., Jiang, S., Skibniewski, M., Man, Q., Shen, L.: A literature review of the factors limiting the application of BIM in the construction industry. Technol. Econ. Dev. Econ. **23**(5), 764–779 (2017)
16. Arayici, Y., Charles, E., Coates, P.: Building information modelling (BIM) implementation and remote construction projects: Issues, challenges and critiques. J. Inf. Technol. Constr. (ITcon) **17**, 75–92 (2012)
17. Cao, D., Li, H., Wang, G., Huang, T.: Identifying and contextualising the motivations for BIM implementation in construction projects: an empirical study in China. Int. J. Proj. Manag. **35**(4), 658–669 (2017)
18. Ozorhon, B., Karahan, U.: Critical success factors of building information modeling implementation. J. Manag. Eng. **33**, 04016054 (2016)
19. Newton, L., Chileshe, N.: Enablers and barriers of building information modelling (BIM) within South Australian construction organisations (2012)
20. Barlish, K., Sullivan, K.: How to measure the benefits of BIM - a case study approach. Autom. Constr. **24**, 149–159 (2012)
21. Chien, K., Wu, Z., Huang, S.: Identifying and assessing critical risk factors for BIM projects: Empirical study. Autom. Constr. **45**, 1–15 (2014)
22. Coates, P., Arayici, Y., Koskela, K., Kagioglou, M., Usher, C., O'Reilly, K.: The key performance indicators of the BIM implementation process. In: The International Conference on Computing in Civil and Building Engineering (2010)
23. Migilinskas, D., Popov, V., Juocevicius, V., Ustinovichius, L.: The benefits, obstacles and problems of practical BIM implementation. Procedia Eng. **57**, 767–774 (2013)
24. Broquetas, M., Bryde, D., Marc-Volm, J.: The project benefits of building information modelling (BIM). Int. J. Proj. Manag. **31**, 971–980 (2013)
25. Gu, N., London, K.: Understanding and facilitating BIM adoption in the AEC industry. Autom. Constr. **19**, 988–999 (2010)
26. London, K., Singh, V., Taylor, C., Gu, N., Brankovic, L.: Building information modelling project decision support framework (2008)
27. Arayici, Y., Coates, S., Koskela, L., Kagioglou, M., Usher, C., O'Reilly, K.: BIM adoption and implementation for architectural practices. Struct. Surv. **29**, 7–25 (2011)
28. Karahan, U.: BIM implementations in the Turkish construction industry. Dissertation, Bogazici University (2015, Unpublished)

29. Alder, M.: Comparing time and accuracy of building information modeling to on-screen takeoff for a quantity takeoff of a conceptual estimate. Dissertation, Birmingham Young University (2006, Unpublished)
30. McGrawHill Construction: Smart Market Report the Business Value of BIM for Construction in Major Global Markets. McGraw Hill Construction, New York (2014)
31. McGrawHill Construction: Smart Market Report BIM. McGraw Hill Construction, New York (2008)
32. Tulenheimo, R.: Challenges of implementing new technologies in the world of BIM - case study from construction engineering industry in Finland. Procedia Econ. Finance **21**, 469–477 (2015)
33. Marshall-Ponting, A., Arayici, Y., Khosrowshahi, F., Mihindu, S.: Towards implementation of building information modelling in the construction industry (2009)
34. Kovacic, I., Dragos, V., Filzmoser, M., Suppin, R., Oberwinter, L.: BIM in teaching—lessons learned from exploratory study (2015)
35. Smith, P.: BIM implementation – global strategies. Procedia Eng. **85**, 482–492 (2014)
36. Giacomo, E.: BIM trends from all around the world. In: European BIM Summit (2015)
37. InfoComm International: Building information modeling (BIM) (2013)
38. Eastman, C., Teicholz, P., Sacks, R., Liston, K.: BIM Handbook: A Guide to Building Information Modeling for Owners, Managers, Architects, Engineers and Contractors. Wiley, Hoboken (2011)
39. Krygiel, E., Nies, B.: Green BIM: Successful Sustainable Design with Building Information Modeling. Wiley, Hoboken (2008)
40. Luo, L., Yan, Z., Yang, D., Xie, J., Wu, G.: BIM application in the whole life cycle of construction projects in China, pp. 189–197 (2018)
41. Kovacic, I., Filzmoser, M.: Designing and evaluation procedures for interdisciplinary building information modelling use - an explorative study. Eng. Proj. Organ. J. **5**, 14–21 (2015)
42. Kymmell, W.: Building Information Modeling: Planning and Managing Construction Projects with 4D CAD and Simulations (2008)
43. Alazmeh, N., Underwood, J., Coates, P.: Implementing a BIM collaborative workflow in the UK construction market. Int. J. Sus. Dev. Plann. **13**(1), 24–35 (2017)
44. World Economic Forum: Shaping the future of construction: an action plan to accelerate building information modeling (BIM) adoption (2018)
45. Liu, F., Jallow, A.K., Anumba, C.J.: Building knowledge modeling: Integrating knowledge in BIM (2013)
46. Nanajkar, A., Gao, Z.: BIM implementation practices at India's AEC firms, pp. 134–139 (2014)
47. Syazwani, W., Mohammad, W., Abdullah, M.R., Ismail, S., Takim, R.: Overview of building information modelling (BIM) adoption factors for construction organisations (2017)
48. Singh, M.M., Sawhney, A., Sharma, V.: Utilising building component data from BIM for formwork planning. Constr. Econ. Build. **17**, 20–36 (2017)
49. Mostafa, K., Leite, F.: Evolution of BIM adoption and implementation by the construction industry over the past decade: a replication study (2018)
50. Tereno, S., Anumba, C., Asadi, S.: BIM implementation in facilities management: an analysis of implementation processes (2018)

A Public BIM Project: Cerrahpaşa Healthcare and Education Facility

Cemil Akçay[1(✉)], İlker Ali İliş[2], and Saniye Öktem[2]

[1] Istanbul University, Istanbul, Turkey
cakcay@istanbul.edu.tr
[2] Prota Engineering Project Design and Consultancy, Ankara, Turkey
saniye.oktem@prota.com.tr

Abstract. Building Information Modeling is being rapidly adopted in the Architecture, Engineering and Construction (AEC) industry. Due to its positive impact on project quality, interdisciplinary collaboration and the reduction of construction costs, the BIM adoption rate is even higher in complex construction projects that require hi-end architectural and engineering design solutions. From this perspective, this chapter presents a case study project regarding BIM implementation in a large scale healthcare and medical education facility project. Focusing on the facility design process, the deployment of BIM methods and related techniques are investigated in detail along with significant benefits and implementation issues. The chapter includes a literature review on the advantages of BIM in healthcare and education projects and provides an in-depth inquiry of Cerrahpaşa Healthcare and Education Facility which is under development as one of the largest healthcare and medical education projects in Turkey. The evaluation involves specific design and assessment tasks from the case study such as design reviews, project coordination and immersive VR visualizations. The findings from the case study suggest task-specific advantages of BIM for addressing the complex design problems of large-scale hospitals also significant challenges as compared to conventional design and project development methods.

Keywords: Building Information Modeling · BIM in public projects · BIM in healthcare and education projects

1 Introduction

Building Information Modeling (BIM) is one of the most trending concepts in the Architecture, Engineering and Construction (AEC) industry during the last decade [1]. Through the consistent information exchange between project teams, it improves efficiency and increases productivity during the design, construction and facility management phases. According to the National Institute of Building Science definition, BIM "is a digital representation of physical and functional characteristic of a facility" [2]. Using the data derived from these simulated models and BIM database, AEC teams make better and well-informed decisions that influence the whole building lifecycle. Motivated by these advantages and significant performance gains, the BIM adoption rate is increasing among local and global AEC firms. Like these commercial entities,

© Springer Nature Switzerland AG 2020
S. Ofluoglu et al. (Eds.): EBF 2019, CCIS 1188, pp. 40–53, 2020.
https://doi.org/10.1007/978-3-030-42852-5_4

governments around the world are demanding and embracing BIM and it is very likely to see BIM as the core of governmental strategies for public construction and procurement projects in the near future [3]. On the other hand, BIM is being utilized on different project types such as building, infrastructure, industrial and natural resources projects. According to McGraw-Hill Construction (2014), the rate for the percentage of contractors that are using BIM on institutional projects (such as healthcare, education, religious) over 40% is 77% for the US and 62% for UK respectively. The construction companies have reported a positive Return on Investment (ROI) with the firmwide BIM implementation [4].

Keeping pace with the global developments regarding BIM, the adoption rate is also increasing in Turkey. As the local AEC industry provide a solid ground for BIM related R&D activities, the aim of this study is to evaluate the use of BIM in public projects in Turkey with a large-scale project. Cerrahpaşa Healthcare and Education project in Istanbul is selected as a case study. Focusing on the project design and development phases, task-specific benefits and challenges of BIM use are identified with real-world experience and project outcomes. In order to support the particular study scope, an in-depth literature review is provided focusing on BIM utilization in public projects and existing healthcare and education projects. Based on the case study findings, such advantages and potentials are discussed along with the future implications of BIM in public construction projects, particularly in large-scale healthcare and education facilities.

1.1 BIM in Public Projects

The use of BIM is drastically increasing all over the world. The use is even higher in developed countries and the implementation rates are catalyzed with the industrywide demand and legal requirements from the governmental initiatives. BIM standards are developed and released in the US and UK for the regulation of BIM use in the AEC operations. These standards and legislations are creating a BIM-rich AEC ecosystem as many public and private organizations have their own BIM guides. The interest for BIM can be considered very high in Northern European countries as BIM is implemented many public projects particularly in infrastructure projects. BIM is becoming a global language as it is perceived as the key methodology for increased efficiency between all project parties including large governmental organizations [6, 7]. As an example, the UK's construction strategy requires the use of "fully collaborative 3D BIM" in public projects and has mandated BIM adoption in government projects since 2016 [8, 9]. The European BIM Task Group has been founded and BIM is utilized in large construction projects like Deutsche Bahn's tunnel project in Germany, Grand Paris Express (GPE) metro project in Paris, and Cross Rail project which is the Europe's largest civil engineering project in the UK [10].

In Turkey, BIM adoption is in its early phases [11]. Nevertheless, the demand for BIM in local contracts is increasing specifically in public tenders. Some large public BIM projects are the railway projects which are tendered by İstanbul, İzmir and Kocaeli Metropolitan Municipalities which include more than 150 km railway projects [7]. Istanbul Grand Airport (IGA) is another private joint venture that implemented BIM for one of the largest airports in the world for Istanbul (New) Airport project. Although the project was not contracted as a BIM project, the contractor preferred to use BIM to increase coordination efficiency, reduce costs and facilitate productivity in on-site works [13].

The literature review also shows that BIM utilization in public projects is increasing. As the number of tendered public projects with BIM is increasing in the US, the UK and other European countries, Turkey is no different. Although Turkey is still at the initial stages of industry-wide adoption, there are numerous public projects which were tendered with specific BIM requirements. With the increases in productivity and substantial financial savings in public projects all over the world, it can be expected that BIM demand will increase in local public projects in the near future. With the reported benefits and added value, the public owners are more likely to demand BIM for large-scale public projects to achieve sustainable infrastructure, increase environmental adaptability, minimize construction costs and reduce the taxpayers' burden.

1.2   BIM in Healthcare and Education Projects

The use of BIM in large scale projects are considerably higher. As noted in previous sections the motivation comes from the substantial benefits both in design, construction and facility management phases. McGraw-Hill Construction report states that perceived BIM value by the large-scale US owners increased to 27% in the last five years [13]. Specifically, the use is even more in healthcare and educational facility projects. The need for hi-end engineering and design solutions in these types of projects can only be facilitated through BIM methods but the tasks necessitate organizational and professional know-how and technological capabilities. In order to understand the BIM-enabled transformation in the healthcare and education projects, the following studies were reviewed in detail.

According to Bryde, Broquetas and Volm study, BIM use in large scale projects returned various benefits. This study included 35 large scale projects as example cases including 7 healthcare and 6 education projects. The following Table 1 shows a summary of the healthcare facility projects. The healthcare and education cases were from the US and the UK. The completion dates of the projects are between 2007 and 2013. In this study, both positive benefits and negative issues in each case study were defined based on given success criteria such as coordination, scope, time, cost, quality and organization. According to the result, top positive benefits are (1) cost, (2) coordination and (3) time for healthcare and education projects. In this research, the negative issues reported relatively fewer and they were mainly related to hardware and software problems [14].

In a similar research, Khanzode et al. posited the following benefits of the Virtual Design and Construction (VDC) methods in CMG Medical Office Building project: (1) less rework, (2) labor savings, (3) improved safety performance, (4) less conflicts for installation, (5) accurate as-built model for facility management, (5) time and cost-savings [15]. The authors emphasized that the successful MEP coordination processes during the project were made possible with BIM although the project was highly challenging in terms of technical complexity.

According to McGraw Hill Construction report (2012) focusing on owners' perception towards BIM, healthcare facilities were reported as the complex design and

Table 1. Healthcare and education BIM project examples from the study which was conducted by Bryde, Broquetas and Volm [14]

Project name	City	Country	Size	Type
ESEAN Children's Hospital	Nantes	France	7.000 m^2	Healthcare
CMG Medical Office Building	Mountain View, CA	US	23.000 m^2	Healthcare
Palomar Medical Centre West	Escondido, CA	US	69.000 m^2	Healthcare
St Helens and Knowsley PFI	Merseyside	UK	120.000 m^2	Healthcare
Expeditionary Hospital		Middle East	8.920 m^2	Healthcare
St Joseph Mission Hospital	Orange, CA	US		Healthcare
Sutter Health Medical Centre	Castro Valley, CA	US		Healthcare
Springfield Literacy Centre	Springfield, PA	US	4.600 m^2	Education
Dickinson School of Law	Old Main	US	10.500 m^2	Education
School of Cinematic Art	Los Angeles, CA	US	12.700 m^2	Education
Texas A&M Health Science Centre	Bryan, TX	US	24.000 m^2	Education
University Campus Suffolk	Ipswich	UK	10.500 m^2	Education
Cascadia Centre	Bothell, WA	US	5.000 m^2	Education

construction projects in which the highest value is obtained from BIM. As an example, one of the largest healthcare institutions in the US; Kaise-Permanente Healthcare Consortium took advantage of using BIM throughout the entire building life cycle. The BIM use not only included the expected planning and construction phases but also building operation and maintenance tasks. Kaise-Permanents's suggestion to other owners is the participation of all stakeholders in a BIM-centric project from the planning stage to the maintenance and operational phases of the facility in a seamless fashion [13].

The research studies in the literature clearly show the existence of significant benefits of BIM use in healthcare and education projects. These include such upstream improvements like better interdisciplinary coordination, effective building systems and detail development and precise cost control with data-driven estimations and value engineering. In addition, downstream benefits are equally important as healthcare facilities need multi-faceted operations and maintenance activities due to their spatial, functional and bio-sensitive/hazardous content.

2   Cerrahpaşa Healthcare and Education Facility Project

In order to evaluate and explore the potentials of BIM use in the local AEC context in Turkey, a large-scale healthcare and education facility project is selected as a comprehensive case study. This case study includes specific phases and BIM-enabled tasks regarding the design of the project. The following sections cover the details of the Cerrahpaşa Healthcare and Education Facility and the use of BIM in the various design development stages.

2.1   About the Project

Istanbul University, Cerrahpaşa Faculty of Medicine was established in 1827 at Vezneciler district and continued education in different buildings until 1911. After 1911 the school was moved to its main campus location at Cerrahpaşa, Istanbul. During the 100-year period, numerous small size buildings were constructed at this campus for meeting the new needs. The campus was composed of many disconnected buildings serving approximately 3000 students and more than 2000 patients.

In the year 2010, the design of a new campus became a necessity to provide adequate healthcare services and state-of-the-art medical education. Aligned with the current approaches for modern healthcare facilities the main design concept was based on one single building composed of all specialized units. This core design decision was expected to centralize common services and connected sub-systems also offer specific space needs for each clinic/treatment unit. The facility was planned as a large-scale public hospital and a medical school which were separated on the campus site layout. This provided the functional division of educational facilities, student spaces and healthcare services that are accessible to different user groups.

Campus area was given as approximately 110.000 m^2. Requirements for the new hospital project were 1100 patient bed capacity, 44 operating rooms, 164 intensive care units, 3000 outpatient capacity, ER areas and a closed parking lot for 2000 cars. Educational areas were planned for 450 academic staff and 3000 students. The project also included a medical library, various research laboratories, student dormitories for 520 students and housing units for 160 nurses. Construction area of the healthcare units was 358.000 m^2 and the educational part was 258.000 m^2. The design work was carried out by two different design teams.

The project was awarded by Istanbul University. Prota Engineering was chosen as the design subcontractor of the project as the firm has over thirty years of experience in engineering and architectural design. Although there was no contractual obligation for BIM use, it was Prota's choice to implement BIM as it would be very difficult to coordinate this large-scale project with conventional methods. The design responsibilities included the necessary use of BIM for the coordination of the Mechanical/Electrical and Plumbing (MEP) infrastructure in this highly complicated structure in terms of multi-layered building systems for healthcare facilities. The project owner Istanbul University Directorate of Construction and Technical Works supported BIM use and embraced BIM methods as a strategy for construction projects in the future. After this project BIM requirement was added to the construction technical specifications and it is expected that BIM use may also in the operation phase since the owner has previous experience in building operations and challenges in FM tasks.

2.2 BIM Uses in the Project

Cerrahpaşa Healthcare and Education Facility was composed of two large-scale structures. Along with the architectural design; the mechanical, electrical and plumbing solutions required intensive coordination among the project stakeholders. During the design phase, the following procedures included the wide-range use of BIM: (1) Design authoring, (2) visualization, (3) 3D coordination and (4) interdisciplinary collaboration. During the design phase, the following BIM uses were conducted: (1) Design Authoring, (2) visualization, (3) 3D coordination and (4) collaboration.

Design Authoring
All disciplines create their three-dimensional BIM models in the digital environment with the help of object-oriented BIM design authoring software. Three-dimensional models help better understanding, control and quality. It also provides true collaboration between parties [16]. Autodesk Revit® 2018 was used as a design authoring tool in this project.

Aligned with the best practices in the academic and professional literature, the main objective was to create a robust BIM model for interdisciplinary coordination. These 3D BIM models facilitate better understanding and development of building systems and facilitate true collaboration between project parties [16]. Based on these premises Autodesk Revit® 2018 was used as a design authoring tool in this project. Since the project was not awarded with the BIM requirement, only the architectural team created three-dimensional models at the initial stage of this project (Figs. 1 and 2). All design activities such as architectural design and interior design were carried out using the BIM platform.

During the design phase, Dynamo® was used by the BIM coordination team in order to optimize the design process and eliminate repetitive works. Various algorithmic procedures were created for specific tasks such as interior design development. The architectural team identified the finish materials for the walls, floor and ceiling in each room. This data was embedded as a key schedule in Revit®. With the help of Dynamo, the walls and floors objects were automatically added into the model based on the data in the key schedule. The team leader stated that it would take more than a week for a building block, but it was completed in three days with the help of computational methods through BIM. Dynamo was also used for auto-numbering of structural members such as columns, beams, structural walls and floors.

Architectural models were the basis for visualization and coordination tasks. However, the coordination of MEP systems in suspended ceilings and the technical rooms also required discipline-specific parametric models for mechanical and electrical teams. Revit models were also used by the electrical engineering team for lighting analysis. The team also used Dynamo for optimization and scheduling. Two-dimensional drawings were derived from the BIM models for each discipline. As expected, conventional documentation like plans, sections and elevations from the BIM models significantly decreased the dedicated time and effort. In addition, design revisions were rapidly transferred to the models and the layouts.

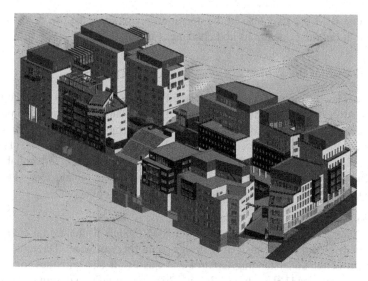

Fig. 1. Axonometric perspective of Cerrahpaşa healthcare and education facility

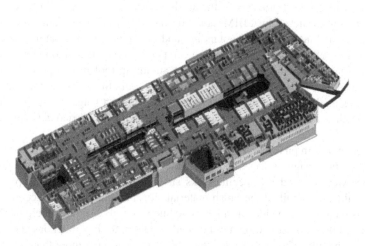

Fig. 2. Cerrahpaşa healthcare and education facility in 3D plan view

Since the facility management team had vast experience in hospital operations, the building operation phase was considered during design. The facility management parameters became as early design inputs. Some operational parameters were created such as component models, date of assembly, maintenance period, etc. The values of these parameters were devised to be defined after the completion of construction.

Visualization

According to Becerik and Kensek study which was conducted to identify the key BIM tasks in AEC projects; visualization was reported as the most common task. BIM users prefer visualization, rendering, 3D model presentation, walk-through analysis for better decision making during design [1]. In order to comprehend spatial environment and building systems, novel visualization technologies are being used such as Virtual Reality (VR), Augmented Reality, Immersive Virtual Environment (IVEs). These technologies help project participants to experience a virtual version of the designed environment and interact with the digital building objects in real-time. Different than conventional visualization purposes, these methods provide better interdisciplinary coordination with the synchronous visualization of multiple building sub-systems models [17].

Parallel to this trend, the use of high-end visualization methods in Cerrahpaşa project increased user involvement and improved the efficiency of the design process. The design team used VR technology to explore the impact of given design decisions and improve the design process. Oculus Rift and HTC Vive headsets were used as a wearable mobile VR devices and Autodesk Revit Live® was used for VR rendering (Fig. 3).

Fig. 3. VR experience

The use of immersive VR technology facilitated the end-user (for example doctors and faculty members) involvement in the project. Decision-making was quicker and effective design decisions were made with the increased cooperation levels. The cloud-based renderings were used for interior design. Stereo panorama renders (360°) significantly helped to explain the design decisions to the owner, academic staff and the hospital management team. The VR system was also available to anyone who was interested in the project. The QR code which is generated by cloud rendering was shared via web page. With this VR feature, the students, faculty members and even the patients had the opportunity to reach a visualization model of the hospital (Fig. 4).

Fig. 4. Lecturer's office render view

3D Coordination

BIM provides parametric building models and system components which catalyze 3D coordination. It helps to detect the system clashes and integrates the entire project team in clash resolution workflows to quickly identify and resolve problems between project parties. This significantly reduces construction costs as the errors are already solved at the design stage [6, 16].

In Cerrahpaşa Healthcare and Education Facility Project, the use of BIM provided better coordination between project stakeholders and contributed to the multidisciplinary coordination process to a considerable extent. Since the project was a healthcare facility, the mechanical, electrical and plumbing layers were highly complex along with the hospital and laboratory-specific sub-systems. At the initial stages of design, only the architectural team was using 3D BIM models without model exchange with engineering teams. As the design progressed, architectural, structural and MEP coordination problems became crucial for the project. In order to solve the coordination problems, mechanical and electrical teams started to work with 3D BIM models for complex spaces in terms of MEP installations (Figs. 5 and 6).

Autodesk Navisworks® 2018 was used as the BIM coordination platform. Coordination meetings were held with 3D BIM models. With the help of 3D BIM models and simultaneous feedback from the project stakeholders, the decision making became more effective without time losses. BIM coordination team detected clashes with the help of clash detection software. These clashes were eliminated by design teams and it was expected to reduce the number of conflicts that would be encountered on the construction site. These clash detections were in paramount importance since the MEP complexity of the project could cause a lot of system clashes during the construction stages which would dramatically increase the costs and the RFI's from the job site. Elimination of those clashes were beneficial to the potential contractor and more to the project owner as they were resolved in the early stages of design without too much effort, resources and time delays.

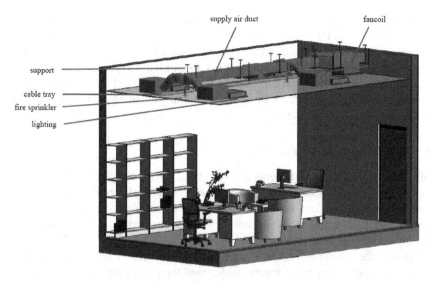

Fig. 5. 3D coordination in a suspended ceiling.

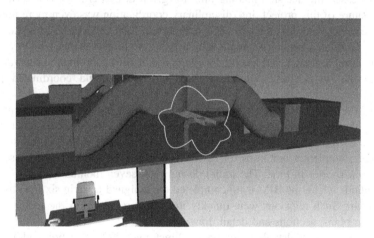

Fig. 6. Clash detection in Navisworks® 2018

Collaboration

In BIM-enabled projects, the success of the project depends on the collaboration of all disciplines. In order to facilitate better collaboration between parties a common data management platform is required. The Common Data Environment (CDE) is a platform for collecting, sharing and managing the project information.

Prota generated the design alternatives in three different offices; Ankara (head office), İstanbul and İzmir. The data exchange between architectural teams was made possible using Autodesk BIM 360 Docs. The use of this CDE tool increased the efficiency between team members, improved process quality and coordination. The owner also had access to the CDE environment including process BIM models and all documentation. This made all project data available to all stakeholders anytime and anywhere since the CDE was a web-based cloud platform. The coordination meetings were enhanced with the collective assessment of the latest BIM models and project documentation. The CDE platform enabled the instant access to the project and building object properties with a user-friendly model viewer. This front-end interface was also beneficial to communicate the project with the non-technical project stakeholders without any BIM literacy.

2.3   BIM Benefits and Future Works

While there were significant benefits from the BIM use for all stakeholders, there were also process specific benefits for the different project task groups. The significant benefits for the design firm were (1) reductions in design decision times, (2) interdisciplinary coordination and clash elimination and (3) time savings in the schedule due to rapid and consistent project documentation.

Since all the project stakeholders were not BIM capable, it was a challenging task to ensure that all participants correctly understand the project for decision making. 3D visualization made the project more legible and comprehensible for any participant which decreased the decision-making time for given design criteria. Due to the complicated nature of this project, interdisciplinary coordination was even more important and the necessary coordination was achieved through BIM methods. BIM collaboration tools also facilitated better communication among the project teams. The system clashes were also eliminated and resolved with the use of BIM coordination software. This shortened the whole design duration with more robust and coordinated project documents.

All of the design works of the project were carried out by two different design groups. Although Prota carried out the project with BIM, the other designer did not implement BIM during the design stage. For this reason, there were different schedules and project completion durations for each design team. BIM-enabled processes comparably took shorter in time. The initial design took seven months with conventional CAD methods where the BIM team completed the assigned tasks in six months with a smaller team. Such revisions were quickly made and reflected on the required deliverables like plans, sections and detail drawings.

The project owner, Istanbul University Directorate of Construction and Technical Works supported the BIM process at the beginning of the project. From the perspective of the owner, the most significant benefit was increased legibility of the project and shorter decision times for the project parties. The design process was revised according to the expert feedback from the university and the hospital management. 3D BIM models and immersive VR technology helped the university and hospital staff to better understand the concept and make the important decisions at the right stage.

The following Table 2 shows the relationships between benefits and BIM use in the project. The shorter decision making periods was an outcome of in-depth visualization and interdisciplinary collaboration. Interdisciplinary coordination and clash elimination were sourced from design authoring with BIM tools and 3D coordination process. Reduction of the project duration is a result of design authoring with the help of parametric design BIM tools. Finally, the increased project legibility was an outcome of immersive VR technology using BIM models.

Table 2. The BIM uses and outcome benefits in the project

#	BIM benefit	BIM uses			
		Design authoring	Visualization	3D coordination	Collaboration
1	Reducing decision time		✓		✓
2	Interdisciplinary coordination and clash elimination	✓		✓	
3	Shortening of project design duration	✓			
4	Increased project understanding		✓		

Relying on the project experience the owner created strategic plans to include BIM in the construction and operation phases of the project. Istanbul University Directorate of Construction and Technical Works added BIM requirements to the organizational construction technical specifications. As the owner's objective was to reduce the cost of the project by utilizing BIM in the construction phase, the expectations were also extended to use the BIM during operation and maintenance phases to control lifecycle costs.

3 Conclusions

BIM use is currently increasing in large-scale public projects in the world. Although Turkey is at the initial stage, there are numerous public projects which were tendered with contractual BIM requirements. Since the benefits and productivity increases from BIM are evident with documented case studies, these gains motivate both public and private owners to use BIM in their projects as well. BIM use is even more popular in healthcare and education facilities. Based on the recent works in the literature, BIM benefits for healthcare and education projects can be listed as (1) cost, (2) coordination and (3) time. Additional value gains are also summarized as (1) less rework, (2) labor savings, (3) improved safety performance, (4) less conflicts for installation, (5) accurate as-built model for facility management, (5) time and cost-savings.

In this chapter, Cerrahpaşa Healthcare and Education Facility selected as a case study. It is a 110.000 m² public project which was composed of a full-fledged hospital and a medical school. In this case study, BIM implementation in a large-scale public project was examined to reveal the BIM benefits along with experienced challenges. Findings from the case study were aligned with the literature in terms of gained benefits and added-value for the owner and the project parties. The developed BIM framework was effective and also became adaptable for future projects. Both time savings, better project control, interdisciplinary coordination were important but the critical project experience turned to BIM know-how both for the project teams and the public owner. Additional studies on this particular project is a possibility for further evaluation of BIM and its impact on the lifecycle performance and operational efficacy.

Cerrahpaşa Healthcare and Education Facility clearly demonstrates the potentials of BIM in complex construction projects in the Turkish AEC context. The case study also showed that the owner involvement is the key to success, increased productivity and added-value. Apart from the mentioned benefits, the case is fairly representative as a well-defined sample for the public projects in Turkey. Both the project contract and content were aligned with the local business schemes and procurement methods along with a special project setting for BIM implementation. Similar project processes and settings may also attract more public and private owners to demand BIM use and tailored delivery methods. With the increase in BIM projects in the local AEC market, it may be expected that BIM know-how will become a vital business asset for Turkish AEC firms.

Acknowledgments. We would like to express our special thanks to Istanbul University Directorate of Construction and Technical Works and Prota Engineering Design Center for their contributions.

References

1. Becerik-Gerber, B., Kensek, K.: Building information modeling in architecture, engineering, and construction: emerging research directions and trends. J. Prof. Issues Eng. Educ. Pract. **136**(3), 139–147 (2010). https://doi.org/10.1061/(asce)ei.1943-5541.0000023
2. NBIMS - National BIM Standard: National Institute of Building Sciences, United States™ Version 2 (2012)
3. Mordue, S., Swaddle, P., Philp, D.: Building Information Modeling for Dummies. Wiley, Hoboken (2016)
4. McGraw-Hill Construction: The business value of BIM for construction in major global markets: how contractors around the world are driving innovation with building information modeling. SmartMarket Report, p. 64 (2014)
5. Underwood, J., Isikdag, U.: Emerging technologies for BIM 2.0. Constr. Innov. **11**(3), 252–258 (2011)
6. Dodge Data & Analytics: SmartMarket report: the business value of BIM for infrastructure, pp. 1–68 (2017)
7. Oktem, S., Akcamete A., Ergen, E.: BIM implementation in infrastructure projects: benefits and challenges. In: 5th International Project and Construction Management Conference (IPCMC 2018), 16–18 November, North Cyprus, pp. 1–9 (2018)
8. Cabinet Office, H.: Government Construction Strategy. Constr. **96**(May), 43 (2011)
9. Hayne, G., Kumar, B.: BIM capability audit of contracting-based organizations. Int. J. 3-D Inf. Model. **5**(4), 12–24 (2016). https://doi.org/10.4018/ij3dim.2016100102
10. EUBIM Task Group: Handbook for the Introduction of Building Information Modelling by the European Public Sector. BIM, P. 84 (2016)
11. Oktem, S., Ergen, E.: Towards developing building information modeling (BIM) guide and execution plan template for Turkish construction sector. In: 12th International Congress on Advances in Civil Engineering (ACE 2016), 21–23 September, pp. 1–8 (2016)

12. Autodesk Istanbul Grand Airport. https://www.autodesk.com/solutions/bim/hub/iga-istanbul-grand-airport. Accessed 03 May 2019
13. McGraw-Hill Construction: The Business Value of BIM for Infrastructure, pp. 1–64. BIM-Infra (2012)
14. Bryde, D., Broquetas, M., Volm, J.M.: The project benefits of building information modelling (BIM). Int. J. Proj. Manag. **31**(7), 971–980 (2013)
15. Khanzode, A., Fischer, M., Reed, D.: Virtual design and construction (VDC) technologies for coordination of mechanical, electrical, and plumbing (MEP) systems on a large healthcare project. J. Inf. Technol. Constr. (ITcon) **13**, 324–342 (2008). Special issue: case studies of BIM use
16. The Computer Integrated Construction Research Program: BIM project execution planning guide. Version 2.1 (2011)
17. Heydarian, A., Carneiro, J.P., Gerber, D., Becerik-Gerber, B., Hayes, T., Wood, W.: Immersive virtual environments versus physical built environments: a benchmarking study for building design and user-built environment explorations. Autom. Constr. **54**, 116–126 (2015)

BIM for Project Management

4D and 5D BIM: A System for Automation of Planning and Integrated Cost Management

Uğur Çelik[(✉)]

EMAY International Engineering and Consultancy Inc., İstanbul 34662, Turkey
ugur.celik@emay.com

Abstract. The construction sector has difficulty in catching the rapidly developing technology era. While the sectors are rapidly adapting themselves to the new era, firms that do not invest in innovation lose their value at a fast pace. When we look at the Fortune 500 list, it is seen that the biggest leap is made by companies in the IT sector. However, the situation is observed to be the opposite for construction companies. Despite the enormous investment costs and the huge risks involved, construction companies are unable to compete with the leaders of the digital world and falling down in the list. The losses of time and cost are increasing in the construction sector which lags behind in the digitizing world. The systematic analysis of these losses with analytical methods remains limited and there are problems in project management approaches. The industry today invests into digital transformation with Building Information Modeling (BIM) to deal with these problems in the construction sector and to produce a solution according to their dynamics in the digital world. BIM is the digital twin model of actual construction consisting of data-rich 3D objects. Accurate management of a data-rich model is possible with data management techniques. In order to fully benefit from this digital reflection of construction projects, the sector needs to establish processes based on basic theories of digital data management. This study is designed to provide a methodology in which the BIM 4D and 5D processes are handled as integrated and business intelligence approaches. While approaching Information Modeling from Building perspective, some basic approaches to data science have been integrated with 4D and 5D processes. The main objective of the study is to contribute to the digitalization process and to present a proposal for the application of the business intelligence in BIM processes.

Keywords: 4D and 5D BIM · Business intelligence · Automation of construction

1 Introduction

The project-based and fragmented structure of the construction industry brings many problems and risks in project and cost management as in every field. In terms of the project management, variable conditions cause big problems between contractors and employers in the process from tender stage to the end of the project. Although the speed of advancing technology is very fast, the studies on the solution of the problems in the construction sector with technological developments have not been widespread

© Springer Nature Switzerland AG 2020
S. Ofluoglu et al. (Eds.): EBF 2019, CCIS 1188, pp. 57–69, 2020.
https://doi.org/10.1007/978-3-030-42852-5_5

enough yet. This has caused the sector to become a sick industry with continuous problems in the growing economy. Despite the high investment costs and high added value in the economy, the construction sector has remained as a sector that has not yet completed its technological evolution in project management. The conservative approach prevents the progress of the sector and restrains the change and management of the work by professionals. While this understanding leads to an increase in time and cost losses in the projects, the irregularities and inconsistencies of the site records is an obstacle to the accurate measurement of losses. Besides the losses in the housing sector as a burden on the consumer with price increases, it is certain that the financial losses in public projects have resulted in a chain loss from the public to the smallest economic element. It has been seen many times that the problems experienced in the construction sector with high investment cost led the states to great economic crises.

With developing technology, all sectors are evolving rapidly. However, the construction sector is resisting to abandon conventional methods. According to McKinsey's research, the construction sector was the least developed sector in digitalization after agriculture and livestock [1]. The heavy loss caused by this inability to digitization was examined in detail by KPMG. Research shows that most of the time and cost losses come from the problems experienced in the design/planning processes [2]. In another study, it was shown that the driving forces for innovation were efficiency, planning and cost reduction [3]. The specific challenges of the construction sector prevent digitization and new ways of thinking and studies have been conducted to increase productivity. In the development of these new ways of thinking and working, it is not possible to change the habits of the sector suddenly. For this reason, it would be useful to produce solutions that are similar to traditional methods in the transition process, which can be easily adapted by practitioners.

It can be said that the best way to solve the challenges facing the industry is digital transformation. The main starting point for this transformation can be Building Information Modeling. BIM is a digital representation of the products and processes of construction in the project lifecycle. BIM, which includes 3D models of the project as the core components; also enables project simulation which contains all the necessary information in the planning, design, construction or operation phases of the project. The simulated 3D model consists of intelligent and data-rich objects. These smart objects are part of a process that allows the right people to reach accurate data at the right time. The integration of all these objects and data actually forms a database of the construction. This database created during the design is an excellent platform for project management with the information added during the construction phase. This database, which was created during design, is an excellent platform for project management with the information added during the construction phase. This platform feeds the data warehouses that are suitable for analytical work and creates an inseparable process with all stages of the project, which can be evaluated according to project forecasts, plans and different scenarios. The analysis of these data by machine learning and artificial intelligence will require the combination of the information developed with the design and construction, and the data collected from the sensors during the operation phase [4].

Data warehouse created in BIM processes is a platform where the data received from the asset information models (AIM) and project information models (PIM) stored, including the design and construction of new assets, the renewal of existing assets, the operation and maintenance of an asset, and the structured repositories of the information required to make decisions throughout the entire life cycle of the asset. As stated in BS EN ISO 19650-2:2018, in BIM, which requires an integrated approach, the methodology should be designed from the first phase of the project to the end of the project's life cycle and the management of the information should be defined [6]. The fact that this integrated design is considered as a comprehensive and complex work from design to construction, even after the operation, and the avoidance of the practitioners from this working style is very common in the construction sector as professionals do not make long-term plans. The inclusion of different stakeholders in the process and the cultural differences of the firms distract the construction sector from standardization. However, it should be noted that there are also processes that can be adopted in the traditional way and integrated with BIM. In particular, publicly funded projects have certain procedures and principles. At this point, designing the processes through BIM and the way in which the project management can stream data to these procedures will provide useful solutions.

Research shows that project offices are progressing rapidly in 3D modelling [7]. However, it is accepted that the practices towards the construction cannot progress at the same pace and using traditional approaches which cannot be changed. In this study, the method which is designed to integrate traditional project management and BIM processes in cost and time management has been explained. This study aims to contribute to the digitalization of the construction sector.

2 Definitions

2.1 5D Cost Management

Model-based cost estimation (5D) provides fast and reliable access to current quantity data it also helps in easily determining the cost changes created by different design alternatives. It is certain that not only for budget estimate purposes but also with parameters defined in smart objects, it is of a great benefit as a method in which progress and money flows can be tracked. Another point to be emphasized is that this benefit is the effect of BIM on all disciplines and all stakeholders due to its nature.

These factors are the strengths of 5D BIM activities against traditional processes. However, the inability to model all construction processes in 5D brings the requirement to continue with 2D drawings to achieve a precise cost estimate. It should be noted that 5D is defined not only as a model-based cost analysis, but also as a Cost-Living Plan where costs are considered integrated [10]. Where cost and time data are evaluated together, critical analyses can be made about the overall project and these analyses will become a digital resource for future work with technologies such as machine learning.

2.2   Work Breakdown Structure

WBS was first developed the formula used to determine the tasks and predict the required effort for a results-oriented project known as the PERT (program evaluation and review technique) by the project team due to the fact that the US Navy lagged behind the ballistic missile program [11]. In the following stages, the PMI (Project Management Institute) has incorporated the term "Work Breakdown Structure" down into business analysis structures for non-military implementation for corporate and other organizational projects. [12] WBS can be defined as a "deliverable orientated" and "hierarchical decomposition of the work" to be carried out to achieve the project objectives [13].

The WBS scheme created varies with the sector and the specific business. However, it should basically represent the overall scope of the project. The WBS level of detail should be determined according to the details requested in the project management. It is important for the specified WBSs to be facilitators in the cost and planning management and to be understood by the project staff in effective project management. The proper design of WBSs will enable the project to analyse the cost, time and construction processes in an excellent manner.

2.3   Business Intelligence

The path from data to information is indicated by the DIKW (Data, Information, Knowledge and Wisdom) hierarchy [14]. *Rowley* defines this process as "data can be used to create information; information can be used to create knowledge, and knowledge can be used to create wisdom" [15]. The basic components of the DIKW hierarchy must be correctly identified and understood in the development of an information system [16]. Information systems are used in multidimensional analysis and synthesis of all activities of a project or organization [16]. Business intelligence systems combine data from different information systems with multidimensional analysis for decision-makers and summarize and ensure that decisions and related reports are generated. Thanks to business intelligence systems, it is provided that the risks are reduced, and the processes of the firm or project are optimized. A data warehouse consisting of various databases is needed to provide this benefit. The data warehouse can be defined as the approach that allows the data from the databases to be converted into information by context queries for analysis and synthesis, and to allow time-based multidimensional inferences from different databases [14, 16]. Data kept in data warehouses are updated from databases in certain periods. While the dynamic structure of construction projects reduces the period of a data warehouse, it is expected that this period will increase in the data warehouse system consisting of data warehouses in different projects of a construction company (Fig. 1).

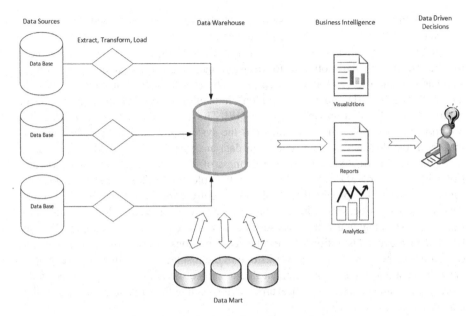

Fig. 1. A basic data warehouse schema

Data in data warehouses can be integrated into different software for graphical analysis, reporting or statistical analysis. Decision-makers can refer to these sources to identify problems at different times. While these decisions may be operational in terms of the project, there may be long-term critical decisions that will change a firm's business approach.

3   Methodology

3.1   Fundamentals of the Methodology

BIM software with 5D support developed by different companies helps in the digitization of cost analysis. Different solutions can be offered according to the selected software. However, the adoption of 5D processes by project staff is much more important than the solutions offered by the software. 3D models created with different software can be imported with the data, work program software and can work with the database to work with are points to take into consideration in the selection of software. The ability of the selected software to be exported directly to the extensions of Excel, which is the most commonly used tool of traditional project management, or to support CSV and XML formats, will facilitate data transfer.

Another important issue in data transfer is that the input can reach the exit point without any intervention. The most basic way to achieve this is that the data should contain a unique key that can be recognized by all software. Correct identification of the data transfer path; will ensure that the right information reaches the right person at the right time.

The identification of the process of transformation of the collected data into the information will make the transferred data meaningful. It is an undisputed fact that the contribution of data that is not transformed into knowledge into project management will be limited. The data collected for decision-making purposes should be organized, summarized, analysed and synthesized [16]. The transformation of multidimensional data collected by "4D and 5D integration" into information will make a significant contribution to decision-making processes [17]. The decision support system (Decision Support System-DSS), which is defined as the system providing support to decision-makers in the decision-making process in data analysis, can be a BIM based system when managed correctly. Not only the richness of data but also the visualization and simulable nature of 3D models strengthen the role of the 3D model in a decision support system. This proves that BIMs are visually enriched databases that support decision-making processes. The database created by 3D models allows multidimensional analysis integrated with databases of different disciplines. For example, DSS can be used to prevent disruption of the other constructions affected by the loss of time caused by the belated excavation works due to the displacements. In another example, the extra cost and time-out assessment due to project revision can be analysed much more quickly, and in the future, measures can be taken in the early stages for issues that may cause controversy (Fig. 2).

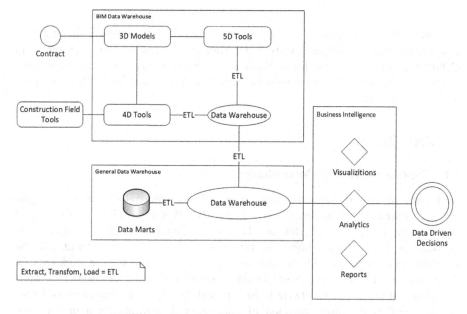

Fig. 2. Data warehouse workflow diagram

Problems in data collection cause serious losses in the construction sector. Irregular and non-updated data does not contribute to the decision support system and may even cause decision-makers to make errors. Choosing the right and available data transmission path will keep the database updated. The labour/human-oriented structure of construction projects prevents full automation. One of the problems faced by the sector is the lack of adoption of innovative approaches by staff and the difficult change of corporate culture [18]. For this reason, another issue to be considered within the scope of this study is the determination of the data transmission path that the site personnel can adapt and integrate this process into classical methods easily. In the project-specific forms, only the WBS codes of the objects are added automatically from the database, and the data produced without distortion of the traditional form.

The project-based fragmented structure in the construction sector hinders standardization in project management [19]. There is also a similar situation in the WBS structure and although there are certain standards, there are changes according to the project. Therefore, no standard has been used for WBSs in the methodology and it is considered to be within the basic principles specified in the PMI. The basic expectation in WBS structure is that it reflects the constructions that are based on payment in a suitable breakdown; WBS codes are suitable for cost codes; designed to be convenient for facility management and to be easily understood by all employees.

The basis of the data flow and analytics for 4D and 5D integration, which is the main purpose of the study, is explained in this section. Considering the data warehouse as a database where the 4D and 5D information is stored will not be sufficient for process management. This approach only provides monitoring of extra cost and delays. However, data warehouses must be multi-dimensional data systems that should be evaluated under the causality principle and support decision-makers [20]. If all the processes of construction can be stored in the same data warehouse, this would enable the determination of the real causes of the problems experienced in the projects and would help in finding solutions. In addition, this data warehouses will be able to stay alive until the destruction of the building if they are also utilized for FM operations.

3.2   Practical Aspect of the Implementation

Process Schema
This section describes the practical implementation of BIM tools and Database tools in a local project.

Integration of WBS Schema to Navisworks Quantification
In the local project the Navisworks *Quantification* tool was used for cost control. The construction procedures, unit prices and calculation methods defined in the unit price descriptions of each item are integrated with the data obtained from the relevant model and the cost analyses are made quickly and easily [21]. At this stage, the equations based on the method described in the unit price description are defined in the resource catalogue.

In order to identify the WBS scheme in the Navisworks *Quantification* tool, the appropriate XML scheme was used. Visual Studio is used to add codes and definitions specific to the project. In the maintained resource catalogue, new parameter columns were defined according to the needs of the project. These columns were 2D quantity survey, construction progress information, total cost and start-end date of construction. It is possible to increase or revise columns specific to the project.

XML can be easily understood by the practitioners with its simple structure and provides the easy applicability requirement that lies at the basis of the methodology. It is also possible to modify the structure of the project, which allows the addition of new codes and columns.

Linking 3D Elements and WBS Code

The model takeoff feature in the *Quantification* tool is used for 3D modelled objects. In order to match the objects with the *Quantification* tool, sets were created according to the codes. The created sets were assigned to WBS sub-breakdown with *Quantification* Model takeoff feature [22]. At this stage, the program automatically creates WBS code for each 3D object. These WBSs together with the Globally Unique Identifier (GUID) will form the identity of each object in the process.

The status feature within the *Quantification* tool is helpful for any revisions of the model. It warns when the object is deleted, replaced, or changed in *Quantification* [23]. The problem of detecting new objects, i.e. another disadvantage of revisions, is solved by the dynamic structure of the Navisworks set system. In the case of revision, set sources will not change and update of the budget estimation will be automated.

Another problem encountered in the 5D process is that the 3D model of some objects cannot be generated. This may be caused by the contract as well as in some cases that 3D model of construction cannot be provided by the design team. For example, the absence of rebar models in reinforced concrete objects is frequently encountered. For the solution of this problem, the values calculated by the traditional method are entered as a parameter to the 3D objects.

The Virtual Takeoff feature of the *Quantification* tool has been used for constructions or payments that cannot be connected to the 3D model [24]. Virtual takeoff is creating viewpoint and sub-breakdown bound to an upper-level breakdown in the catalogue. The value calculated by the traditional method is entered into the parameters 2D budget estimation. In this way, it is possible to follow a single database which is the basis of the methodology. At the end of this phase, WBS code is assigned for each object and budget estimation is calculated. With Excel export, new data has been brought into the format that can be transferred to other software and the first part of organizing the data is completed.

5D: Integration of Cost with 4D

At this stage, the connection between 4D and 5D is established. The WBS code for each object, whose unique ID is identified, is assigned to the object associated with the Navisworks Data Tools. Data Tools allows data to be assigned to objects from the database by defining certain rules and creating new parameter groups. The Globally Unique Identifier (GUID), which the program recognizes as a data ID, is used in the assignment process. With the unique and constant identity, GUID, the error-free transfer of the data is ensured [25]. The GUID, which Industry Foundation Classes (IFC) takes as basic identity, is widely used in operational phases.

The data organized in Excel format is summarized and imported into Ms Project in CSV format. Schedule has been created in Navisworks TimeLiner and after the creation of the schedule, the 5D WBS codes are assigned to the objects as a description through the GUID of each object. The draft schedule exported from Navisworks is detailed in Ms Project. For works that cannot be connected to a 3D object, virtual takeoffs have been created in the *Quantification* tool. In line with the weekly schedules, the identification of new constructions in the *Quantification* tool was used in the preparation of the cash flow and construction control forms.

The Data Warehouse

The fact that 3D models are digital twin of construction will strengthen their usability as a good resource for good planning and budget estimation. In this way, problems encountered during construction are analysed and planned project management can be maintained. Although the top-down data warehouse design process is considered more suitable for construction projects, the dynamic structure of construction projects and the structure affected by a variety of factors also require data marts. For this reason, a hybrid approach was adopted and the 4D/5D data warehouse was designed top-down, and integrated into a business intelligence software, where all of the data warehouses created for multi-dimensional data analysis can be connected.

The excel file, which is exported with the Navisworks *Quantification* tool, is a database that feeds into the data warehouse. This database with WBS code, GUID, 3D object properties is linked to Ms Access, which is used to create the data warehouse. In order to integrate the construction times of objects, the schedule prepared in the Navisworks TimeLiner was exported and linked to Ms Access. At this stage, the queries for the project needs are prepared in the SQL query language. SQL queries are used for linking common parameters of the same objects from a different database [16]. For a multidimensional analysis, time and cost parameters are interconnected in the data warehouse.

The data in the connected databases were used in the preparation of the site forms with the Ms Access forms tool. The Ms Access forms tool has a structure that can be used to extract the desired data in a certain format from the database and to export them in different formats [26]. From the database, WBS code, 3D object properties and scheduled construction time according to the work schedule were placed in the form. The unique IDs of the prepared forms were selected the same as the GUID; in this way, a common ID with 3D objects is provided. It is foreseen that the related forms of the work to be carried out weekly will be assigned to the site engineer as a duty in line with the work program. After completion of the construction, the information in the completed forms can be automatically linked to the relevant columns in the tables of the database.

The way in which the data coming from the site can be changed in terms of the project. What is important here is that the data comes from a database that can connect to the Ms Access data warehouse. Within the scope of this study, PYP, which is used by EMAY Engineering as site tracking software can import the generated forms, assign/follow the task and export its data in CSV format. PYP data is stored in the company's database and there was active data flow from all projects of the company.

Transfer of the Data: Database and Date Warehouse Integration

The seamless and simple transfer of data between different software is the most important part of the methodology. This transfer mechanism should be defined in a plain way and the stages should be automated. This chapter summarizes the general data transfer process described in the methodology. CSV and .xlsx formats where all software has the ability to import and export are preferred as the transfer format. Another important point of the data transfer path is where to store the data. In this methodology, the data is stored in a document management system.

The widespread use of Excel in the construction industry has enabled the transfer format to be easily implemented without extra cost. The data sets created in 3D objects (available in metadata) are the starting point of the process. The WBS codes of 3D object-based constructions and non-object-based constructions defined within the *Quantification* tool are the visible part of the transfer structure and the integration of the programs is provided by GUIDs. The constant nature of GUIDs will ensure that they are not only available for the construction phase, but also in the operational phase. The .xlsx file that is exported from the *Quantification* tool and the CSV file exported from MS Project was linked to Access.

Data cleansing is made with Access queries and connected data were generated according to the customized format. Instructions for, connecting to the data warehouse and match with their GUIDs of the edited data were provided. From this data, forms were created as described above and the connection of forms to the PYP system was made in CSV format.

Construction progress information is linked to the document management system from the PYP system. The system automatically updates the current data every time it is online. The same file is connected to the 3D model with Navisworks Data tools. The rule defined in Navisworks updates the progress information in each object according to the GUID in a new parameter group that was created. The percentage of progress generated in the *Quantification* catalogue, the construction date and the actual construction rate was updated with the parameters generated by the data tools in the *Quantification* tool. Similarly, 4D TimeLiner tool is connected to the same group of parameters and integration of construction date data is provided. Non-conformities encountered during construction in 3D objects are also added as parameters. In this way, a register has been created against future conflicts.

Business Intelligence: Analysis and Synthesis
Human beings cannot always visualize the information in their mind or fully establish the connections between them. Business intelligence tools help us to establish some links that we cannot recognize or detect [27]. In this study, Power BI is preferred as a business intelligence software. This cloud-enabled software is a query-based software that includes professional graphics tools. The multidimensional data generated is converted to visual graphics by connecting Power BI with Ms Access. These graphs are intended to be used for the analysis and synthesis of information in the data warehouse.

Data transformed into information were synthesized in two ways in Power BI. The first one is the progress reports prepared for the progress of the project. These reports are prepared in one format and the number of the reports increase as the project progresses. The aim of these reports is to give brief information to the decision-makers about the progress of the project.

The second way of synthesis is dynamic queries that are prepared to make forward-looking inferences based on insights about the project. These queries provides support for decision-makers and assist them to make critical decisions. Dynamic queries can vary specific to the project and project phase.

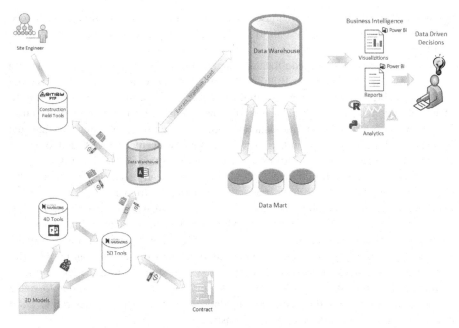

Fig. 3. Data warehouse workflow diagram with tools

4   Conclusion

Construction projects have difficult processes to analyse due to their complex structure and changing conditions specific to the project. Usually, project managers are making critical decisions by using analytical thinking skills developed through their experiences. However, delays in projects and cost increases indicate that decision-makers need a decision support system. In this respect, the digital twin provides a great benefit to the decision-makers with its visual power, multidisciplinary feature and data-rich structure. It is clear that a systematic approach is needed to increase this benefit. Considering the complex and dynamic nature of construction projects, the need for rapid decision-making and implementation of decisions at a fast pace is one of the biggest challenges. Another challenge is the multiplicity of factors that affect the projects. Although the effects are numerous, it is seen that cause-effect analysis is limited and far from the statistical approach.

In this study the data-rich 3D objects that form the basis of the study are used to create data transfer paths and to create project register. The process starting from the objects provides the follow-up of the progress of the project and the cause-effect analysis of the problems (Fig. 3).

Data warehouse and business intelligence approaches reinforce the holistic approach of the process. The different databases connected to the data warehouse provide the project data to be gathered in one place. The data synthesized in the data warehouse become available to use where a clean and simple management approach has been adopted. Construction data can be received digitally from the site and connect automatically with the data warehouse. Business intelligence applications have helped to create a decision support system to increase efficiency and to address project-wide problems.

The study aimed to provide data transfer and analysis methodology for moving from Information Modeling to Building Information Modeling. Data warehouse and business intelligence approaches are multi-dimensional analysis approaches. Multidimensional internal and external factors such as weather, displacement, worker numbers, non-conformities, economic data, and political events can be integrated into the business intelligence model. Furthermore, with the advancement in IoT technology, it is possible to receive live data from the site and to integrate it into the system.

With this approach, time-based analyses in projects can be carried out in a multi-dimensional manner and therefore, productivity is expected to increase. The analysis of the different design alternatives in terms of time and cost will be possible in a multi-dimensional manner to be integrated with other data from the databases. In addition, the adoption of this approach in all projects carried out by a construction firm will form the register of the company, increase the productivity in the work carried out by the firm, and generate resources for the decision support system starting from the tender phase. In the light of this study, further studies should be carried out in order to make statistical analyses with data collected in data warehouses and to determine good practices that will increase efficiency in construction projects.

References

1. https://www.mckinsey.com/industries/capital-projects-and-infrastructure/our-insights/imagining-constructions-digital-future, 04 March 2019
2. https://assets.kpmg/content/dam/kpmg/pdf/2016/04/smart-construction-report-2016.pdf, 04 March 2019
3. https://assets.kpmg/content/dam/kpmg/tr/pdf/2016/11/tr-global-construction-survey-2016.pdf, 21 April 2016
4. https://www.thenbs.com/knowledge/nbs-construction-technology-report-2019, 21 April 2019
5. The British Standards Institution: BS EN ISO 19650-1:2018 organization and digitization of information about buildings and civil engineering works, including building information modelling (BIM) - information management using building information modelling part 1: concepts and principles (2018)
6. The British Standards Institution: BS EN ISO 19650-2:2018 organization and digitization of information about buildings and civil engineering works, including building information modelling (BIM) - information management using building information modelling part 2: concepts and principles (2018)
7. https://www.thenbs.com/knowledge/the-national-bim-report-2018, 21 April 2019
8. The British Standards Institution: PAS 1192-2:2013 specification for information management for the capital/delivery phase of construction projects using building information modelling. Incorporating Corrigendum No. 1 (2013)
9. Associated General Contractors of America: The contractors' guide to BIM, edn 1 (2005)
10. Mitchell, D.: 5D – creating cost certainty and better buildings. In: RICS Cobra Conference, Las Vegas (2012)
11. https://www.smartsheet.com/getting-started-work-breakdown-structures-wbs, 04 March 2019

12. Project Management Institute Standards Committee: The Project Management Body of Knowledge (PMBOK). Project Management Institute, Darby (1987)
13. Norman, E.S., Brotherton, S., Fried, R.T., Ksander, G.: Building high quality work breakdown structures using the practice standard for work breakdown structures—second edition. Paper presented at PMI® Global Congress 2006—North America, Seattle, WA. Project Management Institute, Newtown Square (2006)
14. Akpınar, H.: Data: Veri Madenciliği Veri Analizi, 1st edn. Papatya Yayıncılık, İstanbul (2014)
15. Rowley, J.: The wisdom hierarchy: representations of the DIKW hierarchy. J. Inf. Sci. **33**(2), 163–180 (2007)
16. Çağıltay, N.: İş Zekası ve Veri Ambarı Sistemleri, 1st edn. ODTÜ Yayıncılık, Ankara (2010)
17. Naeem Hasan, A., Rasheed, M.S.: The benefits of and challenges to implement 5D BIM in construction industry. Civil Eng. J. **5**, 412 (2019). https://doi.org/10.28991/cej-2019-03091255
18. Azhar, S., Hein, M., Sketo, B.: Building Information Modeling (BIM): benefits, risks and challenges. McWhorter School of Building Science, Auburn University, Auburn, Alabama (2011)
19. Aapaoja, A., Haapasalo, H.: The challenges of standardization of products and processes in construction. In: Proceedings of the 22nd Annual Conference of the International Group for Lean, Olso, Norway, 25–27 June 2014, pp. 983–993 (2014)
20. Faisal, S., Sarwar, M., Shahzad, K., Sarwar, S., Jaffry, W., Yousaf, M.M.: Temporal and evolving data warehouse design. Sci. Program. **2017**, 18 (2017). Article ID 7392349
21. https://knowledge.autodesk.com/support/navisworks-products/learn-explore/caas/CloudHelp/cloudhelp/2017/ENU/Navisworks-Manage/files/GUID-B1140D6D-8832-42BB-971E-7AE07 CF4216F-htm.html, 10 April 2019 (QA Workbook)
22. https://knowledge.autodesk.com/support/navisworks-products/learn-explore/caas/CloudHelp/cloudhelp/2017/ENU/Navisworks-Manage/files/GUID-18F054C9-B414-4BA3-B97A-56F08 66DCF69-htm.html
23. https://knowledge.autodesk.com/support/navisworks-products/learn-explore/caas/CloudHelp/cloudhelp/2017/ENU/Navisworks-Manage/files/GUID-1DD771DC-837E-44AF-86A2-470A FF0CD44A-htm.html
24. https://knowledge.autodesk.com/support/navisworks-products/learn-explore/caas/CloudHelp/cloudhelp/2017/ENU/Navisworks-Manage/files/GUID-C95DE000-D84E-459E-B249-C43FA 2F7FE2F-htm.html, 10 April 2019 (Virtual Takeoff)
25. http://www.buildingsmart-tech.org/implementation/get-started/ifc-guid
26. https://support.office.com/en-ie/article/create-a-form-in-access-5d550a3d-92e1-4f38-9772-7e 7e21e80c6b
27. Liew, A.: DIKIW: data, information, knowledge, intelligence, wisdom and their interrelationships. Bus. Manag. Dyn. **2**, 49–62 (2013)

Comparison of BIM Based Alternative Scheduling Workflows for Confined Wall Systems

Eylem Zorlutuna[1]([⊠]), Uğur Kaya[1], and Sinan Düz[2]

[1] EMAY International Engineering and Consultancy Inc., İstanbul, Turkey
{eylem.zorlutuna,ugur.kaya}@emay.com
[2] Turkey Istanbul Metropolitan Municipality, İstanbul, Turkey
sinanduz@ibb.gov.tr

Abstract. Management of running costs to approach productivity indices between planned and actual is an important topic for BIM-based cost management systems. In the context of conventional BIM management, it is expected to get more detailed models as the design decisions developed. On the other hand, in the complex structure of project deliveries, where the construction phase is started and the design decisions are not completed yet, alternative procedures are required to manage outputs for both early and detailed stages of the design in the same model environment. In this chapter, the M9 Ikitelli-Ataköy underground line project was analyzed to decide the most proper scheduling workflows to generate survey reports of confined wall systems. While the length value is required to estimate cost alternatives of interior cladding, bill of quantities are going to be measured for calculation of surface area completed from the same model assembly. On the contrary, the system is assembled with both architectural and structural model elements, thus, the measurement data from length and area values cannot be pulled out to table list by default scheduling features of modelling software. When the BIM model elements hold the data, but those can not be inferred as required information, alternative information acquirement methodologies were reviewed and compared. During the study, the scope of BIM ontology was formed by such BIM platforms as Revit and its associated extensions Dynamo and Roombook. At the end of the study, it is aimed to present practical advantages of extensions at the automation of cost estimation and preparing bill of quantities in the BIM environment.

Keywords: BIM · Quantity survey · Confined wall · Visual programming

1 Introduction

Management of running costs for achieving good productivity indices between planned and actual is an important topic for the cost management systems within the BIM-based projects. During the construction process, accurate analysis on scheduling and cost estimation is also important to meet the requirements of the project. At previous practices and studies, it is also pointed out that digitizing surveying process with BIM-based systems have both effective and efficient results on saving time and preventing

S. Ofluoglu et al. (Eds.): EBF 2019, CCIS 1188, pp. 70–79, 2020.
https://doi.org/10.1007/978-3-030-42852-5_6

loss of information between project deliverables [1]. However, while expecting beneficial results, BIM management scenarios must be well defined for specific requirements of each unique project.

In the context of conventional BIM management approach, it is expected to get more detailed models as the design decisions mature. On the other hand, in the concurrent structure of project deliveries, where the construction phase is started and the design decisions have not made yet, alternative procedures are required to manage outputs for both early and detailed stages of design in the same model environment. Requirements for exceptional design deliverables propagates new management workflows, where modelling techniques and model qualities must be defined properly during the automation of the scheduling process. In such cases, more than one solution can be used to reach the required information, such as the diverse data of BIM may be manipulated with alternative workflows in an existing working environment or the lack of information in model can be resolved outside of the native software [2, 3].

In this study, the M9 Ikitelli-Ataköy underground line project was analyzed to reach the most proper scheduling workflows to generate survey reports of confined wall systems. The M9 Ataköy-Ikitelli Underground Line project is the second underground line construction project in Istanbul that is tendered by the Istanbul Metropolitan Municipality (IMM). The project has been benefiting from BIM workflows since 2016. At the beginning of the project, information modelling aspects are elaborately defined in a BIM Execution Plan (BEP). The BEP outlines the structure of the information to be reported for cost estimation. The reporting process has been carried out simultaneously during the design decision-making processes (Fig. 1, Process Overview Map). In terms of cost estimation, data extracted from MTO and QTO are essential to compare

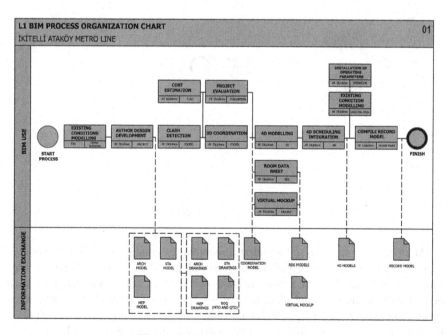

Fig. 1. BIM process overview map

alternative design solutions. Due to scope of the BEP, MTO and QTO for bill of quantities are planned, but the execution methods have not defined in detail yet (Fig. 2, Progress Payment Steps) [9].

The construction decisions can change due to geographical conditions in infrastructure projects, which directly affect the spatial organization in architectural design. Thus, the design and construction phase of interiors proceeds concurrently. Therefore, the submission of construction documents was divided into two phases in order to manage scheduling for different approval processes. At the first approval phase, finishing materials of technical areas, which are not affecting the conceptual design of stations, were approved according to their priority for procurement and process billing. Additionally, in the second phase, most proper claddings for passenger areas are determined based on various feasibility aspects including cost. Cladding material takeoff in a passenger area is needed to compare the impact of cladding material alternatives on the total project cost. In such a case, room-based scheduling is required to get walls and their claddings associated with passenger areas. However, the relationship between the wall elements and rooms cannot be established in Revit software by default.

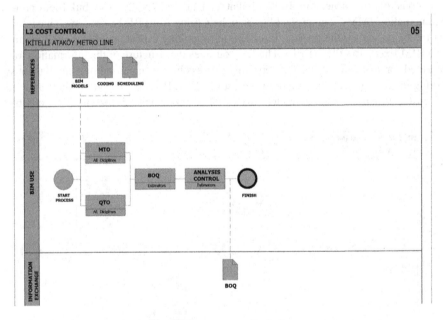

Fig. 2. Progress payment steps

At the first phase, where information is required to contain installation methods, the brick walls have been modelled with reinforced concrete frames which all elements bring into confined walls. In such a case, detailed wall models, assembled with both architectural and structural model elements are not able to deliver overall measurements directly to table list by default scheduling features of the modelling software. While the length value is required to estimate cost alternatives of interior cladding, bill of quantities are going to be measured for calculation of the surface area from the same model assembly. When the BIM elements hold the data, but those can not be inferred as required information, alternative information acquirement methodologies were reviewed and compared. During the study, the scope of BIM ontology was formed by such BIM platforms as Revit and its associated extensions Dynamo and Roombook (Fig. 3).

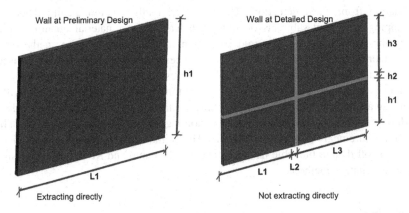

Fig. 3. Detail differences between core wall elements in design development

2 Literature Review

BIM-based quantity takeoff may report geometry parameters in the model such as length, area, volume, weight, and the number of objects [4], as well as object information such as category, name, and placement information. Defining a methodology to report geometry parameters, Olatunji claims that the automatically extracted takeoffs indicate not the actual quantity of materials used in construction, but the quantities of materials contained in the 3D model [5]. Due to the lack of some elements and materials not shown in 3D model may lead to the omission of some materials and labour [6].

Numerous studies have been conducted on enhancing BIM-based quantity takeoffs. Bylund and Magusson [7] claims that there are three types quantity information, which is explicitly represented in the model, components that are not explicitly represented but can be inferred, components that are not represented in the model and cannot be inferred. Bylund and Magusson proposed three types of quantity survey methods to extract quantities of all building elements in finishing works. In an automatic process, geometric data in the model can be listed directly with BIM software and directly accessed to the information. In case of the absence of intelligent objects containing quantity data or insufficient, some measurement data is manually entered in the BIM software to access the information, and this is called as semi-automatic. In the third method, all measurements made manually and listed in different software, where it is not possible to obtain new data by BIM software and in the absence of intelligent objects containing quantity data. Monteiro and Martins suggested using another modelling tool as an add-in to a native software when some components cannot be extracted from the BIM model with the semi-automatic method [6].

In the modelling phase of this study, room tags were defined for rooms in the model manually to link the associated walls with the rooms for calculation of wall cladding materials. Later on, in the decision-making process of cladding materials takeoff materials are calculated with the semi-automatic method.

Khosakitchalerta [8] proposed a method within the concept of a BIM-based clash detection to enhance the accuracy of the architectural wall quantity takeoff by using the information from clash detection. The proposed method automatically detects the overlapping areas and subtracts or adds each wall layer's material quantity without editing the BIM model by Dynamo Extension in a selected room or in the overall project. During the early stages of the design process, accurate quantities can be used in the selected project delivery method where cost estimation feedback is needed.

In this study, we aimed to provide an automated extracting workflow without interfering any manual data input until getting the takeoff. As mentioned above, default scheduling features of modelling software don't grant permission the user to deliver overall measurements directly to a table list. Hence the native software is insufficient to extract takeoff data to the table list automatically, Dynamo and Roombook add-ons are used as alternative methods.

3   Methods

In this study, automated scheduling workflows are designed to get (listed) values for both bricks and cladding materials on interior wall assemblies. Schedules for both components are generated in Dynamo with separate workflows. Subsequently, a single workflow is defined in Roombook to schedule both brick and cladding components to acquire reports for room-based takeoff.

Dynamo is a visual programming extension developed by Autodesk for Revit [10, 11]. Dynamo gives users an opportunity to create algorithms using data or geometry from a Revit model. Functions such as modelling and QTO and MTO in Revit can also be achieved with Dynamo Nodes which represent every function and variable in Dynamo. Each node can be wired to another node to perform operations. A group of nodes elaborate packages. Packages can be published and shared with the online community on the Dynamo website. The proposed method is implemented using Autodesk Revit 2018 with an extension of Dynamo. The workflow in Dynamo begins with the input of element categories from the Revit model. Two different workflows are designed to generate the required information about the different components of wall assemblies. Both results obtained are scheduled in Revit inherently.

3.1   Calculation of Area of Brick Walls Through the Surface of the Confined Walls

This workflow is used to calculate area values of brick walls in confined wall systems. The input categories are brick walls, structural columns, reinforced concrete frame, rooms and room names in the workflow in Dynamo. The development process is shown in Fig. 4. The brick walls, structural columns, the reinforced concrete frame will be combined and converted into geometry and exploded into surfaces in selected areas.

After selecting all the surfaces and then listing, the core brick wall area will be calculated for room-based takeoff.

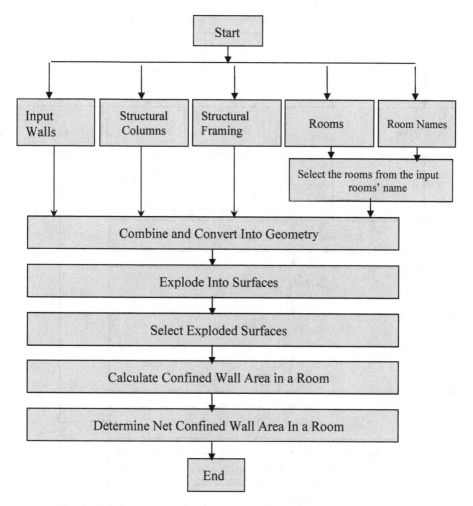

Fig. 4. Calculating the area of bricks through the surface of confined walls

3.2 Calculation of Area of Cladding Materials Through the Length of Confined Walls in a Room

In the scope of the studied project, height of cladding materials were not equal to the adjacent core surface of wall systems. While the core structure of the wall is constrained between floor levels, the height of claddings was limited with the height of the false ceiling level. The inputs categories are the brick walls, structural columns in the workflow of in Dynamo. The overall process is shown in Fig. 5. The brick walls and structural columns combined and converted into geometry in selected areas. After selecting the length of geometry by multiplying the custom height input (defined manually by the user), the area of the walls through the length of confined walls was calculated. The area of the cladding materials through the length of confined walls was calculated for the room-based takeoff.

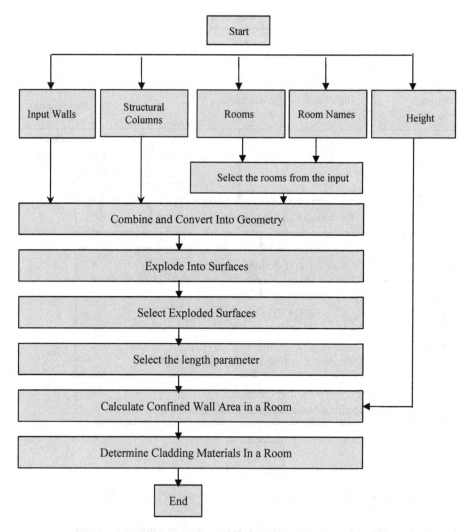

Fig. 5. Calculating area of confined walls through length in a room

3.3   Calculation Area of Both Bricks and Cladding Materials Through Quantification of Confined Wall

The Roombook Revit add-on is called a computer programming - based Revit API (Application Programming Interface). According to Autodesk, the add-on "helps calculate the surface area of walls, floors and ceiling elements, room circumferences and the total number of furnishing elements within a project". It utilizes to obtain quantities of room-specificic information available in the model. The extension can specify various analytical settings and add materials that can be used for rooms [12].

After configuring the settings in the surface materials of cladding, "Calculate Room Quantity" function is selected. After selecting the rooms to be analyzed and then running the Calculate function, the results are reviewed in a dialogue box. The Roombook Extension – Room Quantities dialogue box has an option to display all of the individual

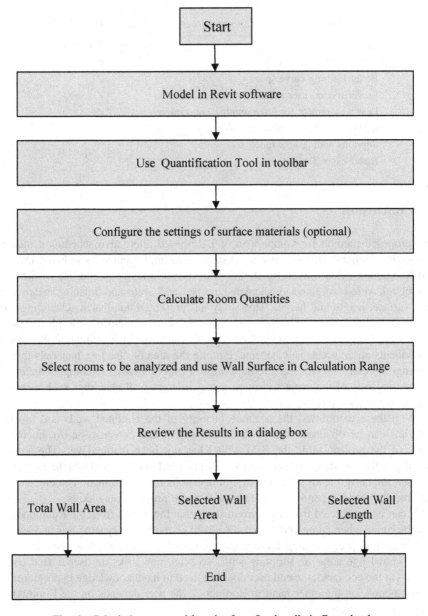

Fig. 6. Calculating area and length of confined walls in Roombook

element listings by selected room of wall surfaces. When selecting the "Wall Surfaces" option, it lists each wall in/around each selected area. It lists the wall type along with the information regarding structural elements of the wall, area of the wall, height of the wall, total area for all walls(if all rooms areas were selected). The results are exported to a Microsoft Excel spreadsheet. The default template provides a table listing of all desired information on a "selected area basis" for each confined wall (Fig. 6).

Table 1. Comparison of dynamo and roombook workflows

Findings	Dynamo	Roombook
Better takeoff accuracy		✓
Better learning curve speed		✓
Lower risk on user related errors		✓
Less requirement for programming knowledge		✓
Open source application capabilities	✓	
Supports adding new functions	✓	
Better execution speed		✓

4 Conclusion

The proposed method for comparison of BIM-based alternative scheduling method-ologies for confined wall systems in the study, was implemented by utilizing Dynamo and Roombook extensions in Revit. Two workflows in Dynamo and one workflow in Roombook were configured to calculate confined wall areas and finishing materials by their surface, length and height. This study has presented automated scheduling solu-tions for the brick walls modelled with structural support elements. Besides, different options are compared to optimize the accurate results for cost estimation of cladding components on adjacent wall systems. Finding the area of cladding materials through the length of confined walls in a room workflow makes it easier to compare the impact on the total cost of the project through using different wall claddings such as acrylic and coloured glass panels.

With these workflows, the accurate quantity of the confined walls and finishing materials can be obtained both in schematic design and construction documentation phase of the project while the BIM model has not been matured yet. The accurate quantity of the confined walls and finishes can be used to estimate the building cost and to assist the design team make the design decisions more informed. The efficiency of the process would depend on the learning curve at programming skills.

It can be interpreted from the current study that the results from the Roombook are more accurate when compared with results from Dynamo. In Dynamo it is necessary to have sufficient programming knowledge for debugging to correct any errors. Addi-tional knowledge areas on scripting will also bring new risks on user related coding errors. On the one hand, the end user does not need to have knowledge in programming in Roombook, on the other hand in Roombook the user depends on the Roombook's encoding capabilities.

MTO and QTO information can be extracted in every BIM based project. While comparing the execution speeds, authorized processing of API based addins, such as Roombook renders faster results. Despite the fact of open source programming capabilities, Dynamo can interfere with end-user programming tools for distinctive needs of the project, it cannot be possible in the Roombook extension. Table 1 provides a comparison of the workflows in Dynamo and Roombook.

In future research, Dynamo execution will necessitate more case studies for validation and improvements in the Dynamo scripts. In the near future, it is possible that there will be an increase in the number of architects and engineers who know to code, and the knowledge of visual programming will be widespread. Thus, the automation of the takeoff process in the AEC sector will be achieved at high efficiency and automation of the takeoff will be achieved in an easier and less time-consuming way. In order to avoid difficulties in such applications, BIM definitions in different design phases and scheduling of takeoff requirements have to be taken into consideration and clarified in BEP and other guidelines at the start of the project.

References

1. Bečvarovská, R., Matějka, P.: Comparative Analysis of Creating Traditional Quantity Takeoff Method and Using a Bim Tool Construction Macroeconomics Conference (2014)
2. Małgorzata, G., Marek, S.: Challenges in Takeoffs and Cost Estimating in the BIM Technology, Based on the Example of a Road Bridge Model (2017)
3. Olsen, D., Taylor, J.: Quantity takeoff using building information modeling (BIM), and its limiting factors. Proc. Eng. **196**, 1098–1105 (2017)
4. Royal Institute of Chartered Surveyors (2013)
5. Olatunji, O.A., Sher, W.D., Ogunsemi, D.R.: The impact of building information modelling system on construction cost estimating. In: CIB 2010 World Congress, 2010c, Salford, UK (2010)
6. Monteiro, A., Martins, J.P.: A survey on modeling guidelines for quantity takeoff-oriented BIM-based design. Autom. Constr. **35**, 238–253 (2013)
7. Bylund, C., Magnusson, A.: Model based cost estimations - an international comparison. Masters thesis. Faculty of Engineering, Lund University, Lund, Sweden (2012)
8. Khosakitchalert, C., Yabukib, N., Fukudac, T.: The accuracy enhancement of architectural walls quantity takeoff for schematic BIM models. In: 35th International Symposium on Automation and Robotics in Construction (ISARC 2018), pp. 777–784 (2018)
9. Ataköy İkitelli Metro Line BIM Execution Plan
10. Dynamo BIM: http://dynamobim.org/. Accessed 19 Feb 2019
11. CRAFTAI. http://www.craft.ai. Accessed 15 Feb 2019
12. https://www.autodesk.com. Accessed 12 Feb 2019

BIM-Based Automated Safety Review for Fall Prevention

Gokhan Tekbas[1] and Gursans Guven[2(✉)]

[1] Department of Civil Engineering, Engineering Faculty, Ozyegin University,
#235, Cekmekoy, 34794 Istanbul, Turkey
gokhan.tekbas@ozu.edu.tr
[2] Department of Civil Engineering, Engineering Faculty, Ozyegin University,
#105, Cekmekoy, 34794 Istanbul, Turkey
gursans.guven@ozyegin.edu.tr

Abstract. The construction industry is globally known as one of the most hazardous industries. Safety in construction is affected by many factors such as the behavior of workers, site conditions, the design and the implementation of the safety measures. Falls from height and hits by moving or falling objects are the most common types of accidents at construction sites and lead to serious injuries and fatalities. Researchers have been looking for solutions to reduce fall incidents at construction sites. Health and safety (H&S) experts usually follow traditional methods to plan and employ safety measures at sites. These safety planning methods are mainly based on reviewing 2D drawings to identify the risks and associated hazards and have some important deficiencies. First of all, the efficiency of safety planning depends on the experience of H&S experts. More importantly, it is difficult to identify the potential hazards from a 2D drawing while the project is progressing. Building Information Modeling (BIM) can overcome the challenges observed with the traditional safety planning processes. Hazards in a project and the related safety measures should be continuously identified throughout the construction. Since BIM is a 3D model-based process that assists the stakeholders not only to construct and manage but also to plan and design structures; BIM can provide an efficient solution to plan and design the safety measures of a construction project both during the design and construction phases. In addition, the safety review of buildings can be more effectively performed with a 3D building information model. In this study, "Automatic Fall Safety Review (AFSR)" rule checking tool is developed by using Dynamo, the open-source visual programming add-in for Autodesk Revit. This tool analyzes a 3D building model in Revit, and automatically identifies the hazardous places in a building and shows the related safety measures for preventing falls from height in particular. This paper presents the details of the AFSR tool and demonstrates its application for an 8-storey residential building.

Keywords: Falls from height · Fall-related hazards · Building Information Modeling · Visual programming · Safety review

© Springer Nature Switzerland AG 2020
S. Ofluoglu et al. (Eds.): EBF 2019, CCIS 1188, pp. 80–90, 2020.
https://doi.org/10.1007/978-3-030-42852-5_7

1   Introduction

The construction industry is considered as one of the hazardous industries. According to the Occupational Safety and Health Administration (OSHA), 20.5% of fatalities occurred in the construction industry in 2014 [1]. International Labour Organization (ILO) indicates that 25–40% of all fatal workplace accidents occur at construction sites in industrialized countries [2]. Moreover, it has been identified that mostly new and young workers are likely to get hurt while working [3]. There are various risks associated with construction works and the followings are among the most common types of hazards in the construction industry: falls from height, falling objects, contact with electricity, heavy equipment accidents, traffic accidents on site, building or structure collapses, cave-ins, fire or explosions [4, 5]. Although all types of hazards must be noticed and handled properly, falls from height and hits by moving or falling objects are the most common type of accident at construction sites and leads to serious injuries and fatalities. There are many conventional safety measures to prevent such hazards: Personal Fall Arrest System (PFAS), guardrail and safety net systems [6]. Although the importance of safety measures is known by the construction professionals and it is straightforward that the related safety measures should be used at hazardous places; one can fail to recognize all of the fall hazards in a project, and therefore not use the proper safety measures where necessary. The main reason for this is that 2D drawing-based traditional methods are still used to plan and design safety measures, although construction projects, nowadays, have become more complex and larger. In addition, technology has been developed expeditiously throughout the years, enabling the use of new techniques and methods for construction which might pose new challenges in terms of safety. It is difficult to identify the potential hazards from a 2D drawing while the project is progressing because it is common that frequent changes in the safety design of a construction project are implemented as the construction continues. The current safety planning methods that are largely used in the construction industry are still mainly based on reviewing 2D drawings to identify the risks and associated hazards. Moreover, in the current practice, the efficiency of the safety planning of a project depends on the experience of the Health and Safety (H&S) experts. Building Information Modeling (BIM) can assist the H&S experts and construction professionals to overcome the challenges observed with the traditional safety planning process.

BIM digitally represents a building in 3D and provides a significant advantage over the 2D traditional representation in terms of visualization and understanding of a built environment. It enables a 3D model-based process that assists the stakeholders not only to construct and manage but also to plan and design structures. Therefore, BIM can provide an efficient solution to plan and design the safety measures of a construction project both during the design and construction phases. In addition, it can minimize the time spent on manual safety reviews of buildings, and eliminate the human error when identifying the risks and hazards by means of automated rule-checking and safety review. Since frequent changes in the safety design of construction projects are commonly needed throughout the construction, BIM can ease the process of adjusting to the changes in safety measures while construction projects are progressing.

The objective of this study is to review a given project and to identify the related fall hazards automatically by using its BIM model. In this study, an "Automatic Fall Safety Review (AFSR)" rule checking tool is developed by using Dynamo, the open-source visual programming add-in for Autodesk Revit. This tool analyzes a 3D building model in Revit, and automatically identifies the hazardous places on a building and shows the related safety measures for preventing falls from height in particular. It is especially aimed to work during the structural works are performed in the project, and can directly run within a Revit project by using the Dynamo Player. The next sections describe the methodology of this study and the implementation of the developed tool over an 8-storey building as the case study.

2 Literature Review

H&S risks in a project are minimized by the efforts of the H&S experts during the construction stage. Designers also have an important role in reducing the risks of a construction project. This is because the decisions of designers during the planning and design stages can decrease the risks even before the construction starts and during the construction, as well. The "Design for safety" subject in the construction has been studied for a long time, and initial practical studies on a computer were in the early 2000s [7]. The authors created a design tool to enable efficiency for project stake-holders in obtaining knowledge about the frequent changes in construction projects, having a control mechanism that is able to assess the risks in projects.

Researchers follow the lead to create practical solutions to enable design for safety in the construction industry. For example, Hadikusumo et al. studied the design for safety subjects in a Virtual Reality (VR) environment and developed a tool. The tool first gets the name of a building component, which also includes the type of the building component, such as "Slab216" [8]. After that, it matches the type of the building component with the possible types of hazards related to this building component. Hazard information is provided as an input to the tool. Finally, the user is informed about the possible safety measures according to the identified hazards about the building component. The main limitation of this study is that the related safety measure for the identified hazards is not presented visually to the user but the possible solutions are provided to the user in written format. In addition, the user needs to change the design of the building manually according to the suggested safety solutions by the tool developed by the researchers. In another study, Chantawit et al. developed a 4D CAD-Safety application to detect fall safety hazards and the related measures [9]. This application combines a building component and its tasks, as in the case of creating a 4D model. The identified safety measures are also presented to the user only in written format. To automatically quantify the safety risk levels for concrete formwork construction, a method was developed by other researchers as well [10].

In more recent designs for safety studies performed by researchers in construction, the developed solutions are more advanced in terms of visualization. For instance, a visual programming tool was developed by researchers in a study to visually show the fall safety measures to the user [11]. The developed tool detects the fall hazards of the building components according to the related parameters and shows the related safety measures. In another study, Zhang et al. developed a 4D-based tool that is called "RAPIDS Safety Rule Checker" [12]. It gives the schedule of installation and removal of safety measures exclusive of the project schedule. Besides, it informs the user about the appropriate fall safety measures in both written and visual format. The RAPIDS tool also enables the user to change thresholds in accordance with the safety standard that is used. This is similar to the method used in the AFSR tool that is developed in this study. Moreover, AFSR does not necessitate working with a specific schedule, and therefore, the user could identify the necessary fall safety measures at any stage of a project before the schedule is provided by the contractor. In addition, to assist the H&S experts and the project stakeholders, the AFSR tool visually demonstrates the necessary safety measures and also automatically modifies the 3D building model accordingly.

3   Methodology

Figure 1 demonstrates an overview of the AFSR tool. As a BIM-based rule checking tool, AFSR consists of a Dynamo script to identify the safety measures needed in a building design and automatically places the necessary safety measures on the 3D model in Revit to the locations that are deemed hazardous. The user is asked to enter some data regarding the type of safety measure that will be used or to change some of the thresholds manually. The following paragraphs explain in more detail how the AFSR tool works and the steps it follows below.

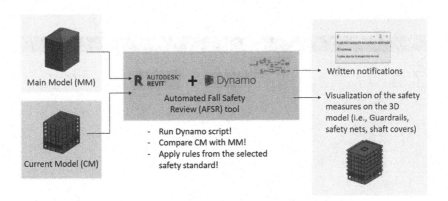

Fig. 1. The Automated Fall Safety Review (AFSR) tool overview

(1) Comparison with the main model: There is a main model (i.e., MM) that represents the final view of the project, and a current model (i.e., CM) that can be at any given stage of a project throughout its construction. When the CM is opened in Revit; the MM should be linked to it so that the AFSR tool can run the Dynamo script to compare the CM with the MM.

(2) Application of the rules: Countries might have different standards defined by different safety agencies such as OSHA (Occupational Health and Safety

Association) in the USA and HSE (Health and Safety Executive) in the UK. Therefore, the limits and thresholds could differ from one country to another. For instance, different standards might suggest different height limits or different guardrail types to be implemented during the safety design of buildings. The tool leaves it to the user to define the thresholds that will be used to identify the hazards related to falls from height in the building. By using the Dynamo Player in Revit, the user enters the desired thresholds and runs the script; the tool checks the fall-related hazards in accordance with the entered threshold and shows the associated safety measures floor by floor in the building model.

The Dynamo Player is a user interface to run Dynamo scripts in Autodesk Revit (Fig. 2). Script files, which are prepared by using Dynamo, should be imported in the Dynamo Player. After the script prepared for the AFSR tool is imported into the Dynamo Player file, it is visible among the Dynamo Player list. The user should check the "Edit Inputs" list on the AFSR to identify the thresholds according to the limits of the selected standard. For example, there is a height limit for the fall hazard. This checks all the levels for the height value entered in the "Elevation Limit to Check (mm)" in the form of millimeters. The floor of the project to be checked for the height threshold is selected from the "Levels" category, which shows the floors of the CM in terms of Revit levels. Additionally, the AFSR tool checks the elevations of the window openings from the level of the floor, named the window opening base offset limit. In addition, the area of the shaft openings is measured to identify the type of safety measure that will be used at a particular shaft opening (i.e., guardrail or shaft cover).

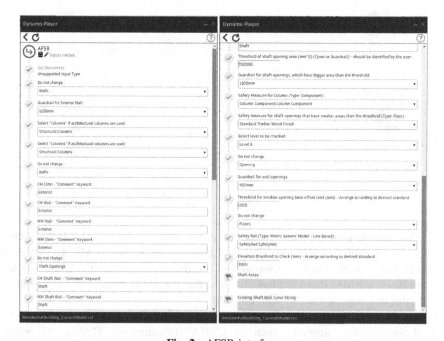

Fig. 2. AFSR interface

The shaft opening area limit is left for the user to decide, depending on the type of preferred safety measure to include in the model. Moreover, the user can change the type of safety measures that will be viewed in 3D from the Dynamo Player interface. For instance, the user can change the guardrail type from the "Railing Types" category, to select among a list of different rail types, such as 1100 mm, 900 mm pipe.

(3) Written notifications through pop-up messages: Users get a pop-up message once the threshold entered by the user is within the limits of the selected safety standard. For example, if the user prefers to use OSHA as the safety standard, the floor needs to be checked in terms of the fall-related hazards if the floor height is more than 6 ft (1.82 m). More information that help to reduce fall-related hazards, such as the related personal protective equipment, is shown to the user through these pop-up messages, as well.

(4) Visualizing the safety measures: Once the user is notified by a pop-up message, the AFSR continues the process and presents the safety measures visually to the user in different types and shapes (e.g., guardrails, safety nets, shaft covers). These are automatically placed at the locations that are deemed hazardous.

AFSR tool can perform the rule checking and identify the related safety measures for the hazardous locations of a building at any stage of the construction of the building. There are three main locations in the construction projects that are identified to cause fall incidents the most: (1) slab edges, (2) shaft openings, and (3) external wall openings. Therefore, the AFSR tool focuses on these locations in building designs and check these locations. The components to represent the safety measures are either created as new Revit Families or modified from existing ones. Figure 3 shows the safety measures that are added to the 3D model as needed.

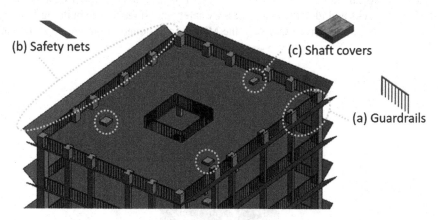

Fig. 3. Components used in Autodesk Revit as the safety measures: (a) guardrails, (b) safety nets, (c) shaft covers.

For the slab edges, AFSR automatically places guardrails if it identifies that the slab edge is not enclosed with a wall or a column. Guardrail application can be seen in Fig. 3a. Similarly, it places safety nets along the slab edges to reduce the risk of falls from height, and also hits by moving or falling objects. Safety nets are created by the authors in Revit by using the Metric Generic Model line based family template for the purposes of this study. The created safety net family is parametric and it adjusts its length based on the length of the slab edge where the safety net is to be placed in the model. The application of the safety net can be seen in Fig. 3b. For the shaft openings, the AFSR tool first identifies the boundaries of the shaft opening. There are two types of safety measures that can be viewed in this case: shaft covers and guardrails. AFSR automatically places one of these safety measures according to the area limit of the shaft opening that is requested by the user: If the area of the shaft opening is smaller than the limit, then the tool places a shaft cover that is modified from Floor family in Revit, and otherwise, it uses guardrails. The shaft covers can be seen in Fig. 3c. Finally, for the wall openings, the AFSR tool checks the elevations from their levels in the current model given by the user. If the elevation is lower than the limit that is requested by the standard and entered by the user manually; it is deemed hazardous and a related safety measure is placed at that location. The case study section provides details on the implementation of the developed ASFR tool.

4   Case Study

A residential building was modeled in Autodesk Revit 2018 and used as the case study. It is an 8-storey building. The Main Model (i.e., MM) of the building is given in Fig. 4, that is the completed version of the project. At any stage of the project, another model of the building called the Current Model (i.e., CM) is used to compare it with the MM. AFSR tool checks and identifies the necessary safety measures for the building floor by floor by comparing the given CM with the MM, as mentioned in the previous section.

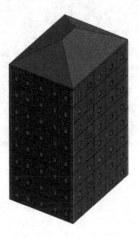

Fig. 4. Main model (i.e., completed project) of the building.

In the following paragraphs, different CMs were reviewed to represent different conditions of the case study building as different examples, and to demonstrate how AFSR identifies the necessary safety measures in each example:

(1) 1st floor of the CM has the slab and columns completed, but the walls are not completed when the safety review was conducted (Fig. 5a). When the Dynamo script of the AFSR tool was run for this particular CM, it was identified that the height of the 1st floor was less than 4.00 m, which was entered as the threshold by the user. Therefore, there will be no safety measures needed for fall prevention in this case. This is communicated with the user through pop-up messages (Fig. 5b).

(2) The 2nd and 3rd floors are reviewed in this example. 2nd and 3rd floors of the CM have slabs, columns, shaft opening walls, and some of the exterior walls at the time of the performed safety review. AFSR tool warned the user through a pop-up message to refer to the 3D model to view the necessary safety measures shown on the Revit model (Fig. 6a). Safety nets were placed on the model at hazardous locations as identified by the AFSR tool and shaft covers were placed on the shaft openings (Fig. 6b). Safety nets and shaft covers were placed on both the 2nd and 3rd floors but not to the 1st floor. Moreover, guardrails were placed on the slab edges at the location of the incomplete exterior walls.

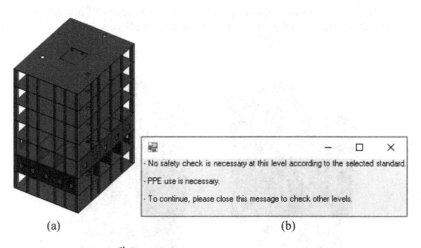

(a)   (b)

Fig. 5. (a) CM for the 1st floor, and (b) pop-up message created after the safety review.

(3) The 4th, 5th, 6th and 7th floors of the CM were reviewed in this example. At the time of the safety review, the exterior walls were not constructed and there were no shaft covers on these floors. The pop-up message is the same as in Fig. 6a, while the shafts and slab edges that were covered with guardrails at these floors are shown in Fig. 7a.

(4) The 8th floor of the building was reviewed in this example and there were no columns but only a slab in this case. This situation had the same solutions as the

3rd case, however, new Revit components were used to place the guardrails. These components are automatically placed on the location of the columns and served as an installation interface for the guardrails. Figure 7b shows the safety measures on the 8th floor of the building.

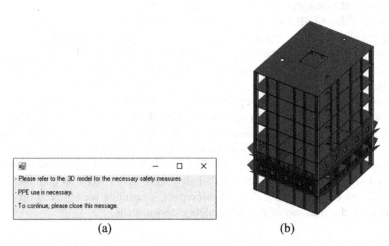

(a)   (b)

Fig. 6. (a) The pop-up message created after the safety review of the 2nd and 3rd floors of the CM, and (b) visualization of the necessary safety measures in 3D view.

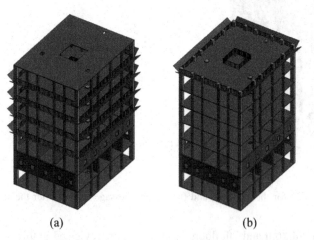

(a)   (b)

Fig. 7. Visualization of the necessary safety measures (a) for the 4th, 5th, 6th and 7th floors, and (b) for the 8th floor of the CM in 3D view.

5 Conclusions

There are many factors that affect construction safety and one of them is the improper implementation of safety measures. Tasks in a typical construction project include various hazards and it is vital to perform a frequent safety review in every construction project to ensure proper measures are taken to avoid accidents. H&S experts still mostly follow traditional safety planning methods which are mainly based on 2D drawings and it is difficult to identify the potential hazards from these drawings. Furthermore, construction projects are frequently changing and being modified. Therefore, it is difficult to determine the up-to-date needs for safety measures while the project progresses. Since identifying and applying the necessary safety measures in a project is not solely the responsibility of the H&S experts but also the responsibility of all stakeholders in a project; all project members will need to have an understanding of the required safety measures and a useful method to view and share the related details in the forms of project drawings. Thus, BIM can overcome the problems observed with the traditional methods as it can view a project and the related safety measures in 3D while providing collaboration among project participants, and enabling automated safety review.

The BIM-based Automated Fall Safety Review (AFSR) rule checking tool is presented in this study. Dynamo, which is the open-source visual programming add-in for Autodesk Revit, was used to create this tool particularly with a focus on fall-related hazards (i.e., falls from height and hits by moving or falling objects). The main principle is to compare two building models to identify the hazardous locations and to place the necessary safety measures at these locations in the 3D model. While one of these models is the complete design of the building, the other model can represent the status of the building at any stage throughout the construction. After performing the safety review, it notifies the user with messages about the required level of safety according to the thresholds that are either manually entered by the user or applied by default. The necessary safety measures are automatically added to the BIM model and the user can visualize these safety measures in a 3D view of the building in Autodesk Revit.

There are some limitations to this study. First of all, this study focuses on fall-related hazards but there are other serious hazards in the construction industry. Future work includes exploring the application of the AFSR tool on other common construction hazards. In addition, the authors will work on enabling the AFSR tool to calculate the amount of the safety measures added in the 3D model by creating schedules in Revit. These schedules will list the necessary amount of safety components such as the safety nets or guardrails, floor by floor. This will help with the planning ahead and ordering of the necessary safety measures for the upcoming days in a construction project.

References

1. Kang, Y., Siddiqui, S., Suk, S.J., Chi, S., Kim, C.: Trends of fall accidents in the U.S. construction industry. J. Constr. Eng. Manag. **143**(8) (2017)
2. Suraji, A., Duff, A.R., Peckitt, S.J.: Development of causal model of construction accident causation. J. Constr. Eng. Manag. **127**, 337–344 (2001)
3. Ontario Ministry of Labour: Health & Safety at Work: Prevention Starts Here: Worker Health and Safety Awareness in 4 Steps (2013). http://www.e-laws.gov.on.ca/html/statutes/english/elaws_statutes_90o01_e.htm
4. Gürcanli, G.E., Müngen, U.: An occupational safety risk analysis method at construction sites using fuzzy sets. Int. J. Ind. Ergon. **39**, 371–387 (2009)
5. Perlman, A., Sacks, R., Barak, R.: Hazard recognition and risk perception in construction. Saf. Sci. **64**, 22–31 (2014)
6. OSHA: Fall Protection in Construction (OSHA 3146-05R 2015), p. 48 (2015)
7. Gambatese, J.A., Hinze, J.W., Haas, C.T.: Tool to design for construction worker safety. J. Archit. Eng. **3**, 32–41 (2002)
8. Hadikusumo, B.H.W., Rowlinson, S.: Integration of virtually real construction model and design-for-safety-process database. Autom. Constr. **11**, 501–509 (2002)
9. Chantawit, D., Hadikusumo, B.H.W., Charoenngam, C., Rowlinson, S.: 4DCAD-safety: visualizing project scheduling and safety planning. Constr. Innov. **5**, 99–114 (2005)
10. Hallowell, M.R., Gambatese, J.A.: Qualitative research: application of the delphi method to CEM research. J. Constr. Eng. Manag. **136**, 99–107 (2010)
11. Hongling, G., Yantao, Y., Weisheng, Z., Yan, L.: BIM and safety rules based automated identification of unsafe design factors in construction. Procedia Eng. **164**, 467–472 (2016)
12. Zhang, S., Sulankivi, K., Kiviniemi, M., Romo, I., Eastman, C.M., Teizer, J.: BIM-based fall hazard identification and prevention in construction safety planning. Saf. Sci. **72**, 31–45 (2015)

An Investigation into Improving Occupational Health and Safety Performance of Construction Projects Through Usage of BIM for Lean Management

Nur Efsan Erusta[1(✉)] and Begum Sertyesilisik[2]

[1] Istanbul Technical University, Taşkışla, 34367 İstanbul, Turkey
nurefsanerusta@gmail.com
[2] Department of Architecture, Faculty of Architecture,
Izmir Democracy University, Uckuyular Mahallesi,
Gürsel Aksel Bulvari, No:14, 35140 Karabaglar, Izmir, Turkey
begum_sertyesilisik@hotmail.com

Abstract. Low performance in occupational health and safety can result in accidents having severe consequences or in near-misses. Furthermore, it can distract a smooth, efficient and effective workflow as well as reducing workers' motivation. Based on lean principles, accidents or near-misses can be described as waste. BIM can be a potential tool for enhancing lean as well as occupational health and safety performance in construction sites. Based on an in-depth literature review, this paper aims to investigate the role and ways of usage of BIM in the construction project management processes to reduce accident rates in construction sites and to increase efficiency through the elimination of wastes in the processes in sites based on the lean management tools and principles. This paper is intended to be beneficial for both building professionals and academics.

Keywords: Occupational health and safety · BIM · Lean construction

1 Introduction

1.1 Need for Enhancing Occupational Health and Safety Performance in the Construction Industry

As the construction industry (CI) is a driving industry in national economies, its development and competitiveness can directly contribute to the development of countries. From this perspective, all approaches having a potential contribution to the efficiency of the CI is important. Occupational health and safety (OHS) related issues play an important role in the problem areas in construction project management. The importance of the OHS is increasing due to the high accident rate in the CI and its adverse consequences affect workers, institutions, society and all stakeholders [1]. CI is the riskiest industry among all other industries with respect to its working conditions [2]. In Turkey, the rate of deadly accidents is the highest in the CI compared to other industries [3]; 1.6% of all occupational accidents result in deadly consequences whereas in the CI 4.7% of the accidents are fatal [4]. Analysis of the accidents that occurred in

© Springer Nature Switzerland AG 2020
S. Ofluoglu et al. (Eds.): EBF 2019, CCIS 1188, pp. 91–100, 2020.
https://doi.org/10.1007/978-3-030-42852-5_8

Turkey between the years of 2012–2016 reveals that 14% of all occupational accidents have occurred in the CI [5]. CI appears to be the most fatal accident intensive industry in Turkey [6]. The OHS issues in the CI cover accidents, occupation caused diseases and near-misses related issues. Construction accidents can have severe consequences. These accidents can result in death and injuries as well as disruption in the workflow, delay, increased cost, reduced efficiency, and harm in the company's prestige [7]. Furthermore, accidents can reduce workers' motivation. Many workers may die or get injured due to construction accidents resulting in social and economic problems [8].

Despite the fact that precautions taken for improving OHS can be perceived as time-consuming and cost increasing activities, their cost remains generally lower than the cost which can be caused due to an accident [9]. In spite of the high accident rate in the CI, there is low awareness in this field [10]. For this reason, there is a need for enhancing the health and safety performance of the CI.

1.2   Enhancing OHS Performance Through the Usage of BIM as a Lean Tool in the Construction Industry

Lean management is known as a strategy for enhancing the efficiency of the systems which eliminate or reduce waste. CI can gain a competitive advantage in the global market by adopting lean management principles and tools. Lean can enhance companies' performance focusing on added-value activities [11]. The lean production concept aims a continuous improvement in the processes to enable a reduction in the cost, and an increase in customer satisfaction [12]. Muda, Mura and Muri in the workflow, lack of standardization and rationalization can pose an obstacle for the zero-defect target which is fundamental in the lean production [13]. Toyota Production System has identified the waste categories [13] as overproduction, waiting, transportation, overprocessing, inventory, movement, defective production.

As all activities which do not add value are described as waste, occupational accidents and injuries can be classified as waste too. All potential risks for accidents on site need to be identified by taking the entire construction process into consideration. Failure in identifying the risks of construction sites accurately can result in the failure of taking all necessary precautions. Near-miss events need to be considered in the risk identification process as well as in the continuous improvement process. The majority of the accidents in the CI are mainly caused due to: dangerous movements (88%), dangerous conditions (10%) and disasters (2%) [6]. Accidents caused due to inappropriate precautions can result in adverse situations on sites (e.g. suspension of the work on-site). The usage of lean principles and tools can enhance OHS performance and contribute to the efficiency in the CI.

BIM can be a potential tool for enhancing lean as well as OHS performance in construction sites. Among other technology tools, BIM is a remarkable one that has the potential to increase OHS performance in the CI. There is a need for enhancing the potential of using BIM technology to prevent accidents and for improving site safety [14].

The usage of BIM technology can enable management and visualisation of actual plans and site layout information management through the integration of safety requirements to the construction planning, site layout, and safety plans [14]. BIM, as a real-time interactive and collaborative communication system tool, has a potential for waste minimization from a lean and sustainability point of view through improved construction performance, design, construction and its entire lifecycle [15]. The usage of BIM as a lean tool can help the integration of all stakeholders with the help of the integrated project delivery, offering a reduction in work hours of the workers and material waste [16, 17]. BIM can support visualisation of the production process through KanBan and Andon and the pull system based production [18]. For this reason, even if at the beginning, lean construction principles have emerged independently from BIM technologies, their integration can contribute to their improvement [19]. BIM enables all details of the project to be determined in the pre-construction phase. BIM enables different disciplines to work together in a coordinated way in all details of the project. BIM usage is important for enhancing health and safety performance on sites. BIM-based construction site layout can be prepared and construction activities/work items related risks can be planned. Risk analysis can be done in an effective way with the help of BIM. BIM can provide a new way of solving health and safety problems [20]. Modeling the projects with BIM helps professionals identify risks on-site and to manage them [21]. Modeling of the site can contribute to the planning of the logistics, access to the site, and controlling of the risks [22]. Information in BIM models can facilitate the decision-making process and can contribute to the reduction in risks of construction activities and to increase efficiency [23].

2   Research Method

This paper aims to investigate the role and ways of usage of BIM in the construction project management processes to enhance OHS performance and to reduce accident rates in construction sites by increasing efficiency through the elimination of wastes in the processes on sites based on the lean management tools and principles. With this aim, a literature review was carried out. Furthermore, the literature review based case studies were investigated. Following the literature survey, a brainstorming session was performed with the participation of eight CI professionals who attended the "Leagility in Construction Project Management" Ph.D. course lectured by the second author of this paper. The brainstorming focused on the relationship between BIM and lean management tools as well as whether or not BIM can be assessed as a lean tool.

2.1   Cases on the Usage of BIM for Improving OHS Performance

BIM can be considered as an important tool for assessing and reviewing designs. All potential problem areas which can be overlooked in the plans and cross-sections which are two-dimensional drawings can be seen more clearly when they are modeled in three dimensions. This can improve the identification of all risks which can emerge throughout the entire project life cycle in which health and safety performance can be enhanced. Cases on the usage of BIM for improving OHS performance were given below:

- BIM's usage for site layout planning and crane plans [24]: Thanks to BIM, all risks can be determined in advanced through models of the site layout plans. For example, BIM can control crane movements and crane access to assess the risks related to falling loads and to establish crane plans [24]. Furthermore, measures can be taken against the risks by modeling the forms of construction equipment [24].

- Integration of rule-checking method and BIM [25]: Rule-checking, which is a legally defined set of rules, is a method for enhancing the OHS practices on the site. The Rule-checking method can be applied to be integrated with BIM so that the legal aspects and requirements of the OHS which can vary from country to country can be modeled and adapted to each country [25]. Thus, a country based rule control system can be developed to manage the legal rules and technical practices concerned with falls from above [25].

- BIM-enabled parametric modeling of scaffolding design [26]: Parametrical designs can be created with BIM. BIM can enable scaffoldings to be designed, assembled fast and easily so that the installation time can be reduced and productivity can be increased [26]. Furthermore, parameters can enable the control of project requirements and contractor preferences as well as the scaffolding specifications [26].

- The usage of BIM for prevention of falling and for identification of different opening types automatically [26]: All openings can be calculated and a detailed fall plan can be modeled with BIM to determine all fall risks. Upon the identification of all fall risks, a model is established and analysed through automatic rule checking so that the remaining risks can be observed and appropriate protection methods can be developed [26].

- The usage of BIM for storage of data [Health and Safety Executive (HSE), published in the Improving Health and Safety Outcomes in Construction booklet]: The Thames Estuary Asset Management 2100 (TEAM2100) Project which has been performed under the leadership of the Environment Agency aims to protect 1.25 million people and 200 billion euros worth properties under the risk of flooding. The need for enabling access to the data stored plays an important role and it is achieved through BIM.

- The usage of BIM for investigation of constructability [Health and Safety Executive (HSE), published in the Improving Health and Safety Outcomes in Construction booklet]: 4D modeling has been done for all project phases in the National Grid. Project stakeholders could investigate and discuss the construction process. Site planning enabled them to identify all risks from the beginning of the project so that the failures could have been prevented before being occurred. 4D enabled the integration of time constraints and assessing the risks based on these time constraints resulting in work programmes to be prepared. Stakeholders could have a chance to understand the work to be accomplished, to take decisions fast and to carry out the work more effectively. All risks could have been identified earlier enabling a proactive approach.

2.2 Brainstorming Session on the Usage of BIM and Lean Tools for Enhancing OHS Performance in the Construction Industry

A brainstorming session was performed in the classroom with the participation of eight CI professionals (experts, civil engineers and architects) who took the "Leagility in Construction Project Management" Ph.D. course. At the beginning of the brainstorming session, the participants were given a brief presentation on the topic as well as about the scope of the brainstorming. The participants have brainstormed on the relationship between BIM and lean management tools, BIM's potential for improving the OHS performance as well as whether or not BIM can be assessed as a lean tool. The findings have been written and Table 1 has been prepared.

The brainstorming session supported that BIM can be considered as one of the lean tools or it can be used integrated with lean tools. BIM can contribute to the OHS performance in case it is integrated into the lean tools. Furthermore, the brainstorming session focused on how each lean tool can enhance OHS performance as a result of its integration with BIM. The points emphasized in the brainstorming session have been briefly summarized in the following paragraphs and Table 1:

- Last Planner System: The Last Planner system can be perceived as a production planning approach with a holistic system towards planned success [27]. The last planner system enables the determination of deadlines for project milestones, and phases. When integrated into these deadlines the requirements of the OHS related milestones can contribute to the OHS performance.

- 5s [Seiri (sort), Seiton (flow optimization), Seiso (clean), seiketsu (standardize), shitsuke (sustain)]: Seiso is important for keeping the site clean which can have an influence on the risks of accident and near-misses. Seiri can contribute to the OHS performance on-site enabling the working area to be free of obstacles as it requires sorting of materials and equipment. Seiton supports the occupational health and safety performance further as it requires materials and equipment to be arranged in a way to facilitate their usage. Furthermore, the availability of studies recommending Safety to be integrated as the 6th s to this lean tool [28] further supports the 5s tool's important role in the OHS.

- Plan, Do, Check, Act: PDCA emphasizes that the change needs to be carried out repeatedly in four stages in the circle [29]. The usage of PDCA in the construction processes can contribute to the reduction in waste and to the continuous improvement in the processes. Furthermore, it enables all employees to participate. In this way, all employees working on-site can participate in the occupational health and safety performance improvement process and they can contribute to the identification of risks related to their specialization area.

- Total quality management: Total quality management enables continuous and complete control of the quality of all procedures from design to delivery [28]. Total quality management advocates that processes should be handled systematically and that all employees' ideas can contribute to these processes. The integration of all employees to the system can contribute to the identification of all occupational health and safety risks and take precautions on time.

- Just-in-time: JIT aims the desired product to be produced at the desired time and in the desired quantity [30]. JIT aims zero inventory by enabling the material needed at the correct place at the time required. JIT further enables the site to be free of unnecessary materials and it can contribute indirectly to the OHS performance.

- Poka-yoke: It aims to prevent errors which can affect the system [12]. Poka-yoke aims to eliminate errors and not to perform the processes which have not been verified. On the basis of these principles, poka-yoke can contribute to the OHS performance through the establishment of a control mechanism in case of a risk of an accident on-site.

- Jidoka: Jidoka enables the machine/operators to detect the error and stop the production immediately upon an error that occurs [30]. Jidoka enables the production line to stop in case of an erroneous production in the system. Jidoka can contribute to the OHS performance on sites in various ways. For example, the usage of smart elevators which only open the doors when they see the floor pavement can reduce the risk of falling from a height.

- Heijunka: Heijunka is about leveling production type and quantity within a certain period of time [31]. Heijunka aims to streamline the Value Flow by using the resources in the production more efficiently by smoothing the production plan and shortening the set-up times between them [30]. Heijunka aims to reach the ideal production system through the production level. In this way, the information becomes clear on the following aspects: which equipment to be used in what frequency and the time when it should be maintained. Possible adverse consequences can be prevented with the periodic maintenance of vehicles and equipment.

- SMED: SMED is focused on reducing the setup time to reduce installation times [32]. It aims at minimizing the effort and complexity in terms of keeping dismantling and installation operations at a minimum level, encouraging the use of standard tools and molds, and shortening transport distances. In this way, it can contribute to the OHS performance on site.

- Kanban: The Kanban system is a pull mechanism built upon limiting the work being done based on the work capacity [33]. Kanban is used to manage material flow on-site and to facilitate communication between managers and the workers on site. It enables works to be organized and planned more clearly with the help of conscious communication. Human resources management and teamwork are valued in the construction. All employees can express their ideas about the processes. For example, situations with accident risks can be identified in advance and precautions can be taken. In this way, it can contribute to OHS performance.

- Five Why: The main principle of Five Why is to identify the problem and its reasons to solve the problems [34]. Five why is a simple, basic and effective system for identifying the root cause of a problem. In this way, the root causes of past accidents and near-misses can be identified. Accident risk analysis can be performed more accurately. It can be considered as an effective lean tool for reducing the risk of accidents.

- Gemba: Gemba is where the production is performed [35]. Accident risk analysis, site layout plans and designs need to be done at the Gemba (site) considering site-specific aspects so that they are performed accurately.

- Team-based management: Team-based management is based on teams rather than on individuals [36]. A team-based management system cares and respects all employees' contributions to the value creation for the product. Respecting people and educating them are among the main principles. It prefers a flat hierarchy where all employees can have a high awareness of adding value to the system. In this way, employees can have a high awareness of accidents and near-misses. They can be more proactive in taking precautions so that OHS performance can be enhanced.

- Total Productive Maintenance: The TPM philosophy aims at perfect production [37]. Total Productive Maintenance can contribute reaching to zero fault and zero accident targets. It gives priority to the prevention of problems. It also gives priority to keeping the machines and equipment operating safely and effectively with the help of maintenance. In this way, it can be useful for enhancing OHS performance on sites.

Table 1. The relationship among lean tools, BIM and OHS.

Lean tools	Lean tool and BIM integrability	Impact on health and safety performance
Last Planner System	✓	✓
5S	✓	✓
Plan-Do-Check-Act	✓	✓
Total Quality Management	✓	✓
Just in Time	✓	✓
Poka-Yoke	✓	✓
Jidoka	✓	✓
Heijunka	✓	✓
SMED	✓	✓
Kanban	✓	✓
Five Why	✓	✓
Gemba	✓	✓
Team-based Management	✓	✓
Total Productive Maintenance	✓	✓

The brainstorming session revealed that each lean tool can be individually integrated with BIM and each lean tool can improve OHS performance in construction. The last planner system can be used with BIM for planning when determining deadlines for project milestones and phases. Arrangement of the work area and equipment (5S) can be used with BIM to reduce accident risks. All lean tools (e.g. PDCA, TQM, JIT, Poka-yoke, Jidoka, Heijunka, SMED, Kanban, Five Why, Gemba, Team-based management and Total Productive Maintenance) can be used more efficiently in BIM technology.

The brainstorming session emphasized the possibility of using lean tools integrated into BIM as well as the possibility of enhancing the effectiveness of these lean tools with the help of BIM. Assessing BIM and lean tools in an integrated and holistic way has been considered as important. BIM has been suggested to be considered as a lean tool. Furthermore, the brainstorm session revealed that accurate adaptation of BIM and lean tools to the CI can enhance OHS performance.

3   Discussion and Limitations

This study investigated the role and ways of usage of BIM in the construction project management processes to reduce accident rates on construction sites. It identified accidents as waste and focused on increasing efficiency through the elimination of wastes in the processes in sites based on lean management tools and principles.

The poor performance of the OHS can result in severe consequences (e.g. deathly accidents) including the reduced motivation of the workers, and suspension of works on site. These consequences can hinder the smooth flow of work. They can result in loss of time, an increase in cost and reduced quality. In other words, they can cause waste (based on lean principles). Damages caused by accidents can also be subject to legal sanctions affecting the workflow. Workers' deaths or injuries can affect workers' motivations and productivity adversely. In the case of near-misses and accident risks, analysis needs to be checked and effective precautions need to be taken based on the continuous improvement principle. This process can be supported by BIM. It can be further enhanced with the help of the integration of lean tools to the BIM. In this way, accidents can be expected to be reduced and the OHS performance on-site can be expected to be enhanced. Despite these improvements, in case of the occurrence of accidents, an agile approach and principles can be used to manage the post-accident phase and to reduce the adverse consequences of accidents. The adoption of agile tools and principles in the post-accident phase can contribute to fast recovery. The focus of this study was on the pre-accident phase where lean principles can be applied to reduce accident occurrence risk.

4   Conclusion

This study highlighted the usage of BIM and lean management tools in an integrated way to reduce accident rates in construction sites. Accidents have been classified as waste due to their adverse consequences complying with the lean philosophy. For example, in addition to other adverse consequences, accidents can result in the suspension of work on-site which can be classified as 'waiting' waste based on lean management principles. All eight waste types of lean management can occur as a result of an accident. Based on the literature review, this study provided cases on the usage of BIM in enhancing OHS performance. Furthermore, this study suggested that the OHS performance of the CI can be enhanced with the help of integrated usage of BIM and lean tools. As accident risks cannot be eliminated entirely, agile principles and tools can support the post-accident phase in case accidents occur despite all these precautions taken. This study is expected to be beneficial to the professionals and academics in the field of BIM usage for enhancing OHS performance in the CI.

References

1. Sanchez, F.A.S., Pelaez, G.I.C., Alis, J.C.: Occupational safety and health in construction: a review of applications and trends. Ind. Health **55**, 210–218 (2017)
2. Zorluer, İ., ve Eleren, A.: İnşaat Sektöründe İş Güvenliği ve Sağlığı Üzerine Risklerin Belirlenmesi ve Örnek Bir Uygulama, 3. İşçi Sağlığı ve İş Güvenliği Sempozyum, pp. 185–193. TMMOB İnşaat Mühendisleri Odası, Çanakkale (2011)
3. Ceylan, H.: Türkiye'de İnşaat Sektöründe Meydana Gelen İş Kazalarının Analizi. Int. J. Eng. Res. Dev. **6**(1), 1–6 (2014)
4. Müngen, M.U.: İnşaat Sektörümüzdeki Başlıca İş Kazası Tipleri. TMH **469**(5), 32–39 (2011)
5. Bilim, A., Çelik, O.N.: Türkiye'deki İnşaat Sektöründe Meydana Gelen İş Kazalarının Genel Değerlendirmesi. Omer Halisdemir Univ. J. Eng. Sci. **7**(2), 725–731 (2018)
6. Hacıbektaşoğlu, S.E.: Analysis of work accidents in construction industry and investigation of the causes of these accidents. Stratejik ve Sosyal Araştırmalar Dergisi **2**(3), 159–177 (2018)
7. Kartam, N.A.: Integrating safety and health performance into construction CPM. J. Constr. Eng. Manag. **123**(2), 121–126 (1997)
8. Çavuş, A., Taçkın, E.: Investigation of the reasons for the accidents in the construction sector in Turkey. Akademik Platform Mühendislik ve Fen Bilimleri Dergisi **4**(2), 13–24 (2016)
9. Köksal, K.N., Gerek, İ.H.: Health and safety practices in building information model. Uluslararası Katılımlı 7. İnşaat Yönetimi Kongresi, pp. 55–62. TMMOB İnşaat Mühendisleri Odası, Samsun (2017)
10. Erusta, N.E.: An investigation on lean mobilization and site waste management in Turkish construction industry. Master thesis. Istanbul Technical University Institute of Science (2018)
11. Mayr, A., Weigelt, M., Kühl, A., Grimm, S., Erll, A., Potzel, M., Franke, J.: Lean 4.0 - a conceptual conjunction of lean management and industry 4.0. In: 51st CIRP Conference on Manufacturing Systems, vol. 72, pp. 622–628 (2018). https://doi.org/10.1016/j.procir.2018.03.292
12. Öksüz, M.K., Öner, M., Öner, S.C.: Yalın Üretim Tekniklerinin Endüstri 4.0 Perspektifinden Değerlendirilmesi. In: 4th International Regional Development Conference (IRDC 2017), Tunceli, Türkiye (2017)
13. Ohno, T.: Toyota Ruhu, Toyota Üretim Sisteminin Doğuşu ve Evrimi, 8th edn. Translater: Feyyat, C., Skala Yayıncılık, İstanbul (2018)
14. Sulankivi, K., Kähkönen, K., Mäkelä, T., Kiviniemi, M.: 4D-BIM for construction safety planning, pp. 1–12 (2010). https://www.researchgate.net/publication/228640694_4D-BIM_for_Construction_Safety_Planning
15. Liu, Z., Osmani, M., Demian, P., Baldwin, A.N.: The potential use of BIM to aid construction waste minimalization. In: Proceedings of the CIB W78-W102 2011: International Conference, pp. 1–12. Centre Scientifique et Technique du Batiment (CSTB), Sophia Antipolis, France (2011)
16. Khodeir, L.M., Othman, R.: Examining the interaction between lean and sustainability principles in the management process of AEC industry. Ain Shams Eng. J. **9**(2018), 1627–1634 (2018)
17. Hamid, Z.A., Zain, M.Z.M., Roslan, A.F.: Sustainable construction waste management. Ingenieur **66**(2016), 62–70 (2016)

18. Dave, B., Kubler, S., Framling, K., Koskela, L.: Opportunities for enhanced lean construction management using internet of things standards. Autom. Constr. **61**(2016), 86–97 (2016)
19. Gerber, D.J., Gerber, B.B., Kunz. A.: Building information modeling and lean construction: technology, methodology and advances from practice. In: 18th Annual Conference, International Group for Lean Construction, Haifa, Israel, 14–16 July, pp. 683–693 (2010)
20. Kiviniemi, M., Sulankivi, K., Kahkönen, K., Makela, T., Merivirta, M.L.: BIM-based safety management and communication for building construction. VTT Technical Research Centre of Finland (2011). https://www.vtt.fi/sites/bimsafety/en/bim-technology-enabled-construction-safety-management
21. Health and Safety Executive Homepage. http://www.hse.gov.uk/construction/index.htm. Accessed 01 May 2019
22. Safety, health and welfare at work (construction) regulations 2013. https://www.hsa.ie/eng/Legislation/Regulations_and_Orders/Construction_Regulations_2013/
23. Health and safety executive: improving health and safety outcomes in construction (2018). http://www.hse.gov.uk/construction/lwit/assets/downloads/improving-health-and-safety-outcomes-in-construction.pdf
24. Khoshnava, S.M., Ahankoob, A., Rostami, R., Preece, C.: Application of BIM in construction safety. In: Management in Construction Research Association (MiCRA) Postgraduate Conference, UTM Razak School of Engineering and Advanced Technology, pp. 155–160 (2012). ISBN 978-983-44732-0-4
25. Rodrigues, F., Estrada, J., Antunes, F., Swuste, P.: Safety through design: a BIM-based framework. In: Calautit, J., et al. (eds.) GeoMEast 2017. SUCI, pp. 112–123. Springer, Cham (2018). https://doi.org/10.1007/978-3-319-61645-2_9
26. Shou, W., Hou, L., Wang, J., Wang, X.: Case studies of BIM-based dynamic scaffolding design and safety prevention. https://sbenrc.com.au/app/uploads/2013/10/Publication-3-27-2_CASE-STUDIES-OF-BIM-BASED-DYNAMIC-SCAFFOLDING-DESIGN-AND-SAFETY-PREVENTION.pdf
27. Lean Construction Blog Homepage. http://www.springer.com/lncs. Accessed 06 May 2019
28. Li, S., Wu, X., Zhou, Y., Liu, X.: A study on the evaluation of implementation level of lean construction in two Chinese firms. Renew. Sustain. Energy Rev. **71**, 846–851 (2017)
29. American Society for Quality Homepage. https://asq.org/quality-resources/pdca-cycle. Accessed 06 May 2019
30. Yalın Danışman Homepage. https://yalindanisman.com/just-in-time-2/. Accessed 06 May 2019
31. Yalın Enstitü Homepage. https://lean.org.tr/heijunka-nedir/. Accessed 06 May 2019
32. Lean Six Sigma Definition Homepage. http://leansixsigmadefinition.com/glossary/smed/. Accessed 06 May 2019
33. Listelist Homepage. https://listelist.com/kanban-nedir/. Accessed 06 May 2019
34. Poli Tercüme Homepage. http://www.politercume.com/5-neden-sorusu-ile-kok-neden-analizi/. Accessed 06 May 2019
35. BTOES Homepages. http://insights.btoes.com/resources/what-is-going-to-gemba-lean-kaizen-definition-introduction. Accessed 06 May 2019
36. Effectivestates Homepage. http://effectivestates.org/wp-content/uploads/2017/04/Team-Based-Performance.pdf. Accessed 06 May 2019
37. Lean Production Homepage. https://www.leanproduction.com/tpm.html. Accessed 06 May 2019

Domain Knowledge Representation Languages and Methods for Building Regulations

Murat Aydın[(✉)] and Hakan Yaman

Department of Architecture, Istanbul Technical University, Istanbul, Turkey
{aydinmurat12,yamanhak}@itu.edu.tr

Abstract. The development of computable building regulations is an important factor for shortening the communication of building code provisions and automated code compliance checking. The representation of building regulations plays an important role in a computer-readable format which recognizes and understands certain aspects of the domain knowledge in compliance checking of building regulations. It allows compliance checking of a building model according to building regulations, codes and standards, and it evaluates the building model with its building elements. The studies have continued to the present to obtain data from legal sources and to create an appropriate computable representation of building regulations. In this research, the studies on domain knowledge representation of computable building regulation compliance checking are reviewed in detail based on the literature in the last 50 years. It also discusses the languages and methods of the studies under common titles such as Human Languages, Formal Languages, Artificial Intelligence Methods, Markup Language Methods and Semantic Web Methods and also reviews the languages and methods which are used in the representation of building regulations.

Keywords: Domain knowledge representation · Automated Code Compliance Checking · Building Information Modeling

1 Introduction

1.1 Domain Knowledge Representation

In the recent years, many researchers have concentrated on engineering information systems for providing effective methods and tools for domain knowledge representations of the construction industry. Such problems are in focus like storing, retrieving, transferring, indexing, sharing and using the data in order to improve and accelerate the design and construction process. The domain knowledge has many facets regarding the building lifecycle tasks, but code checking and agency review processes deserve a special focus due to their content and information complexity. The current research in this domain includes Architecture, Engineering and Construction (AEC) Codes and Regulations and Automated Code Compliance Checking (ACCC).

AEC Codes and Regulations are legal documents written and authorized to be understood and implemented by legal experts and construction professionals. These are not definitive as formal logic. The flexibility of expression is important for an information retrieval system. Only experts can interpret these documents and translate them

© Springer Nature Switzerland AG 2020
S. Ofluoglu et al. (Eds.): EBF 2019, CCIS 1188, pp. 101–121, 2020.
https://doi.org/10.1007/978-3-030-42852-5_9

into formal notations and software applications. They can select and use all kinds of information which they need and use them at various levels of accuracy. These are the practical tasks in which these extractions and applications are carried out, and where researchers and professionals are trying to develop automated or semi-automated methods for many years.

Most of the early studies in this specific research field focus on the conversion of the domain knowledge from natural language into a formal language such as First-Order Logic (FOL). In FOL, a predicate is a well-defined term (or a function) that can be evaluated as True, False or Unknown (if the terms are not defined). In addition, the quantity of predicate logic is related to the emerged logic statements or the application of expressions to all cases. There are general techniques developed for converting logic claims into executable statements, including Prolog Computer Language. The implementation of these methods in AEC regulations is laborious, and it has many limitations. For example, the interpretation of the rules for buildings and how many models should be applied to the rules are important issues. Furthermore, many subjective provisions cannot be translated into FLO.

One of the first implementations of FLO is the decision tables representing AISC specifications which was introduced in 1969. The decision logic tables approach has contributed to a technical standard with many objective data such as AISC specifications. Various applications based on this approach were used as a design tool for steel structures for at least fifteen years [1]. Other studies in this area include one of the most important early standard SASE (Standards, Analysis, Synthesis, and Expression) representation system developed by the NIST in 1984 (National Institute of Standards and Technology formerly known as the US National Bureau of Standards). SASE was used to establish and maintain the structure of decision tables and standards [2].

Other studies focus on using expert systems or AI (Artificial Intelligence) methods to encode regulatory data for use in building design [3–6]. These systems are only useful when basic information is kept up to date with regulatory provisions. Despite the intrinsic ineffectiveness and dependence on manual updates, the use of AI to transfer information from other computable objects and regulatory texts as automated or semi-automated has been utilized until today [7–10].

Other approaches to computerized building code checking include markup document modeling and the use of hypertext to represent regulatory provisions [11, 12]. The concept of marking regulatory texts in order to create a regulatory text are reconsidered in numerous studies [13–15]. Extensible Markup Language (XML) was proposed to represent regulations such as legal documents due to XML's ability to process semi-structured data in 2004 [14]. The studies have continued to the present for obtaining data from legal sources and to create an appropriate computable representation of the building regulations, codes and standards. The search for solutions continues in the AEC industry for more practical computable representation of the regulations, codes and standards.

1.2   Background of Automated Code Compliance Checking

Automated Code Compliance Checking (ACCC) is used for the computable representations of the building regulations. ACCC is a computational procedure for handling the manual regulation verification problem in a limited number of reasoning steps. It includes deduction, induction, abstraction, generalization with a structured logic. It is a systematic extraction of logical rules from written documents and the development of a general implementation plan. ACCC also encompasses algorithmic strategies to search for repetitive patterns, universal principles, modifiable modules, and inductive connections. The rational strength of such systems lies in their ability to allow machine interpretation for building regulations, to obtain results that have missing data, and to expand certain limits of human intellect. Thus, ACCC shows rationality, consistency, coherence, organization and systemization.

The first step of the ACCC process is the creation of a computable representation of the content and context of building regulations. This involves an interpretation process in which the semantic structure of each arrangement is translated into rules or parametric models using certain formal languages. Following this procedure, the information including parametric data structures or rules are queried and activated using specific software tools. The next step includes the connection between these representations and the Building Information Modeling (BIM) data for interpretation. The ACCC process aims to improve the actions of manual design review by rationalizing the knowledge of a predictable result. It includes the actions to extract the necessary information automatically and verify particular details. This task is usually very time-consuming when applied manually to the initial data set of properties and conditions. Here, the computable models serve as a vessel to carry out automated code compliance checking processes.

In the second half of the twentieth century, various formal language models were developed to represent building codes and regulations. These models have been useful to handle various aspects of the knowledge domain. However, none of them is sufficient enough to address all the issues regarding ACCC. The development of computable building regulations is an important asset for the development of existing provisions by shortening the communication of code provisions and ACCC. The representation of building regulations and standards in a machine-readable format that recognizes and reads certain aspects of the knowledge domain plays an important role in the automated validation process of building regulations. The computable numerical scheme of building rules and specifications allows automated code compliance checking without changing building design. The scheme evaluates the compliance design principles of parametric objects, their relationships or their attributes. It contains a code-compliant building design framework for rule-based systems, and results are produced in the form of Success, Failure, Warning, Unidentified.

It is clear that computable building regulations focus on data preparation and rule development. Each of these factors has its own characteristics and limitations. The difficulties are sourced from the nature of building regulations and standards. For example, building regulations are not private documents and they are often referred to as other sources. This means that all professionals must be familiar with most of the regulations in a building code or standard. However, such data is not always represented in a formal form. Furthermore, understanding a design standard requires the knowledge of the relevant design area. In AEC disciplines, basic professional knowledge (basic knowledge acquired by engineers and architects) is expected to benefit from architectural engineering design standards [16]. In addition, both knowledge and tacit experience are required to decide whether a standard is audited and proceeded.

1.3 Building Regulations

People naturally live and carry out various activities together. Laws are required to regulate these activities socially and personally in order to ensure mutual living. Laws are also written rules that always show the necessary importance to maintain unity among people, to ensure harmony in the society and to preserve shared values. Specifically, codes, regulations and standards ensure the health, safety and welfare in the built environment and also contribute to the quality of life. Today, most of the information needed can be accessed through codes, regulations or standards. Codes, regulations and standards are created and updated by authorities, taking all necessary measures to prevent unwanted, unpredictable or controversial issues. They define the minimum requirements for the design and construction features of buildings and other structures that create the built environment. However, it is clear that the requirements of rules, regulations and standards are sometimes insufficient due to the unexpected situations that may cause loss of life and property. The concept of having minimum requirements for buildings and other structures is important for determining the acceptable level of living quality for users [17].

The construction laws and regulations are implemented in federal, county, city, state and local government levels to protect the health, safety and welfare of the society and to ensure the integrity of the completed construction projects. One of the most important challenges is the fact that the codes, regulations and standards are effective locally and different from each other in every specific authority. In general, each country has its own legal practice and local rules and regulations may not be applicable for other countries or domains. In order to address this issue, International Organization for Standardization (ISO) develops universally applicable codes, regulations and standards around the world. The sub-headings of codes, regulations and standards according to the CSI (The Construction Specifications Institute) are given below [17]:

- Codes
  - Design and Construction Requirements
  - Fire and Life Safety Requirements
  - AHJ Plan Reviews and Permits for Construction
  - Evaluation Reports
- Regulations
  - Zoning, Deed Covenants, and Regulations
  - Site Use and Environmental Requirements
  - Occupational Safety and Health Requirements
  - Accessibility Requirements
  - Health and Sanitary Requirements

- Standards
  - Standards Development Process
  - Standards Development Organizations
  - Governmental Standards Development Agencies

Clauses of Building Regulations. Regulations, sometimes known as rules, are developed and written by Authorized Having Jurisdictions (AHJs) for specific purposes. For example, a widely known Zoning Regulation is designed to regulate and determine the use of land within the city boundaries. Likewise, building regulations provide the necessary conditions for safe, healthy and optimum performance of buildings. These include specific issues such as fire protection, accessibility, energy performance, acoustic performance, elevator safety, electrical and gas safety, etc. Regulations also include sanctions or fines in case of non-compliance with the required conditions.

The content of building regulations is of great importance in the practical methods applied to the computerization of building regulations. The main objective of the existing practical methods is to digitize the building regulations through a computable model with clear syntax and semantics. This can be used to represent and justify building rules and clauses. Here, the provided model must comply with the general requirements of digital content providers. For example, an object-based schema of building codes should be represented with the minimum of data as possible in order to check the suitability of the building codes automatically. This amount may vary depending on the content of the specific building regulation. According to the content, some clauses may include short, concise, and quantitative statements, and some other clauses may contain expressive statements. These clauses can also be associated with other clauses by referring to each other. The clauses of a building regulation are classified into four main categories as shown in Fig. 1. These are:

- Conditional Clauses: Conditional clauses are applied to interpret a set of formal rules directly from textual documents. Examples of these are very common, and these clauses often contain rules with numerical values.
- Content Clauses: Contents clauses cannot be converted into TRUE or FALSE statements. These clauses usually include expression with definitions such as a definitions of a firewall, a fire stair, fire speed, smoke evacuation, or a high-rise building etc.
- Ambiguous Clauses: Ambiguous clauses are subjective. These clauses contain unstable or unclear words such as normally, approximately, mostly, nearly, maybe, etc.
- Dependent Clauses: Dependent clauses indicate that a section of a building regulation is related to one or more clauses. If some provisions fully meet the other provisions, it means that it complies with a certain condition. In general, it is somewhat difficult to convert these clauses into a set of formal rules. Therefore, it may be necessary to check compliance of dependent clauses manually.

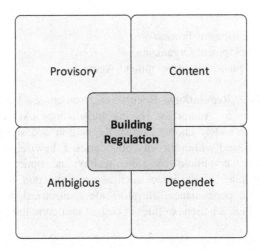

Fig. 1. Clause categories of a building regulation.

2 Domain Knowledge Representation Languages and Methods

The majority of the previous studies on modeling formal language representations of building regulations have focused only on syntax and grammar of rules. Understanding the meaning of a rule considered to be the most important task. This requires experts to have the knowledge and experience to interpret the meaning of the rules of a regulation. For example, CORENET uses a logic-based interpretation approach to translate provisions from natural language into a formal language. During the interpretation process, there are implied assumptions and expectations that provide an understanding of what needs to be examined.

Due to conventional methods in the review process, many inconsistencies, mismatches, human errors, and abuses more likely to occur in manual building regulation compliance checking. As a result of checking, uncertainties arise based on experience. Setting standards for building code ontology and BIM data can be listed as solutions to these particular types of problems. In order to create consistent, accurate and measurable conditions and constraints, the suitability of each rule must be checked by machine-oriented automated processes. The current research studies largely include different modeling techniques for creating a formal language (computer-readable rules of regulations written in human language). Below is a summary of domain knowledge representation languages and methods which are used to automate building regulation compliance checking. As seen in Fig. 2, the most effective way is to apply modeling languages that are capable of generating rules that can be interpreted by computers. According to Fig. 2 workflow, transformation of a building regulation into a building code that is parsed and controlled by a computer is carried out in 3 stages:

- Decomposition (Raw Data/Building Regulation)
  At the initial stage, the relevant building regulation is analyzed and decomposed into the smallest base unit in the decomposition phase. Data tree structure related to the Regulation, Part, Clause, Statement and Textual Expression of Statement is formed until the stage of decomposition into statements. The second stage includes the examination of statement structures. These statements are generally grouped into two types of classification as a Clarification or a Rule. As a result of this classification, a statement is determined which can be a rule. As seen in Fig. 3, the regulation statement is detailed as the following:
  - Building Regulation Name: Planned Area Zoning Regulation (PAZR)
  - Part No: Part 05 (P.05.)
  - Part Heading: Provisions for Building
  - Clause Heading: Doors and Windows
  - Clause No: Clause 39 (C.39.)
  - Statement ID: PAZR.P.05.C.39.ST.(01).a).
  - Textual Expression of Statement: All door heights cannot be less than 210 centimeters.
- RASE Method (Translation/Formal and Logic Languages)
  The decision tables proposed by Nyman and Fenves for steel structures are handled for the representation of the relevant building regulation in the digital environment. According to Nyman and Fenves, a regulation statement is defined as a rule in 4 basic features. These are Requirement, Applicability, Selection and Exception. They suggested this model as a RASE Method. As seen in Fig. 3, the regulation statement "Statement ID: PAZR.P.05.C.39.ST.(01).a)." according to RASE Method is defined as a rule:
  - Building Code Name: Planned Areas Zoning Regulation Code (PAZRCode)
  - Part No: Part Five (RSG.05.)
  - Part Heading: Provisions for Building
  - Clause Heading: Doors and Windows
  - Clause No: Clause 39 (RS.39.)
  - Rule ID: PAZRCode.RSG.05.RS.39.R.(01).a).
  - RASE Method Expression of Rule:
    - Requirement: Door Height $\geq$ 2,10 m
    - Applicability: <IfcDoor> <DOO - ...> <Door> <Door>
    - Selection: <IfcDoor> <OverallHeight> $\geq$ 2100 mm
    - Exception: Null
- C# Language (Encoding/Computer-Readable Statement)
  C# Object-Oriented Programming Language is used to encode the selected rule in the relevant building code. C# is a powerful, modern, object-oriented and type-safe programming language. At the same time, C# provides both the strength of the C++ language and the convenience of Visual Basic. The C# language is used in the Microsoft Visual Studio environment. C# language is a popular programming

language mainly preferred by the AEC industry. It also provides easy operations for standard data formats. IFC is among the standard data format that can be further processed with C#. IFC.XML format is selected as standard data. It is checked in the following coding whether it is selected from IFC.XML data for the related feature to be controlled by the related rule and provides the numerical value specified in the regulation statement. As seen in Fig. 4, the representation of "Rule ID: PAZRCode.RSG.05.RS.39.R.(01).a)." in C# language is as follows:

```
— #region PAZRCode.RSG.05.RS.39.R.(01).a).
  if (Convert.ToDouble(element.height) >= 2100)
  {text = "' compliance with door statement. " }
  else
  {text = "' not compliance with door statement. "
```

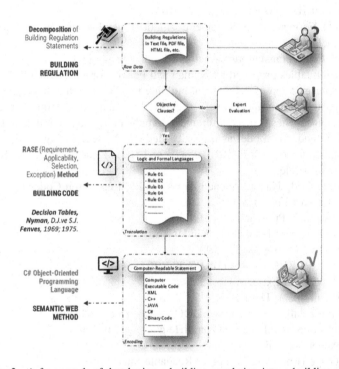

Fig. 2. A framework of developing a building regulation into a building code

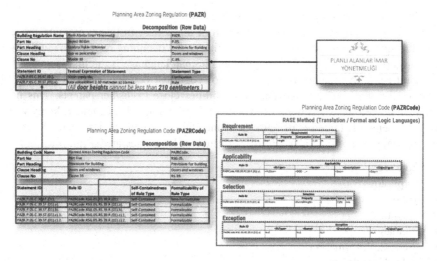

Fig. 3. Decomposition (raw data/building regulation) phase and RASE method (translation/ formal and logic languages) phase

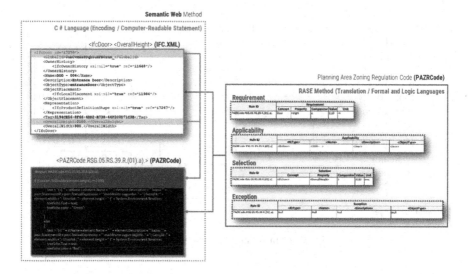

Fig. 4. C# language (encoding/computer-readable statement) phase

2.1 Human Languages

Human is a social entity as all individuals communicate with each other. A language is method of communication between people in written and spoken form. Various arguments were made about the emergence of this tool which provides unity, order and mutual agreement between people. Although these arguments cannot be proved, but, it is widely accepted that the body language emerged and then the speech-language was formed as a result of the human need for communication.

Human languages are easy to learn by children. The learning occurs during the one ended transmission of verbal expressions from the adults. In this expression process, the adult speaks the human language according to the breathing rate and the limitations of short-term memory [18]. This implies that human language is the first language that an infant can comprehend. In the process of cognitive development, a child quickly acquires the speaking and understanding abilities close to his/her parents. This illustrates the numerous extensibility of expressions with a limited vocabulary. Many words have an open-ended number of senses and uncertainty in a human language. As seen in Fig. 5, some of the basic characteristics of human languages are as follows:

- Phonology
- Morphology
- Syntax
- Semantics
- Pragmatics
- Discourse Information
- Realm Knowledge

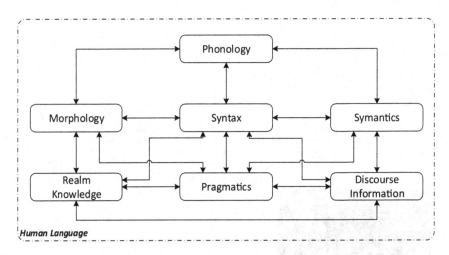

Fig. 5. Human language characteristics.

Rules, which combine sounds and words together, create new sentences of a language grammar. A language grammar is equally complex and logical. It can produce an infinite set of sentences to express any thought. Therefore, it is very difficult to talk about a single meaning for a sentence in human language. Instead, there are numerous possibilities of different meanings within a single sentence. In addition, human languages are constantly changing over time and it is impossible for a person to understand every text or dialogue in his/her language. Taking this complexity into consideration, it is unrealistic to expect a computer to overcome this problem with acceptable levels of effort and computation power.

2.2   Formal Languages

A formal language is a set of symbols' strings that can be limited to specific rules in mathematics, computer science and linguistics. The alphabet of an official language is a set of symbols, letters, or markers. The strings of a particular alphabet are called words. The words of a formal language are sometimes referred to as well-formed words or well-formed formulas. A formal language is often referred to as a formation rule through a formal grammar or context-free grammar.

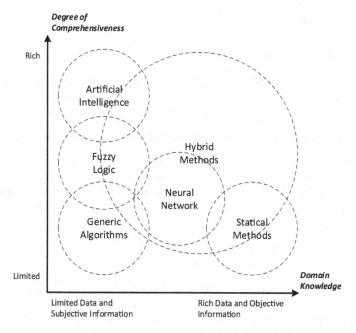

Fig. 6. Application areas of formal languages.

The aim of formal languages is to represent existing problem areas as much as possible to predict objective functions. Some of the major formal languages, which have been developed over the years, show the efforts of researchers to develop a formal language to understand and comprehend the complexity of real-world systems. These include statistics, syntax, binary and fuzzy logic, lexical semantics, neural networks and genetic algorithms. In the 1950s, Claude E. Shannon's knowledge theory and other statistical methods were popular in both linguistics and psychology. But, the speed and storage capacity of the first computers were not sufficient to handle the required data volumes. Towards the end of the century, the increase in computer power made it possible to processes large volumes of data using different methods. Many of these formal languages try to represent the problem area knowledge as adequately as possible to better predict the target function. These languages attempt to develop processes by using heuristic rules and data.

Figure 6 shows the main application areas of these formal languages. Each of these modeling languages is based on a specific technology. These are mathematical statistics, grammar rules, dictionary formats, fuzzy logic and networks of neurons. These formal languages are given below:

- Hybrid Methods
- Statistical Methods
- Generic Algorithms
- Artificial Intelligence Methods
- Neural Networks
- Fuzzy Logic Approaches

2.3   Artificial Intelligence Methods

The aim of Artificial Intelligence (AI) is always to simulate human intelligence, knowledge and perception. This simulation focuses on two main domains:

- The first domain is associated with learning relationships
- The second domain focuses on encapsulating and reusing information.

From the ACCC perspective, the AI methods aim to fully automate a building code compliance checking process by extracting and coding legal requirements to ensure computer processing. These methods are generally based on Natural Language Processing (NLP) models, which predict the probability distribution of language expressions. It includes two main types:

- A rule-based approach and
- A machine learning (ML)-based approach

A rule-based approach uses manually developed rules to process documents. A machine learning (ML)-based approach refers to a system learned from existing data or previous experience and it uses ML algorithms to process text. An ML-based approach may be one of the following types:

- Supervised,
- Unsupervised and
- Semi-supervised.

Supervised ML-based algorithms require intensive manual effort for preparing a data set. However, their sensitivity and performance are relatively higher than other methods. In general, a rule-based approach provides better text processing performance than an ML-based approach [19].

NLP methods can be classified into shallow and deep approaches. These are distinguished by their different emphasis on text processing. If an emphasis is placed on the analysis of missing sentences or specific topics, the NLP method is considered shallow. On the other hand, if an emphasis requires full sentences, the NLP method is considered deep [20]. An NLP method that achieves the most reasonable performance results is shallow. Utilization of a deep NLP method is relatively difficult due to the requirement of detailed information and efficient reasoning about a domain in AI [21].

There have been many research studies focusing on NLP techniques in the AEC. Caldas and Soibelman conducted an ML-based text classification study of construction documents [22]. As seen in Fig. 7, Zhang and El-Gohary proposed several approaches to automate building regulation compliance checking using NLP methods. These approaches include semantic modeling and semantic NLP techniques to facilitate the automatic processing of building regulation documents to extract regulatory rules in computable formats [23–25]. Typically, they involve a set of algorithms on a computable platform. These are Text Classification (TC), Information Extraction (IE) and Information Transformation (IT).

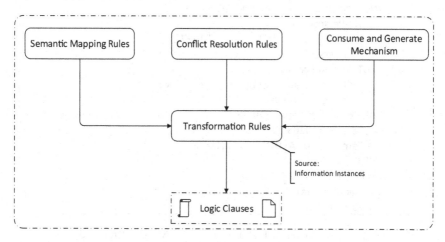

Fig. 7. Transformation rules study of Zhang and El-Gohary [25].

2.4   Markup Language Methods

A markup language is a system used to note attributes of a document. Historically, the term "marking" has been used to refer to the process of marking a string. It usually contains fonts, dimensions, spaces, letters, and other formatting features. Marking specifies the order of characters or other symbols that are placed in a text or a word to define the logical structure of the document or to specify how the document should appear when viewed or printed. Markup languages are static, unlike programming languages. Programming languages process data through various operations in a dynamic fashion. Basically, a markup language defines similar units of information in a document. It enables them to read and to process applications more effectively by introducing a form of into a document.

Hypertext Markup Language (HTML). Hypertext Markup Language (HTML) is a standard text markup language used to create web pages. HTML cannot be defined as a programming language. Because HTML contains no programming logic and it doesn't have common conditional and flow control statements. Basically, HTML is necessary to simply connect different data such as text, image, video and a page together for the proper viewing by a web browser software. As shown in Fig. 8, HTML commands are written between <and>. They are often used to indicate the beginning and the end of the highlighted text (<FamilyName>AYDIN</ FamilyName>). However, they can also be used individually if a sign is placed in the text (<ThePerson>). Most of the building regulations and standard documents are obtained in addition to a printed copy with an HTML.

```
<IfcPersonAndOrganization id="i1643">
   <ThePerson>
     <IfcPerson xsi:nil="true" ref="i1637"/>
   </ThePerson>
   <TheOrganization>
     <IfcOrganization xsi:nil="true" ref="i1639"/>
   </TheOrganization>
</IfcPersonAndOrganization>
<IfcPerson id="i1637">
   <FamilyName>AYDIN</FamilyName>
</IfcPerson>
<IfcOrganization id="i1639">
   <Name>Murat</Name>
</IfcOrganization>
```

Fig. 8. An example of HTML text in IFC.XML of a BIM model.

Extensible Markup Language (XML). Extensible Markup Language (XML) is a markup language for creating documents that can be easily read by both humans and computer systems. The XML standard is defined by W3C. Figure 9, shows the "xmlns: xlink" referenced to this standard. In addition to data retention, it also serves as an intermediate format for exchanging data between different systems. For example, Lau and Law proposed an integrated format to represent Extensible Markup Language (XML) regulations. Because XML is capable of modeling semi-structured data such as legal documents [26]. In fact, XML has a binary property as a markup language and a Web standard.

```
<?xml version="1.0" encoding="UTF-8"?>
<ex:iso_10303_28       xmlns:xsi="http://www.w3.org/2001/XMLSchema-in-
stance"                  xmlns:xlink="http://www.w3.org/1999/xlink"
xmlns:ex="urn:iso.org:standard:10303:part(28):version(2):xmlschema:com-
mon"          xsi:schemaLocation="urn:iso.org:standard:10303:part(28):ver-
sion(2):xmlschema:common ex.xsd" version="2.0">
    <ex:express id="exp_1" external="" schema_name="IFC2X3">
    <!--external: When the EXPRESS schema is represented 'by-reference', the
external XML attribute shall be present and its value shall identify a resource that
contains the EXPRESS schema (text).-->
    <!--schema_identifier: For an EXPRESS schema that is defined by a Part of
ISO 10303 schema_identifier shall contain the ASN.1 (official identifier for a part
of 10303 ) identifier value associated with that schema by that Part of ISO 10303-
->
    <ex:uos id="uos_1" description="" schema="exp_1" configuration="i-
ifc2x3" edo="" xmlns="http://www.iai-tech.org/ifcXML/IFC2x3/FINAL" xsi:sche-
maLocation="http://www.iai-tech.org/ifcXML/IFC2x3/FINAL ifc2x3.xsd">
```

Fig. 9. A short example of an IFC.XML format.

LegalRuleML and LegalRuleML Modeling Languages. In the last few years, several legal XML standards have been proposed in order to identify and present legal text information with XML-based rules [27–30]. Other studies have focused on Legal Ontology Research, which is combined with Semantic Web to model law concepts and provisions [31–33]. Many of these studies have used the Expressive XML Annotation, combined with Semantic Web technology, to meet the unique features of legal rules and norms. Examples of these efforts have resulted in RuleML and LegalRuleML Modeling Languages [30, 34–36]. The purpose of LegalRuleML is to determine the characteristics (comprehensive, articulated, and meaningful markup) of legal rules and norms.

2.5   Semantic Web Methods

The Semantic Web is an internet add-on that aims to enable web content to be understood, interpreted and used not only by natural languages but also the related software. This software can easily find, share, and integrate data. The semantic web essentially consists of a philosophy, a set of design principles, collaborative working groups and assistive technologies. Some components of the semantic web are not yet developed or implemented but these are more likely to be achieved in the near future. The other parts are expressed in official descriptions. All of these parts are expected to formally describe the concepts, terms and connections in a particular problem space. These parts are:

- Resource description framework (RDF)
- Various data conversion formats such as XML, N3, Turtle, N-Triples.

- Notations like resource description framework Diagram (RDFs)
- Web ontology language (OWL)

The Internet (World Wide Web) was originally designed as a content service for documents shown by web browsers. It is a content service that is meaningful to users rather than machines [37]. The data and meanings expressed in web pages are difficult for a computer to extract, understand and process automated information [38]. It is recommended to solve the problem by adding contextual information to the existing information in order to gain meaning on the internet with the Semantic Web approach. This semantic approach is the key concept underlying web marking including:

- Web coding
- Information processing
- Universal usability
- Search engine visibility
- Maximum display flexibility

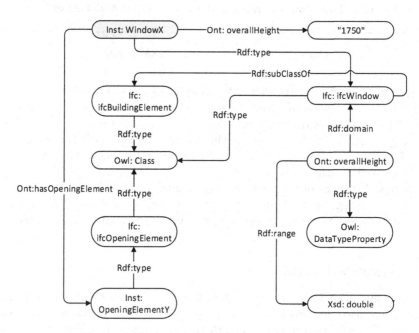

Fig. 10. Semantic network study of Pauwels et al. [39].

The semantic web method is focused on the development of an IFC model based on logic theory and rules by using a descriptive language. One of the earliest studies belongs to Pauwels [39]. The study concentrated on semantic web technologies for building code compliance checking. The main purpose of this study was to provide building acoustic regulation compliance checking using detailed BIM models. The concept of the study was based on a semantic network. This semantic network defines concepts through a directed, labeled graph. Each node represents a concept or an object, and each arc represents the logical relationship between these two concepts or objects [39]. The graph shown in Fig. 10, is an instance of a combination of logic-based declarative sentences, each of which consists of two nodes and a relational arc. The semantic of a particular concept is defined by a graph associated with this concept.

3   Evaluation

The above-mentioned domain knowledge representation methods and languages are used during automated code compliance checking process. Figures 2, 3 and 4, show the three stages of checking and transforming an example regulation. The first stage is the decomposition of the building regulation written in human language. The second stage is the RASE method proposed by Nyman and Fenves, one of Formal Languages, and the last stage is the semantic web method with C# programming language. Preferred languages and methods have advantages and disadvantages according to time, cost, programming labor and their impacts. The most important implication of these approaches is the digital transformation of building regulation checking processes using available technological methods.

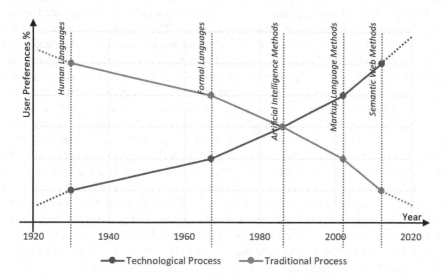

Fig. 11. Traditional and technological checking process of building regulation according to domain knowledge representation languages and methods by year.

As shown in Fig. 11, the traditional checking process of building regulations written in human language had been carried out exclusively by human experts using analog methods. In the late 60s, the development of formal languages provided the opportunity for checking building regulations in using technology through the conversion of regulations into logic building rules. The AI methods which came in the mid-80s initiated the transformation of building regulation checking from conventional to computerized methods. With the increased technological capabilities at the beginning of the 2000s, Markup Languages Methods made it possible for computers to digitally parse and process logic representations of building regulations. As a continuation stage of these advancements, the semantic web methods enabled the specific software to understand and interpret building regulations and perform automatic checking. Currently, web-based systems are being developed for better accessibility and platform-free operations for ACCC. These developments clearly demonstrate the current trajectory of ACCC approaches as they are being rapidly transformed from analog to digital.

4   Conclusion

In this research, the studies on domain knowledge representation of computable building regulation compliance checking are reviewed in detail focusing on the last fifty-year research work. Existing languages and the representation methods are discussed under common categories such as Human Languages, Formal Languages, Artificial Intelligence Methods, Markup Language Methods and Semantic Web Methods. This extensive literature review helped to illustrate the potentials and limitations of the existing methods and the markup languages for Automatic Code Compliance Checking.

In summary, building regulations and standards are legal documents created by the legislation experts and used by AEC professionals. These texts are generally in the form of natural language. They usually include texts, mathematical formulas, tables and other legal provisions. These expressions are as precise as official languages. The flexibility of a text is very important for an information retrieval system. Engineers and architects can use these documents and translate them into formal scientific representations and software applications. This may reduce the complexity of code checking procedures where experts can extract any data type, find problems regarding code checking and apply them in various application stages. The existing methods allow automated or semi-automated code checking procedures using specific software tools. The current literature documents novel research studies on this domain in order to provide more effective methods and approaches the are capable of creating rules and semantic links through new modeling languages. Due to the increasing complexity of construction projects, it can be argued that both research and practical applications of ACCC will increase in the near future using data derived from advanced BIM models and databases. Here, the link between ACCC and BIM methods will be the key to more advanced and effective applications.

References

1. Fenves, S., Goel, S., Gaylord, E.: Decision Table Formulation of the 1969 AISC Specifcation. University of Illinois, Urbana (1969)
2. Fenves, S.J., Garrett, J.H., Kiliccote, H., Law, K.H., Reed, K.A.: Computer representations of design standards and building codes: U.S. perspective. Int. J. Constr. Inf. Technol. **3**(1), 13–34 (1995)

3. Eastman, C., Lee, J., Jeong, Y., Lee, J.-K.: Automatic rule-based checking of building designs. Autom. Constr. **18**(8), 1011–1033 (2009)
4. Frye, M., Olynick, D., Pinkney, R.: Development of an expert system for the freprotection requirements of the national building code of Canada. In: Proceedings of CIB W78 Conference, Montreal, Canada, pp. 215–226 (1992)
5. Mugridge, W., Hosking, J., Amor, R.: Adding a Code Conformance Tool to an Integrated Building Design Environment. Auckland Uniservices, Auckland (1996)
6. Rosenman, M.A., Gero, J.S., Oxman, J.: An expert system for design codes and design rules. In: Sriram, D., Adey, R. (eds.) Applications of Artificial Intelligence in Engineering Problems, vol. II, pp. 745–758. Springer, Heidelberg (1986). https://doi.org/10.1007/978-3-662-21626-2_60
7. Hjelseth, E., Nisbet, N.: Overview of concepts for model checking. In: 27th International Conference–Applications of IT in the AEC Industry, CIB W78 2010, Cairo, pp. 16–18 (2010)
8. Kiyavitskaya, N., Zeni, N., Mich, L., Cordy, J.R., Mylopoulos, J.: Text mining through semi automatic semantic annotation. In: Reimer, U., Karagiannis, D. (eds.) PAKM 2006. LNCS (LNAI), vol. 4333, pp. 143–154. Springer, Heidelberg (2006). https://doi.org/10.1007/11944935_13
9. Zhang, J., El-Gohary, N.: Automated information extraction from construction related regulatory documents for automated compliance checking. In: Proceedings of the 28th International Conference of CIB W78, Sophia Antipolis, France, pp. 1–10 (2011)
10. Zhang, J., El-Gohary, N.: Extraction of construction regulatory requirements from textual documents using natural language processing techniques. In: Issa, R., Flood, I. (eds.) International Conference on Computing in Civil Engineering, pp. 453–460. ASCE American Society of Civil Engineers (2012)
11. Turk, Z., Vanier, D.: Tools and models for the electronic delivery of building codes and standards. In: Proceedings of CIB W78 Conference, Stanford, CA, pp. 20–30 (1995)
12. Vanier, D.: Computerized building regulations. In: Proceedings of the International Conference on Municipal Code Administration Building Safety and the Computer, pp. 43–62. National Research Council Canada, Winnipeg (1989)
13. Bolioli, A., Dini, L., Mercatali, P., Romano, F.: For the automated mark-up of Italian legislative texts in XML. In: Bench-Capon, T.J.M., Daskalopulu, A., Winkels, R. (eds.) Legal Knowledge and Information Systems: Jurix 2002: The Fifteenth Annual Conference, pp. 21–30. IOS Press, Amsterdam (2002)
14. Lau, G., Law, K.: An information infrastructure for comparing accessibility regulations and related information from multiple sources. In: The Proceedings of 10th International Conference on Computing in Civil and Building Engineering, Weimar, Germany, p. 11 (2004)
15. Hjelseth, E., Nisbet, N.: Capturing normative constraints by use of the semantic mark-up (RASE) methodology. In: Proceedings of CIB W78-W102 International Conference, Sophia Antipolis, France, pp. 1–10 (2011)
16. Nawari, N.O., Alsaffar, A.: Methods for computable building codes. J. Civil Eng. Archit. **3**, 163–171 (2015)
17. Construction Specifications Institute: The CSI Project Delivery Practice Guide, Chapter 4, Codes, Regulations, and Standards, pp. 51–63. Wiley, Hoboken (2011)
18. Sowa, J.F.: The challenge of knowledge soup. In: Ramadas, J., Chunawala, S. (eds.) Research Trends in Science, Technology and Mathematics Education. Homi Bhabha Centre, Mumbai (2006)

19. Crowston, K., Liu, X., Allen, E., Heckman, R.: Machine learning and rule based automated coding of qualitative data. In: Proceedings of 73rd ASIS&T Annual Meeting: Navigating Streams in an Information Ecosystem, pp. 1–2. Association for Information Science and Technology, Silver Spring (2010)
20. Zouaq, A.: An overview of shallow and deep natural language processing for ontology learning. In: Ontology Learning and Knowledge Discovery Using the Web: Challenges and Recent Advances, pp. 16–38. IGI Global, Hershey (2011)
21. Tierney, P.J.: A qualitative analysis framework using natural language processing and graph theory. Int. Rev. Res. Open Distance Learn. **13**(5), 173–189 (2012)
22. Caldas, C.H., Soibelman, L.: Automating hierarchical document classification for construction management information systems. Autom. Constr. **12**, 395–406 (2003)
23. Zhang, J., El-Gohary, N.: Automated regulatory information extraction from building codes leveraging syntactic and semantic information. In: Proceedings of 2012 ASCE Construction Research Congress (CRC), West Lafayette, IN (2012)
24. Zhang, J., El-Gohary, N.M.: Semantic NLP-based information extraction from construction regulatory documents for automated compliance checking. J. Comput. Civil Eng. **30**, 04015014 (2013)
25. Zhang, J., El-Gohary, N.: Automated information transformation for automated regulatory compliance checking in construction. J. Comput. Civil Eng. **29**, B4015001 (2015)
26. Lau, G.T., Law, K.: An information infrastructure for comparing accessibility regulations and related information from multiple sources. In: Proceedings of 10th International Conference on Computing in Civil and Building Engineering, Weimar, Germany (2004)
27. Lupo, C., et al.: General XML format(s) for legal sources: Estrella European Project IST-2004-027655. Deliverable 3.1, Faculty of Law. University of Amsterdam, the Netherlands (2007)
28. Boer, A., Radboud, W., Vitali, F.: MetaLex XML and the legal knowledge interchange format. In: Casanovas, P., Sartor, G., Casellas, N., Rubino, R. (eds.) Computable Models of the Law. LNCS (LNAI), vol. 4884, pp. 21–41. Springer, Heidelberg (2008). https://doi.org/10.1007/978-3-540-85569-9_2
29. Sartor, G., Palmirani, M., Francesconi, E., Biasiotti, M.: Legislative XML on Semantic Web. Springer, Heidelberg (2011). https://doi.org/10.1007/978-94-007-1887-6
30. Palmirani, M., Governatori, G., Rotolo, A., Tabet, S., Boley, H., Paschke, A.: LegalRuleML: XML-based rules and norms. In: Olken, F., Palmirani, M., Sottara, D. (eds.) RuleML 2011. LNCS, vol. 7018, pp. 289–312. Springer, Heidelberg (2011). https://doi.org/10.1007/978-3-642-24908-2_30
31. Mazzei, A., Radicioni, D.P., Brighi, R.: NLP-Based Extraction of Modifcatory Provisions Semantics, pp. 50–57. ACM Press, New York (2009)
32. Francesconi, E., Montemagni, S., Peters, W., Tiscornia, D.: Semantic Processing of Legal Texts: Where the Language of Law Meets the Law of Language. Springer, Heidelberg (2010). https://doi.org/10.1007/978-3-642-12837-0
33. Palmirani, M., Brighi, R.: Model regularity of legal language in active modifcations. In: Casanovas, P., Pagallo, U., Sartor, G., Ajani, G. (eds.) AICOL 2009. LNCS, vol. 6237, pp. 54–73. Springer, Heidelberg (2010). https://doi.org/10.1007/978-3-642-16524-5_5
34. Boley, H., Tabet, S., Wagner, G.: Design rationale for RuleML: a markup language for semantic web rules. In: Cruz, I.F., Decker, S., Euzenat, J., McGuinness, D.L. (eds.) Proceedings of SWWS 2001, the First Semantic Web Working Symposium, pp. 381–401 (2001)
35. Wagner, G., Antoniou, G., Tabet, S., Boley, H.: The abstract syntax of RuleML: towards a general web rule language framework. In: Proceedings of Web Intelligence 2004, pp. 628–631. IEEE Computer Society (2004)

36. RuleML. The Rule Markup Initiative. http://www.ruleml.org. Accessed 01 Apr 2018
37. Cardoso, J.: Semantic Web Services: Theory, Tools and Applications. IGI Global, Hershey (2007)
38. Berners-Lee, T., Hendler, J., Lassila, O.: The semantic web. Sci. Am. **284**(5), 34 (2001)
39. Pauwels, P., et al.: A semantic rule checking environment for building performance checking. Autom. Constr. **20**(5), 506–518 (2011)

BIM for Sustainability and Performative Design

BIM and Sustainability Integration: Multi-agent System Approach

Bahriye Ilhan[1(✉)] and Faikcan Kog[2]

[1] Istanbul Technical University, Taskisla Campus, 34367 Istanbul, Turkey
ilhanba@itu.edu.tr
[2] Schaeffler Technologies, Industriestrasse 1-3,
91074 Herzogenaurach, Germany

Abstract. The Architecture, Engineering, Construction (AEC) and Facility Management (FM) industry is under pressure to move towards technological innovations as well as sustainability. New technologies are of great importance to sustainable design and construction processes by providing the means to act efficiently. Building Information Modeling (BIM) as the state-of-the-art technology in the industry provides a digital representation of physical and functional characteristics and information resources of a facility by forming a reliable basis to manage the processes and decisions during its entire life cycle. Despite the opportunities and potential advantages of BIM in sustainability for certification and decision-making, there are still challenges of integrated and collaborated systems. This paper addresses a more flexible and dynamic object-oriented approach for successful sustainable project deliveries. The aim is to provide a guideline through the development of an automated solution based on industry foundation classes (IFC) and a multi-agent system (MAS). The proposed approach comprises of three main phases, which are (1) development of sustainability assessment database and library, and extension of the criteria concerning the sustainability assessment methods into BIM software via property sets, (2) generation of the BIM model and its conversion to ifcXML and XML file formats and (3) evaluation of the data and presentation of the potential alternatives by extracting the related data from the converted file. It will support effective decision-making throughout the complete building life cycle by offering the possible criteria selection according to the user-provided project properties and certification level target.

Keywords: BIM · IFC · Integration · MAS · Sustainability

1 Introduction

The recent advancement and growth of building information modeling (BIM) technology has considerably transformed the traditional paper-based practice of the Architecture, Engineering and Construction (AEC) industry [1]. As the integral aspect of the project life cycle for the requirements of planning, programming, cost and time data organisation, performance analysis and the delivery of construction documents, in addition to design and visualisation [2], BIM allows multidisciplinary information to be superimposed within one model [3] so that correct and efficient environmental

S. Ofluoglu et al. (Eds.): EBF 2019, CCIS 1188, pp. 125–136, 2020.
https://doi.org/10.1007/978-3-030-42852-5_10

performance analyses and sustainability enhancement measures can be performed [4]. Since the demand for environmentally friendly buildings that have minimal environmental impacts on society [5] and provide both outperform and economic solutions [6] has increased, the growth of more integrated platforms is now essential to sustain the level of achievement reached so far [2]. In response to this demand and the force on the built environment, several countries have developed and initiated environmental certification systems [1]. BIM is considered to be an appropriate facilitative tool for the support of sustainable design and certification process [1, 2, 7, 8].

The advantages of BIM such as saving time and hence cost, increasing productivity and minimising the conflicts and errors, enable a sustainable built environment. Despite the awareness and positive expansion of sustainability in the AEC industry, certification systems are sometimes unable to go beyond an advertising and marketing tool. The targeted certification level cannot be achieved in most cases. Cost related obstacles are one of the reasons for this problem. Lack of a clear sustainable design goal, mid-stream attempts to incorporate sustainability, decentralized management of the sustainable building process, lack of experience/knowledge with sustainable building and insufficient time/funding are the barriers to controlling costs [9]. Setting a clear sustainable goal based on the budget at the very early stage of the project life cycle can overcome the barriers to manage the certification process efficiently.

This paper focuses on an effective decision-making method in sustainable projects by providing an integrated and automated approach that utilises industry foundation classes (IFC) and a multi-agent system (MAS). The main purpose is to develop a system that presents the alternative certification solutions and facilitates to select the optimal option according to the preliminary project cost estimate.

2   Background

2.1   BIM and Sustainability

The World Commission on the Environment and Development, also known as the Brundtland Commission (1897) defined sustainability in construction as:

"Sustainable development meets the needs of the present without compromising the ability of future generations to meet their own needs".

Considering other factors such as global warming, pollution and the rapid consumption of energy resources, sustainability plays an important role in today's construction industry.

The growing interest in green solutions is driving the AEC industry toward transformations. For more environmentally friendly practices in the industry, legal steps and procedures worldwide are taken action to boost sustainable innovation in terms of products and processes [10, 11]. The Green BIM report 2010 [12] revealed that the strong growth of the green building market can encourage BIM adoption and practitioners believe that BIM has the potential to help achieve sustainable objectives. BIM's increased presence in the market has fuelled greater attention for research into new BIM technology, as well as studies regarding its level of market penetration and benefits in the industry [13]. Various studies examined BIM from the sustainability aspect.

Table 1 presents the studies regarding the impacts of BIM on sustainability in design, construction and facility management. Based on the literature, from optimizing the design to improving operations and maintenance, BIM has substantial impacts on sustainability. The more practicable BIM solutions for any phase of the life cycle of a construction project that aims to be sustainable, the more added-value.

Table 1. BIM impacts on sustainable design, construction and facility management*.

Impact	Research
Integrated project delivery	Nagalingam et al. [14]
Design optimization	Wong and Fan [15], Geyer [19], Zanni et al. [32]
Reduced waste, errors and costs	Azhar [16], Chong et al. [17], Bynum [49], Akinade [50]
Improved energy analysis	Ham and Golparvar-Fard [22], Kim and Anderson [23], Kim et al. [24], Ma and Zha [25]
Collaborative decision-making	Arayici [18], Zanni et al. [20], Inyim et al. [21], Kim et al. [30], Zelkowicz [31]
Certification process integration	Wong and Kuan [1], Ilhan and Yaman [2], Jalaei and Jrade [8], Azhar et al. [7], Wu and Issa [26, 27], Alwan et al. [28], Oti and Tizani [29]
Reduced site-based conflicts, claims and litigation	Hanna [51], Bolgani [52]
Enhanced project safety and health performance	Vacharapoom [53]
More accurate and cost-effective as-built drawings	Akintoye [54], Boktor [55]
Improved operations and maintenance	Azhar [16]

*Adapted from [13, 48]

Despite its rise in importance and prospective use in sustainability, BIM is still assessed as 'immature, ad-hoc and unsystematic' for a green built environment [33]. Based on the literature, the barriers to BIM adoption in sustainable projects can be grouped into six different categories including industry-related, legal and regulatory, monetary, organisational, software related and sustainability-related issues. The main obstacles for each category are given in Table 2.

As a slow adopter of new technologies, the characteristics of the AEC/FM industry make the BIM and sustainability integration harder. Lack of regulations, high-cost investments in new technologies, organisational structures in the industry and difficulty in obtaining sustainable data are the other barriers that the industry faces.

Table 2. Barriers to the BIM usage in sustainability*.

Barrier	Sub-obstacles
Industry-related issues	Fragmented nature of the industry
	Resistance to change
	Domination of the traditional processes, methods and tools
	Lack of qualified staff in BIM
	Insufficient research and development (R&D) in the industry
	Heterogeneous market conditions
Legal and regulatory issues	Inadequate government support
	Lack of legal framework
	Lack of proper contractual agreements
	Lack of standards for sustainability
Organisational issues	Lack of top management support
	Lack of understanding of the procedures necessary for sustainability and BIM
	Difficulty in cooperation amongst project participants
	Long-standing effort in BIM technology adoption
	Absence of execution plan for BIM and sustainability
Software related issues	User-unfriendly BIM software packages
	Lack of open source guides for software development
	Incompatibility problems among different software programs
	Lack of BIM software developer support
	Insufficient tools for supporting sustainability analysis
	Influence of certain BIM software developers in the market
Sustainability related issues	Problems encountered for evaluating the buildings in terms of environmental factors
	Difficulty in obtaining sustainable data
	The complexity of sustainability assessment systems and their criteria
	Lack of semantic data model for BIM and sustainability integration
Other	Lack of owner demand
	Difficulty in assigning and distributing BIM-related responsibilities and risks

*Adapted from [56]

The drawbacks of current sustainable BIM literature can be grouped into (i) inadequate exploration for managing environmental performance at the building maintenance, renovation and destruction phase; (ii) insufficient 'cradle-to-grave' holistic sustainability simulation tools through BIM; (iii) lack of attention given to the trending technologies such as cloud computing and 'big data' within the green BIM tool [34].

Even though there are various difficulties at different levels in BIM and sustainability integration, these can be overcomed by raising awareness through colloquiums, workshops and development of university curriculums as well as government initiatives.

2.2 Assessment Systems

Sustainability assessment methods play a key role in the dissemination of environmentally friendly buildings. Different assessment methods are being used in various nations to measure all dimensions of sustainability. These comprise Building Research Establishment Environmental Assessment Methodology (BREEAM) (UK), Leadership in Energy and Environmental Design (LEED) (US), Green Star (Australia), Sustainable Building Council (DGNB) Certification System (Germany), Comprehensive Assessment System for Building Environmental Efficiency (CASBEE) (Japan), High-Quality Environmental (HQE) (France) and Building Environmental Assessment Method (BEAM) Plus (Hong Kong).

In the assessment methods, the overall goal is to have a common set of criteria and targets and these are typically embodied in design guides that help professionals design, construct and manage the building more sustainably [36]. Their effort is to (a) maximise building performance and minimise environmental impact, (b) measure a building's influence upon the environment and (c) determine reliable standards' by which facilities can be evaluated objectively [36]. Table 3 summarises the general features of the assessment methods that are widely used globally.

Table 3. A general overview of BREEAM and LEED.

Assessment method	BREEAM	LEED
Year	1990	2000
Country	UK	US
Schemes	Communities Infrastructure New Construction In-use Refurbishment and Fit-Out	New Construction Core & Shell Schools Retail Healthcare Homes Existing Buildings Commercial Interiors Neighbourhood Development
Categories	Management (12%) Health and Well-Being (15%) Energy (19%) Transport (8%) Water (6%) Materials (12.5%) Waste (7.5%) Land Use (10%) Pollution (10%) Innovation (10% additional)	Sustainable Sites (21 points) Water Efficiency (11 points) Energy and Atmosphere (37 points) Materials and Resources (14 points) Indoor Environmental Quality (17 points) Innovation and Design (6 points additional)
Ratings	Unclassified (<30) Pass (30) Good (45) Very Good (55) Excellent (70) Outstanding (>85)	Certified (40–49 points) Silver (50–59 points) Gold (60–79 points) Platinum (>80 points)

The inclusion of the BIM model to a decision-making tool and to sustainability metrics facilitates to take strategic decisions and perform environmental analyses in the early design stages through real project data [34]. This approach enables one to model the effects of decisions for the entire project life cycle as well as to encourage a sustainable built environment by using multi-dimensional visualisation technology [35]. Besides, efficient energy solutions and minimised resources can be achieved through the assessment of different options for sustainability [34].

2.3   Multi Agent Systems (MAS) in Construction

An intelligent agent [37] is an autonomous entity, which reacts to its environment by observations and their capabilities. Besides their independent behaviour, agents can interact and co-operate with each other to reach their objectives. A number of intelligent agents construct a multi-agent system (MAS) because of its ability to provide robustness and efficiency; to allow inter-operation of existing legacy systems; and to solve problems in which data, expertise, or control is distributed [38]. Multi-agent frameworks are aimed to model complex problems or to create systems with multiple separately developed agents that enable the acting in the real world.

MAS is a developing information and communication technology. MAS is especially used to solve complex problems in a knowledge-based environment. The AEC/FM industry is one of the most suitable application fields for MAS due to its fragmented, complex and dynamic nature requiring many contributors with different objectives, knowledge, interest, experience and skills. The information is decentralized, and knowledge and experience are unevenly distributed among stakeholders [57].

Many researchers [38–40] express that MAS provide a collaborative and dynamic solution framework for the complex problems of the construction sector. The main areas studied are:

- Design of a project,
- Procurement and
- Coordination of supply chain.

For instance, Chiou and Logcher [41] have proposed an agent-based system for building design process; Kog and Yaman [42] have proposed a MAS based automated contractor pre-qualification and selection model for tendering and negotiation process; and Udeaja and Tah [43] have proposed a MAS in order to improve collaboration in the construction material supply chain. MAS also provide a valuable framework for intelligent control systems to learn building and occupancy trends, negotiate energy resources, and react to real-time environmental conditions [44]. On the other hand, agents have the capability of learning and MAS has flexible, adaptive and interoperable behaviours. Therefore, MAS are also used to support the decision-making process to attain the expected results.

3 Proposed Approach

The proposed system provides a guideline for the project stakeholders to make effective decision-making from the initial stages of the sustainable project aiming at certification. IFC and MAS based approach has three main phases: (1) Development Phase, (2) Generation Phase and (3) Evaluation Phase, see Fig. 1.

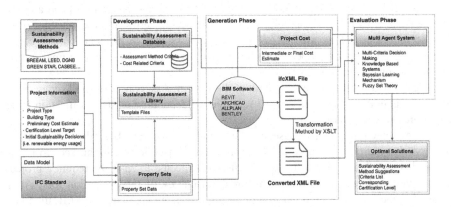

Fig. 1. The IFC and MAS based approach for sustainability assessment.

The development phase includes the following processes:

- Creating the sustainability assessment database: This process comprises creation of a database of the categories and criteria of the assessment methods and analysis of the cost related criteria of each assessment method (i.e. determination of the cost for the criteria that affect the overall project cost).
- Producing the sustainability assessment library: In this process, a sustainability assessment library based on the related criteria of the assessment method is produced and embedded into a BIM software through template files.
- Developing the property sets: The extension of the sustainable data provided by the user within the BIM software is achieved via this process. The property sets are developed in the IFC standard by examining the assessment method criteria and project information. Related assessment criteria and project information including the project and building type, preliminary cost estimate, certification level target and initial sustainability decisions are represented by the property sets that are embedded in the template files. This user-provided data is important for evaluation since each assessment method has a different calculation methodology for different types of projects (i.e. new construction or existing building) and building (commercial or school).

The second phase of the proposed system is generating the input for the next steps. The first process of the generation phase is designing the project in BIM software based on the template file. BIM model is exported to ifcXML file format and then converted to XML file using a transformation method by XSLT. The second process is estimating the cost of the project by computing the cost information provided by the user and the quantity of the related building element/component acquired from the ifcXML file.

In the evaluation phase, the MAS approach is used to support the decision-making process effectively. There are two focuses on the evaluation framework such as intermediate or final cost estimation and criteria evaluation from transformed IFC data. Therefore, the evaluation framework consists of two dimensions that the MAS dealt with. The given criteria evaluation problem is handled as a multi-criteria decision-making (MCDM) [45]. Agents use the Bayesian learning mechanism [46] and a fuzzy set theory [47] to maximize criteria scores and provide certification level objectives. The second approach is used MAS as an expert system to estimate project costs. However, the collaboration between agents provides more realistic and optimal results in comparison to the expert system's results.

The optimal solutions are the output of the system. Assessment method suggestions and corresponding criteria that should be achieved depending on the certification level target are presented based on the evaluation.

As presented in the use case diagram (Fig. 2), the template file including all developed property sets is used for the sustainable project design. In this scenario, it is embedded into ArchiCAD software. The user is expected to enter the required project information and sustainable decisions for the accuracy of the evaluation tool. After generating the model based on the template file, it is then exported as ifcXML file to be transferred into an XML file.

In order to get the optimal solutions, the essential processes are generated within the multi-agent system tool (MAST). All necessary algorithms for these processes excluded in this study are the basis of the validation of the proposed model to be discussed as further research.

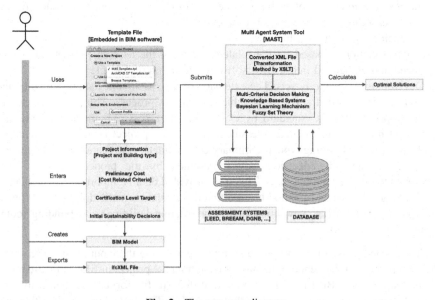

Fig. 2. The use case diagram.

4 Discussions and Conclusion

Even though BIM can provide the improvement of the green building production process via integrated project and certification information, it lacks wider utilisation due to a lack of functional solutions. However, starting from the design of a project, BIM enables visibility of the project data for all relevant parties through a shared model. Accessing the information concerning sustainability evaluation criteria such as geographical, material, layout and so on is of great importance for sustainable construction projects as early decisions affect the overall project performance. This working model not only provides real-time collaboration among the different project stakeholders but also improves the processes by preventing repetitive works and reducing errors. Moreover, the data of the completed project can be easily updated and stored for repairs, renovation and renewals for long-term sustainability. Considering that sustainability is more concerned with the processes of facility management of the buildings, this allows sustainable operational and maintenance schedules.

This study fulfills an automated and integrated sustainability assessment supporting tool by aiming to develop a system that helps decision-making based on cost information at the initial stage of the project so that a successful certification process could be achieved. This study presents an IFC and MAS based automated and integrated approach that helps the decision making during the sustainability certification process by evaluating the targeted certification level and cost estimate. Since cost and time are influential constraints that affect the project decisions, most construction projects aiming to get certification are unable to achieve the goal. With a clear goal and determined cost estimate at the beginning of the project life cycle, the whole process of sustainable project production could be improved. Furthermore, utilising new approaches such as BIM-a collaborative platform and MAS-a computerised decision support system provides accurate solutions on time. The project team then can make the optimal selection among the options. The system may also be useful for comparing the cost of the project at the initial phase and after completion and dealing with further projects depending on this experience. This paper as the basis of such an integrated and automated system emphasizes the decision support system at the early stages of the project. Further research will be the development and validation of the proposed approach.

References

1. Wong, J.K.-W., Kuan, K.-L.: Implementing 'BEAM Plus' for BIM-based sustainability analysis. Autom. Constr. **44**, 163–175 (2014)
2. Ilhan, B., Yaman, H.: Green building assessment tool (GBAT) for integrated BIM-based design decisions. Autom. Constr. **70**, 26–37 (2016)
3. Azhar, S., Brown, J., Sattineni, A.: A case study of building performance analyses using building information modelling. In: Proceedings of the 27th International Symposium on Automation and Robotics in Construction, Bratislava, Slovakia, pp. 213–222 (2010)
4. Schlueter, A., Thesseling, F.: Building information model-based energy/exergy performance assessment in early design stages. Autom. Constr. **18**, 153–163 (2008)

5. Biswas, T., Wang, T.H., Krishnamurti, R.: Integrating sustainable building rating systems with building information models. In: Proceedings of the 13th International Conference on Computer-Aided Architectural Design Research in Asia, Chiang Mai, Thailand, pp. 193–200 (2008)

6. Jrade, A., Jalaei, F.: Integrating building information modelling with sustainability to design building projects at the conceptual stage. Build. Simul. 6(4), 429–444 (2013)

7. Azhar, S., Carlton, W.A., Olsen, D., Ahmad, I.: Building information modelling for sustainable design and LEED rating analysis. Autom. Constr. 20(2), 217–224 (2011)

8. Jalaei, F., Jrade, A.: Integrating building information modelling (BIM) and LEED system at the conceptual design stage of sustainable buildings. Sustain. Cities Soc. 18, 95–107 (2015)

9. Syphers, G., Baum, M., Sullens, W.: Managing the Cost of Green Buildings. http://www.usgbc.org/Docs/Archive/General/Docs5049.pdf. Accessed 21 May 2018

10. Hellstrom, T.: Dimensions of environmentally sustainable innovation: the structure of eco-innovation concepts. Sustain. Dev. 15(3), 148–159 (2007)

11. Steurer, R., Hametner, M.: Objectives and indicators in sustainable development strategies: similarities and variances across Europe. Sustain. Dev. 21(4), 224–241 (2013)

12. Green BIM How Building Information Modeling is Contributing to Green Design and Construction. https://www.construction.com/market_research/freereport/greenbim/MHC_GreenBIM_SmartMarket_Report_2010.pdf. Accessed 05 Apr 2018

13. Oduyemi, O., Okoroh, M.I., Fajana, O.S.: The application and barriers of BIM in sustainable building design. J. Facil. Manag. 15(1), 15–34 (2017)

14. Nagalingam, G., Jayasena, H.S., Ranadewa, K.A.T.O.: Building information modeling and future quantity surveyor's practice in Sri Lankan construction industry. In: Proceedings of the Second World Construction Symposium, pp. 81–92 (2013)

15. Wong, K.D., Fan, Q.: Building information modeling (BIM) for sustainable building design. Facilities 31(3/4), 138–157 (2013)

16. Azhar, S.: Building information modelling (BIM): trends, benefits, risks, and challenges for the AEC industry. Leadersh. Manag. Eng. 11(3), 241–252 (2011)

17. Chong, H.Y., Wang, J., Shou, W., Wang, X., Guo, J.: Improving quality and performance of facility management using building information modeling. In: Proceedings of the International Conference on Cooperative Design, Visualization and Engineering, pp. 44–50 (2014)

18. Arayici, Y.: Technology adoption in the BIM implementation for lean architectural. Autom. Constr. 20(2), 189–195 (2011)

19. Geyer, P.: Systems modeling for sustainable building design. Adv. Eng. Inform. 26(4), 656–668 (2012)

20. Zanni, M.A., Soetanto, R., Ruikar, K.: Defining the sustainable building design process: methods for BIM execution planning in the UK. Int. J. Energy Sect. Manag. 8(4), 562–587 (2014)

21. Inyim, P., Rivera, J., Zhu, Y.: Integration of building information modeling and economic and environmental impact analysis to support sustainable building design. J. Manag. Eng. 31(1), A4014002 (2015)

22. Ham, Y., Golparvar-Fard, M.: Mapping actual thermal properties to building elements in gbXML-based BIM for reliable building energy performance modelling. Autom. Constr. 49, 214–224 (2015)

23. Kim, H., Anderson, K.: Energy modeling system using building information modelling open standards. J. Comput. Civ. Eng. 27(3), 203–211 (2013)

24. Kim, J.B., Jeong, W.S., Clayton, M.J., Haberl, J.S., Yan, W.: Developing a physical BIM library for building thermal energy simulation. Autom. Constr. 50, 16–28 (2015)

25. Ma, Y., Zhao, Y.: Model of next-generation energy-efficient design software for buildings. Tsinghua Sci. Technol. 13(1), 298–304 (2008)

26. Wu, W., Issa, R.R.A.: BIM facilitated web service for LEED automation. In: Proceedings of ASCE International Workshop on Computing in Civil Engineering, pp. 673–681 (2011)
27. Wu, W., Issa, R.R.A.: BIM execution planning in green building projects: LEED as a use case. J. Manag. Eng. **31**(1), A4014007 (2015)
28. Alwan, Z., Greenwood, D., Gledson, B.: Rapid LEED evaluation performed with BIM-based sustainability analysis on a virtual construction project. Constr. Innov. **15**(2), 134–150 (2015)
29. Oti, A.H., Tizani, W.: BIM extension for the sustainability appraisal of conceptual steel design. Adv. Eng. Inform. **29**, 28–46 (2015)
30. Kim, J.I., Kim, J., Fischer, M., Orr, R.: BIM-based decision-support method for master planning of sustainable large-scale developments. Autom. Constr. **58**, 95–108 (2015)
31. Zelkowicz, A., Iorio, J., Taylor, J.E.: Integrating decision support system (DSS) and building information modeling (BIM) to optimize the selection of sustainable building components. J. Inf. Technol. Constr. (ITcon) **20**, 399–420 (2015)
32. Zanni, M.A., Soetanto, R., Ruikar, K.: Towards a BIM-enabled sustainable building design process: roles, responsibilities, and requirements. Archit. Eng. Des. Manag. **13**(2), 101–129 (2017)
33. Wu, W., Issa, R.R.A.: Integrated process mapping for BIM implementation in green building project delivery. In: Proceedings of the 13th International Conference on Construction Applications of Virtual Reality, pp. 30–39 (2013)
34. Wong, J.K.W., Zhou, J.: Enhancing environmental sustainability over building life cycles through green BIM: a review. Autom. Constr. **57**, 156–165 (2015)
35. Bank, L.C., McCarthy, M., Thompson, B.P., Menassa, C.C.: Integrating BIM with system dynamics as a decision-making framework for sustainable building design and operation. In: Proceedings of the First International Conference on Sustainable Urbanization, pp. 39–48 (2010)
36. Reed, R., Wilkinson, S., Bilos, A., Schulte, K-W.: A comparison of international sustainable building tools-an update. In: Proceedings of the 17th Annual Pacific Rim Real Estate Society Conference, pp. 16–19 (2011)
37. Russell, S.J., Norvig, P.: Artificial Intelligence: A Modern Approach, 2nd edn. Pearson Education International, Prentice Hall (2003)
38. Ren, Z., Anumba, C.J.: Multi-agent systems in construction–state of the art and prospects. Autom. Constr. **13**(3), 421–434 (2004)
39. Ritchie, D.: Crane simulators as training tools. CraneWorks, p. 16 (2004)
40. Anumba, C., Ren, Z., Ugwu, O.O.: Agents and Multi-agent Systems in Construction. Routledge, Routledge (2007)
41. Chiou, J.D., Logcher, R.D.: Testing a Federation Architecture in Collaborative Design Process-Final Report. Report no. R96-01. CERL (1996)
42. Kog, F., Yaman, H.: A multi-agent systems-based contractor pre-qualification model. Eng. Constr. Archit. Manag. **23**(6), 709–726 (2016)
43. Udeaja, C., Tah, J.: Agent-based material supply chain integration in construction. In: Anumba, C.J., Egbu, C., Thorpe, A. (eds.) Perspectives on Innovation in Architecture, Engineering and Construction, CICE, pp. 377–388. Loughborough University, Loughborough (2001)
44. Klein, L., Kwak, J.Y., Kavulya, G., Jazizadeh, F., Becerik-Gerber, B., Varakantham, P., Tambe, M.: Coordinating occupant behavior for building energy and comfort management using multi-agent systems. Autom. Constr. **22**, 525–536 (2012)
45. Banaitiene, N., Banaitis, A.: Analysis of criteria for contractors' qualification evaluation. Technol. Econ. Dev. Econ. **12**(4), 276–282 (2006)

46. Zeng, D., Sycara, D.K.: Bayesian learning in negotiation. Int. J. Hum. Comput. Stud. **48**(1), 125–141 (1998)
47. Plebankiewicz, E.: Contractor prequalification model using fuzzy sets. J. Civ. Eng. Manag. **15**(4), 377–385 (2009)
48. Olawumi, T.O., Chan, D.W.: An empirical survey of the perceived benefits of executing BIM and sustainability practices in the built environment. Constr. Innov. **19**(3), 321–342 (2019)
49. Bynum, P., Issa, R.R.A., Olbina, S.: Building information modeling in support of sustainable design and construction. J. Constr. Eng. Manag. **139**(1), 24–34 (2013)
50. Akinade, O.O., Oyedele, L.O., Ajayi, S.O., Bilal, M., Alaka, H.A., Owolabi, H.A., Kadiri, K.O.: Design for Deconstruction (DfD): critical success factors for diverting end-of-life waste from landfills. Waste Manag. **60**, 3–13 (2017)
51. Hanna, A., Boodai, F., El Asmar, M.: State of practice of building information modeling in mechanical and electrical construction industries. J. Constr. Eng. Manag. **139**(10), 1–8 (2013)
52. Bolgani, M.: The implementation of BIM within the public procurement: a model-based approach for the construction industry. VTT Technology Report (2013). https://www.vtt.fi/inf/pdf/technology/2013/T130.pdf. Accessed 23 Sept 2019
53. Vacharapoom, B., Sdhabhon, B.: An integrated safety management with construction management using 4D CAD model. Saf. Sci. **48**(3), 395–403 (2010)
54. Akintoye, A., Goulding, J., Zawdie, G.: Construction Innovation and Process Improvement. Wiley-Blackwell, Hoboken (2012)
55. Boktor, J., Hanna, A., Menassa, C.C.: State of practice of building information modeling in the mechanical construction industry. J. Manag. Eng. **30**(1), 78–85 (2014)
56. Olawumi, T.O., Chan, D.W., Wong, J.K., Chan, A.P.: Barriers to the integration of BIM and sustainability practices in construction projects: a Delphi survey of international experts. J. Build. Eng. **20**, 60–71 (2018)
57. Taillandier, F., Taillandier, P., Tepeli, E., Breysse, D., Mehdizadeh, R., Khartabil, F.: A multi-agent model to manage risks in construction project (SMACC). Autom. Constr. **58**, 1–18 (2015)

A Multi-criteria Group Decision Making Model for Selection of Green Building Project

Daniela Borissova[1,2(✉)]

[1] Institute of Information and Communication Technologies
at the Bulgarian Academy of Sciences, 1113 Sofia, Bulgaria
dborissova@iit.bas.bg
[2] University of Library Studies and Information Technologies,
1784 Sofia, Bulgaria

Abstract. The green building concept is recognized as a sustainable building strategy due to its benefits. Careful selection of sustainable building project has been identified as the easiest way to impose the sustainable building principles. The frame of building information modeling concerns all aspects of building design, construction and operations. In this respect, the current paper deals with design problems related to the selection of the most suitable project for building by group decision making. The proposed combinatorial optimization model for selection is based on the formulation of utility function considering some evaluation criteria corresponding to the green building concept. The experts' opinion is taken into account by weighted coefficients. These coefficients express the importance of experts' opinions corresponding to their experience and knowledge. The practical applicability of the proposed modeling approach is demonstrated in the case of selection of the most appropriate building project among a predefined set of projects. A project evaluation is done by using the given criteria and a group of experts. The final decision for the selection of the building project is a result of the aggregated evaluation of all experts. Each expert takes part in a group decision both through evaluations and the contribution expressed by weighted coefficients for the level of expertise and knowledge. The results showed that using weights for experts influence the final aggregate group decision for the selection of the project for green building.

Keywords: Green building · Group decision making · Multi-attribute utility function · Optimization model

1 Introduction

A key factor to reduce the negative effects on the environment and resources is the usage of green buildings [1]. In order for a building to be classified as green it needs to fulfill certain criteria. It is should be noted that green buildings vary in different countries due to local climatic conditions and requirements. Therefore, the assessment criteria for green buildings can be different [2]. Since 1990 many countries have issued green building assessment standards. A comparison between five aspects of the latest evaluation standards for green buildings in China, the Great Britain and the United States are described in [3]. The green building concerns resource-efficient models of

© Springer Nature Switzerland AG 2020
S. Ofluoglu et al. (Eds.): EBF 2019, CCIS 1188, pp. 137–146, 2020.
https://doi.org/10.1007/978-3-030-42852-5_11

construction, operation, reusing and recycling, renovation, maintenance and demolition, i.e. the whole building lifecycle from the inception to the demolition stages [4, 5]. The green building strategy aims to decrease negative effects on the environment and resources by enhancing the positive effects by the life cycle of building [5]. Different strategies are employed by the governments in major economies to encourage the adoption of green technology and its spreading out in the building sector [6]. The green entrepreneurship could promote and extend the understanding of how entrepreneurs are engaged in the spreading of sustainable technologies [7].

A promising direction for sustainable green strategy implementation is the usage of mathematical modeling to make a modern management strategy that benefits the building industry. In order to do that, different decision-making techniques can contribute to identifying and choosing alternatives based on the performance and preferences of decision makers (DM) [8]. Different approaches are proposed to assess green buildings. For example, Kabak, et al. propose a fuzzy multi-criteria decision making approach to assess building energy performance [9]. On the stage of project approval, different models could be used to comply with the strategy for green building. The green material index is one of the indicators for ranking of building materials to provide the best solution for a green and sustainable project. Therefore, a hybrid multi-criteria decision-making method is proposed to rank such green building materials [10]. The use of proper methods and models ensures resource-efficiency in different building elements and renovation. One-dimensional cutting stock model and combinatorial optimization are proposed for the manufacturing joinery that reduces the overall waste [11, 12]. These models seek to determine the optimal length of the blanks and cutting pattern of each blank to meet the requirement for a given number of elements with different length while minimizing the trim waste.

The evaluation of design, construction and management of office buildings aims to help the public authorities to ensure that projects are selected in accordance with the principles of the sustainable green strategy. A model for evaluation of the whole urban planning situation including neighborhood and transport infrastructure is proposed [13]. This model is based on five criteria such as efficiency, effectiveness, impacts, relevance and sustainability. The assessment of green buildings includes both quantitative and qualitative criteria [14]. Quantitative criteria could be identified as performance-based criteria while the qualitative criteria cannot be measured but could be estimated. Due to the multidimensional nature of green building principles, a group of different experts should be formed. These experts have to assess the diversity of green building aspects with respect to the energy and resource efficiency policy. For purposes of resource efficiency evaluation, the proposed multi-criteria decision methodology could be used. This methodology limits the distance between the suppliers and the construction site, evaluates a reduced subset of potential suppliers are then ranks them [15].

From a theoretical point of view, different multi-criteria decision making (MCDM) methods are proposed to cope with evaluation and selection as SAW, WPM, AHP, ELECTRE, TOPSIS, etc. [8]. The problems of evaluation and selection could be also done by using SMART and combinatorial optimization [16, 17]. Some of these methods are based on absolute or relative performance values. The linguistic DM preferences could be transformed with some rule base simplification [18]. Due to the progress of ICT the processes in planning, design and management of buildings could benefit different Web-based applications or by Web-based decision support systems using [19, 20]. Utilizing advantages of the information technologies contribute to more close cooperation between academia and industry that reflects in sustainable and efficient projects for buildings. The evaluation and selection could be realized by using group decision-making techniques that rely on the compensatory strategy. With this strategy, the high value in one attribute compensates for a low value in another [21]. In group decision making, the experts' knowledge, experiences and preferences influence the evaluation. When forming the final group decision, it is important to consider the opinion of DMs with different importance [22, 23]. To overcome the different levels of competence between DMs, weighted coefficients consisting of objective and subjective parts are proposed [24]. It is possible also to use entropy-based weights on DMs to differentiate opinions of DMs [25]. The weight of DM is based on the consistency of decision information of DM in which the incomplete fuzzy preference relations are provided by DMs.

In group decision making the weights of DMs play a crucial role in establishing the final decision. Taking into account the importance in estimation and evaluation of green building projects, a multi-criteria group decision making model for project selection considering weights for each DM is proposed.

The rest of the article has the following structure: Sect. 2 contains the problem description for building project selection; Sect. 3 describes the proposed mathematical model for selection via group decision making and multi-attribute utility function; Sect. 4 presents the input data used for the numerical application of the proposed model in selection of a building project; Sect. 5 describes and analyses the obtained results, while Sect. 6 contains the conclusion and future directions for investigations.

2 Problem Description

The rapid development of ICT is a prerequisite for the development of various intelligent software solutions with the capabilities of building information models. The availability of different building information models imposes to make a choice for a project that best fits into the available infrastructure and is consistent with the principles of sustainable construction. The benefit of green buildings is related not only to decreasing the negative environmental impacts by using less water, energy or natural resources, but also positively influencing the environmental impact by generating their own energy. The building's environmental impacts could be quantified by using data of all components' materials. Therefore, combining technical data from building information and life cycle assessment models helps to compare different building design projects from an environmental perspective point of view. Well-designed building projects help for reducing the amount of generated waste by providing on-site solutions thus reducing waste. A lot of energy could be saved when centralized wastewater treatment systems are used. Therefore, different aspects should be taken into account in the evaluation of projects for the construction of public buildings. Each of these projects has to be evaluated with respect to meet the green building strategy concept including the urban characteristics of buildings and transport infrastructure.

The choice of a particular project among given projects considering the green building concept is based on some predefined number of evaluation criteria. The input data of this multi-attribute decision making problem are expressed by decision matrix as shown in Table 1.

Table 1. The decision matrix for the multi-attribute decision problem

Projects/Alternatives	Evaluation criteria & coefficient weight for the importance			
	C_1	C_2	C_j	C_N
	w_1	w_2	w_j	w_N
P_1	e_{11}	e_{12}		e_{1N}
.....	.....	.....	.....	.....
P_i	e_{i1}	e_{i2}	e_{ij}	e_{iN}
P_M	e_{M1}	e_{M2}		e_{MN}

The used notations are as follows: P_i denotes i-th project (alternative), C_j expresses the j-th evaluation criterion, w_j is the weighted coefficient for j-th criterion and e_{ij} expresses the evaluation of i-th alternative toward j-th criterion.

For the goal of project selection, a group of DMs with different fields of competency are determined. Each of these experts should evaluate the projects for building public construction toward evaluation criteria corresponding to the sustainable green strategy. There is no limitation about the number of alternatives (projects) or a number of evaluation criteria neither about a number of experts that will form the group.

3   Mathematical Model for Selection via Group Decision Making

One of the most widely used approaches among MCDM is SAW where m alternatives are evaluated toward n criteria and for each criterion a corresponding coefficient weight for importance is determined [8]. For each alternative, the weighted average value is calculated by multiplying the weighted coefficient of each criterion with the evaluation (score) of the alternative against this criterion, and the overall estimates for each of alternatives are determined. The best alternative is the one with the best performance score. This well-structured method is the basis of the proposed mathematical model for group decision making using weights for DMs according to their experience and knowledge.

In accordance with the described problem, the given number of building projects (alternatives) determines the same number of decision variables used to perform the selection and confirming the terms of combinatorial optimization. Considering the classical SAW, requirements for weights on DMs and condition for decision variables, the following mathematical optimization model for group decision making is formulated:

$$\text{maximize} \left(\sum_{k=1}^{Q} \lambda^k \sum_{i=1}^{M} \sum_{j=1}^{N} x_i w_j^k e_{i,j}^k \right) \tag{1}$$

subject to

$$\sum_{k=1}^{Q} \lambda^k = 1 \tag{2}$$

$$\sum_{i=1}^{M} x_i = 1, \, x_i \in \{0, 1\} \tag{3}$$

$$\sum_{j=1}^{N} w_j^k = 1, \forall k = 1, 2, \dots, K \tag{4}$$

where λ^k express the weighted coefficient for k-th experts depending on corresponding level of experience and knowledge; x_i is binary integer variable of i-th alternative (building projects); w_j^k is coefficient for relative importance about j-th evaluation criterion from k-th expert; and $e_{i,j}^k$ express the evaluation for i-th alternative toward j-th criterion from k-th expert.

The relation (1) expresses a modification of the utility function of the classical SAW method. The modification of SAW concerns the additional weighted coefficients λ^k used to express the differences between DMs and additional decision variables x_i to realize the single choice as a result of the optimization task (1)–(4) solving. This makes more accurately the aggregation of assessments in a final group decision.

The coefficients w_j^k can take values within range between 0 and 1, and the greater value means more importance. In addition, the sum of these coefficients for a relative importance between evaluations criteria for each DM has to be equal to 1. The evaluation score $e_{i,j}^k$ for i-th alternative in regard to the j-th criterion by k-th expert are also limited with same range of (0, 1) and again the bigger value means the better performance. It is possible to use another evaluation scale for example the range between 0 and 10 or 0 and 100. Using of a different scale requires the normalization of the estimations to obtain the comparable measure between coefficients w_j^k and evaluation score $e_{i,j}^k$.

4 Numerical Application

The multi-criteria group decision making for selection of building information model (project) is produced from five projects submitted for evaluation in relation to six criteria that include environmental impact (C_1); life cycle cost (C_2); resource efficiency (C_3); performance capability (C_4); social benefit (C_5) and waste minimization (C_6).

The evaluations toward these criteria are realized by a group composed of three experts considered as DMs. This expert group includes an administrative manager (DM-1), a resource utilization manager (DM-2), and an architecture manager (DM-3). The corresponding evaluations score together with coefficients for relative importance between criteria form point of view of three DMs that are shown in Table 2.

For the goal of numerical illustration, the opinions of these experts are considered with different importance expressed by three cases. The Case-1 considers with equal importance opinions of all DMs toward the estimations and weighted coefficients for evaluation criteria. The Case-2 illustrates the situation when the most important is the opinion of DM-2 that is followed by opinions of DM-3 and DM-1. The Case-3 expresses the situation where the opinions of DM-1 and DM-2 are dominant over the opinion of DM-3.

Table 2. Evaluations of 5 building project toward 6 criteria and 3 DMs

Alternatives/Projects	Evaluation criteria & coefficients for their importance						Group of DMs
	C_1	C_2	C_3	C_4	C_5	C_6	
	0.15	**0.28**	**0.08**	**0.3**	**0.11**	**0.08**	DM-1
P1	0.510	0.420	0.780	0.680	0.920	0.800	
P2	0.420	0.370	0.840	0.900	0.910	0.740	
P3	0.380	0.470	0.800	0.760	0.960	0.770	
P4	0.650	0.350	0.890	0.830	0.900	0.820	
P5	0.580	0.400	0.910	0.720	0.870	0.790	
	0.17	**0.2**	**0.14**	**0.16**	**0.15**	**0.18**	DM-2
P1	0.620	0.490	0.840	0.780	0.860	0.810	
P2	0.580	0.470	0.770	0.830	0.880	0.790	
P3	0.690	0.500	0.790	0.940	0.800	0.730	
P4	0.640	0.410	0.800	0.860	0.850	0.800	
P5	0.660	0.430	0.870	0.780	0.900	0.820	
	0.15	**0.22**	**0.11**	**0.2**	**0.17**	**0.15**	DM-3
P1	0.590	0.500	0.790	0.940	0.910	0.770	
P2	0.650	0.410	0.800	0.860	0.960	0.820	
P3	0.580	0.470	0.780	0.780	0.830	0.790	
P4	0.690	0.350	0.840	0.800	0.880	0.800	
P5	0.640	0.400	0.820	0.850	0.800	0.820	

The results for the selected projects as group decisions under different importance for DMs opinions are shown in Table 3.

Table 3. Selected project by using of different weights for DMs

Case	Weights for DMs			Selected project by group of DMs
	DM-1	DM-2	DM-3	
Case-1	0.34	0.33	0.33	P-2
Case-2	0.22	0.41	0.37	P-1
Case-3	0.46	0.40	0.14	P-4

The results in Table 3 are obtained by formulating and solving the corresponding optimization tasks based on the proposed model (1)–(4) and using the input data from Table 2 for three cases of the importance of DMs' opinions.

5   Result Analysis and Discussion

The proposed mathematical optimization model for selection takes with different importance of the individual opinions of DMs in an aggregated group decision. This gives an opportunity to incorporate the views of DMs in accordance with their experience and relevant knowledge in regard to the investigated problem for selection

The formulated and solved three optimization tasks are done by means of Lingo v.12. The obtained results in Case-1 where project P-1 is selected are visualized in Fig. 1.

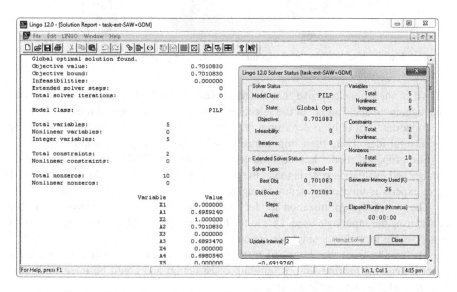

Fig. 1. Solution report in Lingo environment in Case-1 of input data

The solution time for each optimization task is about some milliseconds as a type of the formulated model is pure integer linear programming. Lingo uses the branch and bound algorithm and determines the global optimum solution (see Fig. 1).

The input data for Case-1 determines the optimal alternative the project P-2 as the objective function achieves its maximum at value equal to 0.701083 (Fig. 1). This case is similar to the classical SAW method where all DMs are considered with equal importance. When the selection relies mostly on the opinions of DM-2 and DM-3 as is in the Case-2, the optimal alternative is project P-1 with a maximum value of 0.7082. In Case-3, the selection is based predominantly on the opinions of the DM-1 and DM-2 and the corresponding task solution is determined as the best alternative the project P-4 for which the objective function value is 0.6960.

The comparison of obtained aggregated results for the selection of the building project as group decision making for three cases of DMs' opinions importance is shown in Fig. 2.

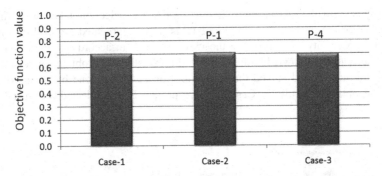

Fig. 2. Building projects selection under different cases of weighs on DMs

All of these results prove that usage of weights for DMs opinions influences the final aggregate decision about the selection of the project for green building. Therefore it is important not only to determine the group of experts for project evaluations, but also careful identifying their importance in aggregating the final group decision.

The proposed model has no limit for the number of DMs or about the project's number and evaluation criteria to get the final group decision. A single condition to add more experts is their competency in regard to the given evaluation criteria.

The use of the optimization model ensures that the resulting solution is the best considering the input data used. Due to the binary integer variables in the model (1)–(4) it is possible to realize a single selection of alternative via a single run of the task.

The results from the described mathematical modeling approach can be used to support decision-making toward building construction and could be integrated into a building information modeling software.

6 Conclusions

The usage of ICT and mathematical modeling contributes to sustainable and modern management strategies that comprise both academia and industry. Under building information modeling, different processes could be identified as planning, design, and construction of buildings. On the design stage, different 3D designs could be contenders and one of them should be selected. This selection process has to be able to cope not only with existing infrastructure but to be consistent with the principles of sustainable construction. For the goal, a mathematical optimization model for selection via group decision making is proposed. This pure integer linear programming model considers the opinions of each DM with different importance accordingly to DM's experience and knowledge related to the investigated problem for selection.

The case study described concerns the selection among five alternative design projects evaluated toward six criteria and a group of three DMs. The different evaluation criteria used reflect the requirements of the strategy for green building. The introduced weight for DMs expertise makes possible to determine more precisely the best selection. The numerical results demonstrated the applicability of the proposed model for group decision making in the selection of green building projects. There is no limitation to use the proposed optimization modeling approach for other areas from the building industry that requires some kind of selection. The described approach could be used as a standalone application or could be implemented as a tool within a software environment of building information modeling.

The evaluation of environmental impacts of buildings requires integration of the models of building information and life cycle assessment to make more transparent the selection of building projects considering the environmental perspective point of view. The use of knowledge from the field of operation research contributes to the realization of new tools for the successful analysis and selection of suitable green projects for building construction. The future directions for investigations concern with the use of other utility functions and their modifications to cope with differences of DMs.

References

1. Akadiri, P.O., Olomolaiye, P.O., Chinyio, E.A.: Multi-criteria evaluation model for the selection of sustainable materials for building projects. Autom. Constr. **30**, 113–125 (2013)
2. Ding, Z., Fan, Z., Tam, V.W.Y., Bian, Y., Li, S., Illankoon, I.M.C.S., Moon, S.: Green building evaluation system implementation. Build. Environ. **133**, 32–40 (2018)
3. Zhang, Y., Wang, J., Hu, F., Wang, Y.: Comparison of evaluation standards for green building in China, Britain, United States. Renew. Sustain. Energy Rev. **68**, 262–271 (2017)
4. Illankoon, I.M.C.S., Tam, V.W.Y., Le, K.N.: Shen, L: Key credit criteria among international green building rating tools. J. Clean. Prod. **164**, 209–220 (2017)
5. Zhang, L., Wu, J., Liu, H.: Turning green into gold: a review on the economics of green buildings. J. Clean. Prod. **172**, 2234–2245 (2018)
6. Hall, J., Matos, S., Bachor, V.: From green technology development to green innovation: inducing regulatory adoption of pathogen detection technology for sustainable forestry. Small Bus. Econ. **52**(4), 877–889 (2019)

7. Darko, A., Chan, A.P.C.: Strategies to promote green building technologies adoption in developing countries: the case of Ghana. Build. Environ. **130**, 74–84 (2018)
8. Triantaphyllou, E.: Multi-criteria decision making methods. In: Triantaphyllou, E. (ed.) Multi-criteria Decision Making Methods: A Comparative Study. Applied Optimization, vol. 44, pp. 5–21. Springer, Boston (2000). https://doi.org/10.1007/978-1-4757-3157-6_2
9. Kabak, M., Kose, E., Kirilmaz, O., Burmaoglu, S.: A fuzzy multi-criteria decision making approach to assess building energy performance. Energy Build. **72**, 382–389 (2014)
10. Khoshnava, S.M., Rostami, R., Valipour, A., Ismail, M., Rahmat, A.R.: Rank of green building material criteria based on the three pillars of sustainability using the hybrid multi criteria decision making method. J. Clean. Prod. **173**, 82–99 (2018)
11. Mustakerov, I., Borissova, D.: Combinatorial optimization modeling approach for one-dimensional cutting stock problems. Int. J. Syst. Appl. Eng. Dev. **9**, 13–18 (2015)
12. Mustakerov, I., Borissova, D.: One-dimensional cutting stock model for joinery manufacturing. In: Mastorakis, N., et al. (eds.) Circuits, Systems, Communications and Computers, CSCC 2014. Recent Advances in Computer Engineering Series, vol. 22, pp. 51–55 (2014)
13. Bohne, R.A., Klakegg, O.J., Lædre, O.: Evaluating sustainability of building projects in urban planning. Proc. Econ. Finance **21**, 306–312 (2015)
14. He, Y., Kvan, T., Liu, M., Li, B.: How green building rating systems affect designing green. Build. Environ. **133**, 19–31 (2018)
15. Borissova, D., Mustakerov, I., Korsemov, D., Dimitrova, V.: Evaluation and selection of ERP software by SMART and combinatorial optimization. Int. J. Adv. Model. Optimiz. **18**(1), 145–152 (2016)
16. Borissova, D., Atanassova, Z.: Multi-criteria decision methodology for supplier selection in building industry. Int. J. 3-D Inf. Model. **7**(4), 49–58 (2018)
17. Korsemov, D., Borissova, D., Mustakerov, I.: Combinatorial optimization model for group decision-making. Cybern. Inf. Technol. **18**(2), 65–73 (2018)
18. Gegov, A., Sanders, D., Vatchova, B.: Aggregation of inconsistent rules for fuzzy rule base simplification. Int. J. Knowl.-Based Intell. Eng. Syst. **21**(3), 135–145 (2017)
19. Mustakerov, I., Borissova, D.: A web application for group decision-making based on combinatorial optimization. In: Information Systems and Technologies, ICIST 2014, pp. 46–56 (2014)
20. Kirilov, L., Guliashki, V., Staykov, B.: Web based decision support system for solving multiple objective decision making problems. In: Dey, N. (ed.) Technological Innovations in Knowledge Management and Decision Support, pp. 150–175. IGI Global, Pennsylvania (2019)
21. Keeney, R.L., Raiffa, H.: Decisions with Multiple Objectives: Preferences and Value Trade-Offs. Cambridge University Press, Cambridge (1993)
22. Borissova, D., Mustakerov, I., Korsemov, D.: Business intelligence system via group decision making. Cybern. Inf. Technol. **16**(3), 219–229 (2016)
23. Korsemov, D., Borissova, D., Mustakerov, I.: Group decision making for selection of supplier under public procurement. In: Kalajdziski, S., Ackovska, N. (eds.) ICT 2018. CCIS, vol. 940, pp. 51–58. Springer, Cham (2018). https://doi.org/10.1007/978-3-030-00825-3_5
24. Borissova, D.: A group decision making model considering experts competency: an application in personnel selections. Comptes rendus de l'Academie Bulgare des Sciences **71**(11), 1520–1527 (2018)
25. Yue, C.: Entropy-based weights on decision makers in group decision-making setting with hybrid preference representations. Appl. Soft Comput. **60**, 737–749 (2017)

Compliance of Software in Thermal Load Calculations in Buildings: The Case of BIM and HAP Software

Melike Özdemir and Salih Ofluoglu[(✉)]

Department of Informatics, Mimar Sinan Fine Art University, Istanbul, Turkey
20182109002@org.msgsu.edu.tr,
salih.ofluoglu@msgsu.edu.tr

Abstract. Compliance of software is an important research issue as increasingly more digital applications are introduced in the area of thermal load calculations and energy analyses. Building Information Modeling (BIM), a relatively recent software technology in the line of such, is gaining more acceptance in energy and other sustainability-related analyses in AEC fields. This study assesses the suitability of BIM software in heating and cooling load calculations in buildings, using a sample building project in which thermal loads were calculated in both BIM software (Autodesk Revit) and industry-based MEP software (Carrier HAP). The results obtained in both software platforms were compared.

Keywords: Heating and cooling loads · BIM · Revit · HAP

1 Introduction

In the determination of thermal loads and energy usage of buildings, manual calculation methods are increasingly replaced by computer software. The use of these software from the early stages of design onwards is strongly recommended by professional organizations for their notable contribution to the energy efficiency of buildings [1].

For thermal load calculations, specialized MEP (Mechanical Electrical Plumbing) software and lately Building Information Modeling (BIM) software are two common approaches preferred in AEC disciplines. These software enable project teams to predict the energy use intensity of a building before its construction and to offer feedback for design decisions.

As the number of energy analysis software is increased, the compatibility of the results obtained from different software and the extent to which they reflect real-world conditions has been one of the research topics [2–4].

In accordance with such theme, this study aims to investigate the compliance between heating and cooling load calculations performed in the Carrier Hourly Analysis Program (HAP), a widely used software in MEP sector and Autodesk Revit, a popular BIM software in Turkey, and it additionally examines why these differences may occur.

© Springer Nature Switzerland AG 2020
S. Ofluoglu et al. (Eds.): EBF 2019, CCIS 1188, pp. 147–157, 2020.
https://doi.org/10.1007/978-3-030-42852-5_12

A very similar topic was also examined by another study conducted for office buildings with both the HAP and Revit software [5]. Office buildings usually differentiate from other building types especially in terms of their high internal loads. In contrast to that, in the proposed study, a residential building type was selected and comparative analyses between the two software were conducted with the inclusion of more space and zone options than the previous research study.

2   Calculations of Heating-Cooling Loads in Buildings

Thermal loads, i.e. heating and cooling loads, are the process of adding and discharging heat energy to maintain thermal stability and control humidity for user comfort. These loads directly affect the choice and sizing of HVAC equipment, energy use as well as initial investment cost.

When calculating thermal loads in buildings, external heat transfer methods (conduction, convection and radiation) and internal heat-generating factors such as people, lights and equipment in spaces are taken into account. Total heating and cooling load calculations are carried out according to the TS 2164 Principles for the Preparation of Central Heating Systems Project Guidelines in Turkey [6].

Choosing appropriate building materials, insulation details, wall openings along with the form and orientation of a building greatly affect the heat transfer. Decisions of such also determine a building's energy-use classification rank in the Energy Identification Certificate, compulsory documentation required for new and existing buildings in Turkey [7].

2.1   Calculating Heating and Cooling Loads in BIM

Heating and cooling load calculations can be performed with different BIM software and supplementary third party BIM applications. BIM can handle these calculations by working with 3D models developed at a different level of detail, from the early to advanced stages of a project.

Due to its three-dimensional simulation and collaboration environment, BIM enables architects and engineers to focus on engineering and design-related tasks rather than mundane drafting works, and it also allows them to prepare a virtual prototype for assessing preliminary design stages [8]. Problems that can be easily overlooked in traditional two-dimensional environments can be spotted in BIM software. Interdisciplinary BIM models can be coordinated in three-dimensions to avoid element clashes and delays on the site.

In this study, Autodesk Revit, a popular BIM software in Turkey and its 2019 version is used. In contrast to many industry-based MEP software, BIM software extract thermal calculation data from 3D models that essentially incorporate both graphical and alphanumerical data. Therefore, graphical construction and attribute definitions of elements in a BIM model are critical affecting the accuracy of heating and cooling calculations.

The basic information that should be defined in the Autodesk Revit environment in the calculation of thermal loads are as follows:

- **Project Location:** It is where the geographical location of the building is specified. According to this location, local meteorological data for the site is retrieved by the software.
- **Space Definition:** All spaces that are intended for conditioning in the building must be defined here. The space type, that is the purpose of use for spaces, should also be identified.
- **Zone Definition:** Zones with similar thermal properties are created in this section.
- **Building Type Definition:** This area determines the purpose of use for the building. Different building types may require different thermal comfort.
- **System Selection:** The heating and cooling system for the building is selected here.

After specifying the information above, Revit generates a heating and cooling load report. In this report, thermal loads for zones and spaces along with loads from all building components can be reviewed.

2.2 Calculating Heating and Cooling Loads in Carrier HAP

The Carrier Hourly Analysis software (HAP) is part of the program libraries of the Carrier's HVAC design program called E20-II. Carrier HAP is designed to advise engineers, construction contractors, mechanical work contractors and other building professionals for the design and analysis of HVAC systems in commercial buildings [9]. Outputs of the program are highly-regarded by international institutions such as the US Green Building Council (USGBC).

The Carrier HAP software calculates the annual heating and cooling loads of a building by taking into account of the number of days per year and full operating state in order to simulate the design of the hourly air flow rate to be blown to a space and the operation of the selected mechanical system devices.

The Carrier HAP program incorporates local information from meteorological stations to make accurate calculations according to the geographical location of a building. The ASHRAE 90.1 [10] standard is used for the thermal load calculations and the HAP software also is kept up to date with the changes in the standard.

In this study, Carrier HAP 5.0 was used. The following information in the program is needed to be specified for the calculations:

- **Location Definition:** The building's location and local weather data information are determined here.
- **Space Definition:** Individual building spaces are defined. The area, height and window data of these spaces are entered. The conditioned airflow in the space, the lighting, electrical equipment and heat gain loads arising from the users are entered according to the design criteria. The window and door areas on the wall in the same direction are defined in this section. The roof area and the skylight area, if any, are entered. The ground characteristics of the space (ground contact, non-heated floor, etc.) and infiltration information that may occur in the space are also defined in this section.
- **System Selection:** The systems to be used in individual and common spaces are specified in this section.

- **Identification of building elements:** Building elements such as walls, doors, windows, roofs and sunshades are defined in the Project Library.

In contrast to BIM software that retrieves information from graphical models, the Carrier HAP software accepts manually entered data. Alternatively, this information can be imported from other software that is capable of exporting gbxml files.

A HAP thermal analysis report includes the performance of selected devices, space-based and zone-based, hourly, daily, monthly and annually heating and cooling load data.

3 Thermal Load Calculations in a Sample Project

As noted above, this study compares the heating and cooling load calculations produced in both Carrier HAP 5.0 and Autodesk Revit 2019 software. In order to achieve that a sample project with the following design criteria, conditions and general system selections was used.

3.1 Project Features

The sample building is a one-story villa project with a (01) Living Room, (02) Dining Room, (03) Kitchen, (04) Kids Bedroom, (05) Bedroom and (06) WC/Bathroom spaces. The building has a total area of 142 m^2 and located in Istanbul. The floor height of the rooms is 3.25 m. The total volume of the building is 461.5 m^3 and the volume to be conditioned is 410 m^3. The building sits on a soil ground. The plan, space and zone information of the building is as follows (Fig. 1 and Table 1):

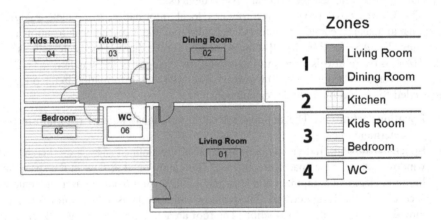

Fig. 1. Spaces and zones in the building

Table 1. Space information in the building

Space no	Space name	Area (m^2)
01	Living Room	45
02	Dining Room	28
03	Kitchen	14
04	Kids Room	13
05	Bedroom	20
06	WC	6

The MMO data was used for the accepted outdoor weather conditions in Istanbul where the project is located [11]:

- Location: Istanbul
- Latitude: 40.91 °K
- Longitude: 38.82 °D
- Summer: 33 °C KT, 24 °C KT, 47.7% BN
- .h = 72 kJ/kg
- .SF = 10.5 °C
- Winter: (−6) °C KT, 90% BN
- .h = 3.6 kJ/kg
- Height: 0 m
- Unheat Space Temperature (Protected): 12 °C
- Underfloor Soil Temperature: 9 °C
- The Soil Temperature Near the Wall: 3 °C

KT: Dry thermometer
YT: Wet thermometer
.h: Enthalpy
SF: Daily Temperature Difference

The atmospheric cleanliness coefficient considered for Istanbul is 1 and the average ground reflectance value is 0.2. The heat conduction coefficient of the soil around the building is 1.4 W/m^{2}K, and this value will be used in areas that come into contact with the soil [12].

The thermal conductivity coefficients (U) of the building elements are determined according to TS825 Thermal Insulation Regulation [13]. Istanbul is in the 'second' zone according to the degree-day climate zone data for the region, and the thermal permeability coefficients (U) to be used in these heating and cooling load calculations are listed below (Table 2). The SHGC (Solar Heat Gain Coefficient) value in the Table indicates the heat permeability coefficient of the glass. It takes a value between 0–1, and the larger this value is the more solar radiation heat enters into spaces.

Table 2. Thermal permeability coefficient of building components to be used

Building elements	U (W/m²K)
Window	2,4- SCH 0,8
Door (Wood)	3,5
Floor	0,6
Wall	0,6
Roof	0,4

The number of building occupants is taken as four for the project. The calculated heating and cooling loads cover 12 months from January to December. The daily usage in percentage for the building by hours are as follows (Fig. 2):

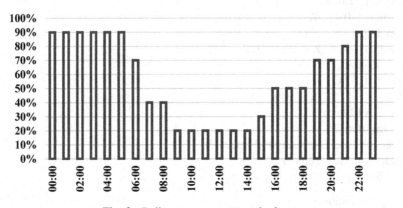

Fig. 2. Daily usage percentages by hours

Indoor Air Conditions: The ASHRAE standard was used for the indoor air conditions of the spaces in the building (Table 3). The zoning was arranged according to the indoor air temperature design criteria. The same type of heating and cooling systems was chosen in spaces belonging to the same zone. There are four zones in the building.

Table 3. Temperature design criteria RH: Relative Humidity

Space no	Space name	Heating (°C)	Cooling (°C)
01	Living Room	22	24-RH %50
02	Dining Room	22	24-RH %50
03	Kitchen	18	24-RH %50
04	Kids Room	20	24-RH %50
05	Bedroom	20	24-RH %50

Lighting and Equipment Loads: The heat loads resulting from lighting and equipment are also based on ASHRAE Standards in W/m². The accepted values are listed below (Table 4):

Table 4. Loads of lighting and electrical equipment

Space no	Space name	Lighting (W/m²)	Electr. equip. (W/m²)
01	Living Room	10	25
02	Dining Room	10	20
03	Kitchen	10	30
04	Kids Room	10	20
05	Bedroom	10	20

Heat Gain from People: The ASHRAE 2013 standard was used as a reference for the heat gain values created by people in spaces. The accepted values can be seen below (Table 5):

Table 5. Sensible and latent loads by human

Room no	Room name	Sensible (W/Person)	Latent (W/Person)
01	Living Room	75	55
02	Dining Room	75	55
03	Kitchen	75	55
04	Kids Room	75	55
05	Bedroom	75	55

Heating Load according to Fresh Air Amount (L/s): The amount of fresh air was calculated according to the ASHRAE standard as well. The amount of fresh air for each space are shown below (Table 6):

Table 6. Fresh air quantity

Room no	Room name	Amount of fresh air per person (L/s)	Number of air change (ACH)
01	Living Room	3,8	–
02	Dining Room	3,8	–
03	Kitchen	–	10
04	Kids Room	2,5	–
05	Bedroom	2,5	–

Inlet Air Flow (L/s) for Infiltration Load: 0.1 $L/s.m^2$ is taken for infiltration load in spaces. Lower infiltration values make the space more comfortable and provide better humidity control.

General System Selections: In order to make accurate comparisons between the two software, the same system was selected for both. The fan-coil system was chosen as the heating and cooling system for the project. Autodesk Revit 2019 refers to this selection as the FC system, and it is called a 4-pipe FC system in the Carrier HAP 5.0 software.

4   Comparison of Calculated Thermal Loads

Calculations are carried out according to the designated design criteria. The WC/bathroom space was not included in the calculations since it is already a cold space; hence there isn't a need for conditioning. Electric underfloor heating or towel warmers can be chosen for heating this space. According to calculations made in Autodesk Revit, there is a need for 338 kW heating in the WC/bathroom space.

In both HAP and Revit software, zonings are determined according to space temperatures. The 24/18 zone covers the kitchen space; the 24/20 zone includes the Kids Bedroom and Bedroom spaces; the 24/22 zone incorporates the Dining and Living Room spaces. In addition, peak times that indicate the maximum cooling load of the zones in the building were calculated in both Carrier HAP and Autodesk Revit (Table 7).

Table 7. Peak times of zones in both software

Zones	Spaces	Peak time/HAP	Peak time/Revit
24/18	Kitchen	June 22:00	June 16:00
24/20	Kids Room	July 22:00	July 17:00
	Bedroom		
24/22	Living Room	August 19:00	August 16:00
	Dining Room		
30/26	WC	June 16:00	June 15:00

For each zone, heating and cooling loads and the percentage of differences between them were calculated and compared. The percentage of difference value was obtained by subtracting the zone's thermal load found in each software from each other, dividing it by the larger one, and multiplying the result by 100 (Tables 8 and 9). The heating and cooling loads generated for the spaces in both software are also shown graphically (Fig. 3).

Table 8. Comparison of heating and cooling loads

Zones	Cooling loads (Watt)			Heating loads (Watt)		
	HAP	Revit	Differ. (%)	HAP	Revit	Differ. (%)
24/18	908	841	7,38	386	410	5,85
24/20	2882	3495	17,54	1733	1675	3,35
24/22	4750	4719	0,65	3157	3764	16,13

Table 9. Cumulative results

Zones	Cooling loads (Watt)			Heating loads (Watt)		
	HAP	Revit	Differ. (%)	HAP	Revit	Differ. (%)
Kitchen	793	796	0,38	386	380	1,55
Kids Room	1315	1539	14,55	781	711	8,96
Bedroom	1586	1754	9,58	952	882	7,35
Living Room	2923	2921	0,07	2015	2134	5,58
Dining Room	1712	1528	10,75	1142	1423	19,75

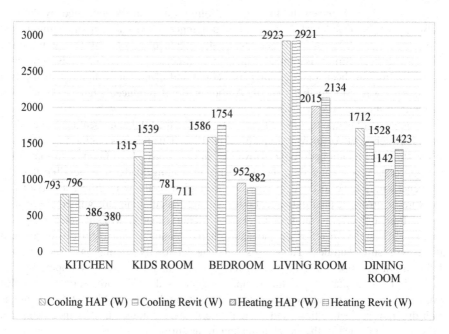

Fig. 3. Comparison of heating cooling loads chart

5   Conclusions

In this study, heating and cooling loads of an Istanbul-based, single-story house project consisting of six spaces were calculated by the Carrier HAP 5.0 and Autodesk Revit 2019 software. As it appears, the two software environments used in calculations have some evident advantages and disadvantages. One of them is that the Carrier HAP software operates with only 50 zones making its use in complex and large building projects impractical. There appears to be no limitation in Autodesk Revit in this regard. As opposed to that, the Carrier HAP software allows a broader collection of MEP systems to be selected than Autodesk Revit. This can be regarded as a disadvantage for the use of Autodesk Revit.

As explained previously, the main interest of this study is to assess the level of compatibility between industry-based MEP software and BIM software in the area of thermal analysis. Based on the results, it appears that thermal load calculations generated in both Carrier HAP and Autodesk Revit are very close to each other.

The difference between the total zone heating load values generated by the two software was found to be 9.80%. Even it is small, one of the possible reasons for this difference may have to do with the thermostat adjustment made in the Carrier HAP software. The thermostat adjustment is used for producing conditioning load calculations with heating and cooling adjustments.

The difference between the total zone cooling loads values generated by the two software was also calculated as 5.69%. This difference is less than that of heating loads. Even though the difference between the results obtained in both software is minimal, this may be even further improved with a more precise definition of walls, windows, doors, infiltration, heat loads emitted by people and electrical equipment in the two software. It was noticed that overall, Autodesk Revit produced higher cooling load results than those of Carrier HAP.

The results illustrate that the differences between the total zone heating and cooling loads between the two software remain below 10%. This result is similar to the finding of the study [5] mentioned above. However, in that study, the difference in total zone cooling loads was greater than the difference in heating loads. It is possible that the differences may have to do with varying calculation methods in different versions of software or errors in data entry. In both software, calculations are vulnerable to user errors. Potential errors can lead to less or higher capacity system selections. The Carrier HAP software relies on the data entered manually and incorrect entries can affect the result. Autodesk Revit uses a 3D model for its calculations. The accurate definition of the model and the parameters of its components are very important.

Within the limitations of the sample project used, this study shows that BIM software can be an alternative to industrial software in the field of MEP. Further studies with different project settings and design criteria are recommended for measuring the software compliance in thermal load calculations further.

References

1. AIA American Institute of Architects: Architecture 2030 commitment progress report (2013) http://content.aia.org/sites/default/files/2016-04/AIA%202030%20Commitment_2013% 20Progress%20Report.pdf. Accessed 11 Oct 2019
2. Kamela, E., Memari, A.M.: Review of BIM's application in energy simulation: tools, issues, and solutions. Autom. Constr. **97**, 164–180 (2019)
3. Jaric, M., Budimir, N., Pejanovic, M., Svetel I.: A review of energy analysis simulation tools. In: 7th International Working Conference on Total Quality Management and Advanced and Intelligent Approaches, 3–7 June, Belgrade, Serbia (2008)
4. Crawley, D.B., Hand, J.W., Kummert, M., Griffith, B.T.: Contrasting capabilities of building energy simulation programs. Build. Environ. **43**, 661–673 (2008)
5. Kurekci, N.A., Kaplan, S.: Isıtma-Soğutma Yüklerinin HAP ve Revit Programlarıyla Hesaplanması. Tesisat Mühendisliği Dergisi **141**, 5–15 (2014)
6. TS 2164 Kalorifer Tesisatı Projelendirme Kuralları. https://intweb.tse.org.tr/Standard/ Standard/StandardAra.aspx. Accessed 11 Oct 2019
7. Enerji Kimlik Belgesi. http://www.yegm.gov.tr/verimlilik/v_mevzuat.aspx. Accessed 11 Oct 2019
8. Azhar, S.: Building Information Modeling (BIM): trends, benefits, risks, and challenges for the AEC industry. Leadersh. Manag. Eng. **11**(3), 241–252 (2011)
9. Alarko Carrier: Hava Koşullandırma "Hourly Analysis Program (HAP)". Teknik Bülten (23), 1–3 (2007). Temmuz
10. ASHRAE Standards. https://www.ashrae.org/technical-resources/standards-and-guidelines. Accessed 11 Oct 2019
11. TMMOB Makina Mühendisleri Odası. MMO Yayın No. 2002-296-2, Tablo: 5-13 A (2002)
12. Dogan, V.: Döşemeden Isıtma Sistemlerinde Hesap Yöntemi. Makine Mühendisleri Odası Dergisi **20**(130), 41–50 (2012)
13. TS825 Binalarda Isı Yalıtım Kuralları. http://www1.mmo.org.tr/resimler/dosya_ekler/ cf3e258fbdf3eb7_ek.pdf. Accessed 11 Oct 2019

BIM and Facility Management and Infrastructural Issues

Analyzing the Benefits and Challenges of Building Information Modelling and Life Cycle Assessment Integration

Botan Azizoglu[1] and Senem Seyis[2(✉)]

[1] Civil Engineering Department, Isik University, Istanbul, Turkey
heval.azizoglu@isik.edu.tr
[2] Civil Engineering Department, Ozyegin University, Istanbul, Turkey
senem.seyis@ozyegin.edu.tr

Abstract. Previous studies show that the architecture, engineering and construction (AEC) industry contributes up to 1/3 of global GHG emissions. With the aim of mitigating negative impacts of AEC industry on the natural environment, the integrated use of advanced technological instruments has been increasing in the last decade. The integration of Building Information Modelling (BIM) and Life Cycle Assessment (LCA), which is one of the cutting-edge technological instruments, provides reduction of the total time spent and the improvement of the application while minimizing the environmental impacts throughout the life cycle of the facility. The main objective of this research study is to identify the benefits and challenges of BIM and LCA integration. In order to achieve the research objective of this study, a comprehensive literature review was conducted. Twenty-two types of benefits and seven types of challenges were identified for the integrated use of BIM and LCA in the AEC industry. The major contribution of this study is a comprehensive identification of the benefits and challenges of BIM-LCA integration. The results of this study may contribute to an increase in the utilization of the BIM-LCA integration in the AEC industry that in return allows decreasing negative environmental impacts of buildings through their life-cycle.

Keywords: Life Cycle Assessment · LCA · Building Information Modelling · BIM · Integration of LCA-BIM

1 Introduction

Previous studies show that the architecture, engineering and construction (AEC) industry contributes up to 1/3 of global GHG emissions [1]. Between 1971 and 2004, CO_2 emissions are estimated to have grown at a rate of 2.5% per year for commercial buildings and at 1.7% per year for residential buildings [2]. Prior research demonstrated that the built environment causes 17% of freshwater consumption, 25% of the wood harvest, 38% of CO2 emissions, 30–40% of energy use and 40–50% of raw material used [3].

Rapid technological innovations in the AEC industry provides new solutions for these environmental problems. With the aim of mitigating these negative impacts of

© Springer Nature Switzerland AG 2020
S. Ofluoglu et al. (Eds.): EBF 2019, CCIS 1188, pp. 161–169, 2020.
https://doi.org/10.1007/978-3-030-42852-5_13

AEC industry on the natural environment, the integrated use of advanced technological instruments in the construction industry has been increasing in the last decade. Building Information Modeling (BIM) and Life Cycle Assessment (LCA) integration is one of the cutting-edge technological instruments that allow decreasing negative impacts of AEC industry on the natural environment in an effective and efficient manner.

Although some previous studies on this research domain have been conducted in the last decade, none of them analyze the benefits and challenges encountered throughout the integrated use of BIM and LCA in the AEC industry. The main objective of this research is to identify the benefits and challenges of BIM and LCA integration. In order to achieve the research objective of this study, a comprehensive literature review was conducted.

This study provides suggestions in order to deal with the challenges of BIM-LCA integration with the aim of promoting its benefits. This paper reviews recent studies on the subject domain and draws common conclusions from them. The study subject of this paper contributes to providing a comprehensive identification of the benefits and challenges of BIM-LCA integration for the AEC industry. The results of this study may contribute to an increase in the utilization of the BIM-LCA integration in the AEC industry.

2   Research Methodology

The research methodology includes a comprehensive literature review with the aim of achieving the benefits and challenges of BIM-LCA integration for the AEC industry. The literature review was chosen as a research technique to obtain information from different perspectives of the previous studies. Comparison of papers was made in the literature to find common points. The main reason for performing the literature review is to collect an adequate amount of useful and reliable data.

In the literature review, studies published between 2008 and 2019 have been investigated using the databases of Elsevier, American Society of Civil Engineers (ASCE), Science Direct, Taylor and Francis and Web of Science. A total of 21 publications have been investigated within the scope of the literature review. The keywords used in these studies were as follows; "Building Information Modelling", "Building Information Modeling", "BIM", Life Cycle Assessment", "LCA", "Building Information Modelling-Life Cycle Assessment integration", "BIM-LCA integration", "Building Information Modelling-Life Cycle Assessment", "linking Building Information Modelling and Life Cycle Assessment", "integration of Building Information Modelling with smart objects".

3   Literature Review

Building industry produces large scale of global greenhouse gas emissions. Most of the percentage of this consumption occurs as part of operations during construction lifetime [4]. Since the negative environmental impact of the construction sector has been understood, the number of the studies to apply sustainability principles to the construction sector in order to reduce the negative effects of the AEC industry are increasing.

Life Cycle Assessment (LCA), an international standard methodology, is able to assess negative environmental impacts of products, materials and facilities throughout their whole lifecycle. Although LCA is commonly used in several industries such as automotive design, equipment manufacturing and consumer product design, this sustainability-oriented methodology has been rarely used in the AEC industry. Researchers and practitioners suggested integrating LCA with Building Information Modeling (BIM) during early-stage decision-making in the design process with the aim of reducing negative environmental impacts of buildings throughout their lifecycle.

BIM is described as a product, process and system by National Building Information Modeling Standard (NBIMS). The reasoning mechanism of BIM is able to generate, store, manage, exchange and share building data. Accordingly, this technology allows creating an accurate three dimensional (3D) digital model of a building using intelligent objects by identification of any potential design, construction or operational issues.

This advanced technological instrument allows designers to share many complex data in a single simple model. Therefore, BIM technology connects different disciplines which in return facilitates them to work in a simultaneous manner. BIM is an emerging technological development that facilitates every stage of construction for the AEC sector. This promising technological instrument coordinates facility management activities, keeps maintenance under control, helps to monitor projects stages easily, enables preparing extensive planning phases, and encourages communication and straightforwardness among partners that altogether promote constructability of the project, increase the productivity. BIM technology provides faster solutions and increases the effectiveness of a project, supports better customer service and better production quality [5]. BIM enables visualization during the design phase, increases communication between other departments and provides cost estimating and material qualification [6].

LCA is defined as a comprehensive methodology which allows determining the environmental and resource impacts of a material, product, or even a whole building throughout its entire life cycle from the extraction of resources to the disposal of the item [7, 8]. The reasoning mechanism of LCA is based on quantifying the energy and resource consumption, emission and waste generation of buildings that in turn provides a healthier construction process for the AEC industry. This internationally standardized methodology enables to examine impacts of material selection decisions by tabulating energy and water demand as well as emissions to air, water, and land over the entity's whole life cycle [8, 9]. LCA tools, such as SimaPro and Athena, are able to calculate the total amount of environmentally hazardous substance generated throughout the construction process of a facility which in return to mitigate negative impacts of buildings on the natural environment.

Although LCA tools are able to fulfil sustainability requirements, these environmentally-oriented tools have some problems with data accessibility. Prior studies show that these environmentally-oriented tools depend on the other technologies for effective and efficient usage in the AEC industry. The application of LCA in the construction sector is not widespread because of (1) lack of specialized professionals on the subject matter, (2) complexity of assessment tools, (3) unpractical manual data input [10].

4 Key Findings

When the previous studies addressing the integrated use of BIM and LCA were reviewed, a total of twenty-five types of benefits and six types of challenges were identified. This section presents and discusses these identified benefits and challenges of BIM-based LCA applications.

4.1 Benefits of the BIM and LCA Integration

Review of the literature showed that the integration of BIM and LCA contributes to the reduction of the total time spent and improvement of its application while minimizing the negative environmental impacts of the buildings throughout their life cycle. With combining these two technological instruments, designers can observe possible embodied energy and global warming potential at the early stages of the planning process inside of the full building analysis [9, 11, 12].

By the use of this sustainability-oriented technological framework, BIM-based LCA is able to eliminate the difficulties of each other with using their valuable features in order to compensate to the missing feature of each other [13]. While BIM technology helps minimization of LCA's challenges and deficiencies (e.g., storage capacity), LCA is able to reduce the negative environmental impacts of the buildings by integrating into BIM. However, Life Cycle Assessment tools without BIM automation can be long and complex due to the requirement of significant time and effort for implementation [14].

The other prominent LCA's software difficulty is the storage capacity. This difficulty can be managed with the integration of BIM technology since BIM provides effective solutions to LCA's storage problem with the ability to work on large files. BIM also allows professionals to organize the project schedule by mitigating the possible design errors that in turn provide LCA to recognize and develop solutions to the challenges which will face throughout the life cycle of the facility. LCA tools enable BIM to be enriched as content. This sustainability-oriented integration provides early decision-making process which helps LCA to be active at the beginning of the building and high potential for assessing decision-making process for early stages [4, 11, 15].

The other significant benefit of BIM-based LCA is that the reasoning mechanism of this integration is able to reduce the environmental expenditure in the early stages of design [15]. The main benefit of this sustainability-oriented platform is to reduce negative environmental impacts. This integration allows finding the main causes of the problems and minimizing these problems. At the beginning of the project, it is made possible to calculate future damages. The integrated use of BIM and LCA is an efficient mechanism for operational carbon emission analyses. The emission of carbon dioxide during construction can be monitored, this feature allows to take precautions and helps to avoid to generate unnecessary carbon dioxide to the atmosphere. Due to the measures taken, the emission of carbon dioxide during construction will decrease.

Additionally, researches support the argument that harmful gas emission reduces with the use of this togetherness [14].

Another important benefit of BIM-based LCA is that this technologically integrated instrument enables monitoring the total amount of energy used during construction, and with this speciality, detailed energy analysis becomes feasible [16]. This collaborative platform helps to detect unnecessary used energy and to regulate this energy usage. Reduction of the unnecessary energy used as well as reduction of the environmental problems decreases the total energy consumption during the project time [9]. The negative impact of the AEC industry on global warming is also able to provide a reduction of carbon dioxide emissions and energy consumption. Total global warming potential decreases with the use of BIM-based LCA platform [12].

Additionally, the other prominent benefit of this integrated platform is that BIM-based LCA is able to create a more effective working platform by avoiding software deficiencies [4]. For example, LCA tools have difficulty in obtaining numerical data single-handedly. When it is used with BIM, this deficiency can be eliminated in an efficient manner. BIM resolves the problems that LCA tools are experiencing to obtain numerical data in the field [16]. Quantitative performance predictions can be available for LCA tools with the use of BIM [16, 17].

The other valuable benefit of BIM-based LCA integration enables determining the properties of the material to be used and adjusting the amount of the material during the construction process; hence, this integrated technological framework helps the selection of the material at the early design stage of the facility. In order to reduce the negative effects of the built environment on the natural environment, a detailed examination can be performed for material selection via BIM-based LCA. This allows designers to prefer (1) less-emitting materials for the construction process at early stages of the design process [18, 19], and (2) more sustainable materials in building production and renovation processes [18, 19].

With the use of BIM and LCA integration, designers gain the opportunity for investigating different alternative materials [15, 20]. Examining different alternatives enables them to make comparisons and accordingly find the best solutions in terms of sustainability, quality, performance and cost.

Based on the results of a comprehensive literature review, the benefits for the integrated use of BIM and LCA are collated and summarized as follows:

- First one is reducing the environmental expenditure in the early stages of design [4, 15]. Predicting the progress of the project is profitable.
- This integration reduces expense and effort by providing a planned work environment. A planned work area facilitates the progress of the project [4, 13, 20].
- This integration facilitates decision-making process [4, 13, 15]. The environment prepared by the software during the decision-making phase offers an easier working environment for designers.
- The combination of BIM and LCA tools can be used effectively in the design phase [15]. The problems experienced by LCA alone in the design phase can be solved by collaborative use with BIM.
- Providing collaborative work between stakeholders, communication and data exchange become easier with different departments [15].

- Possibility of comparing different alternatives is another plus for this technology [13, 15, 20].
- Early-stage design deficiencies of LCA disappears while using information systems [13].
- Improvement of environmental performance can be achieved effectively [9, 10, 12, 14, 15, 17].
- Detailed energy analysis can be performed [4, 5, 10, 11, 13, 14, 17, 20].
- This collaborative technology, which has the potential to reduce the danger of negative impacts of the AEC industry is an efficient mechanism for operational carbon emission analyses [13, 14].
- Even observing carbon emission while transportation of materials is possible (e.g., vehicles) [12, 13].
- Instant feedback about LCA performance for construction [13]. BIM-LCA integration enables reduction of carbon emission in the construction process [9, 11, 13, 14].
- Environmental assessments become possible during the construction process [4, 5, 10, 11, 13, 15].
- Quantitative performance predictions for LCA tools is an important capability of integration [10, 16, 17].
- Conducting daylight analysis and investigating the water harvesting potential are details which the implementation can benefit from. [10, 16, 17].
- BIM-based sustainability software provides very quick results, [10, 14, 16] which help to respond immediately to the progress of the project and to make quick decisions on construction [9].
- Data obtained during design and construction cause a decrease in the total energy consumption [9, 11, 12].
- The environmental problems of the project do not end after the construction process has been completed. When the life of buildings expire, environmental pollution can be minimized by this technology [9].
- Total waste can be minimized after demolition [11].
- Helps in choosing less harmful material for construction process for coating and painting [16, 18, 19].
- Water use consumption can be reduced effectively in the building [16].
- Use of more sustainable materials in building production and renovation can be achieved [11, 12, 18–20].
- The global warming potential related to the facility can be mitigated [9, 11, 12].
- Potential for assessing decision-making process for the early phase of the building can be increased [4, 11–13, 15].

4.2   Challenges of the BIM and LCA Integration

Challenges encountered in the BIM-based LCA applications were examined with the review of the literature. According to the literature review, six types of challenges were identified for the integrated use of BIM and LCA. The challenges of BIM-LCA integration are as follows:

One of the challenges of BIM and LCA integration is the lack of standardization for LCA procedures [10, 11, 15]. Since the AEC sector does not have strict guidelines and standardizations about LCA, that makes difficult to disseminate the use of BIM-based LCA. Creating specific regulations on the subject domain will be beneficial for increasing its usage and accordingly allow to reduce environmental negative impacts of buildings throughout their lifespan [4].

Except some updated software like Revit, other difficulties occur while using tools, because these systems are designed separately and trying to be used simultaneously. The other substantial challenge of BIM-based LCA is that the interoperability is not completely arranged between LCA and BIM [15, 21].

Another challenge of BIM-based LCA occurs due to the lack of sustainability-based BIM tools in the market. This situation creates the difficulty in finding a way of using sustainable BIM-based tools [10, 21]. The potential of working with information systems in the AEC sector is increasing. Although this potential is not entirely be used, it is signalling that the prevalence will increase. As tools are used, their deficiencies will be improved.

One of the other challenges of BIM and LCA integration is that the complexity of the required data and available tools [10]. BIM also can be used for increasing the storage capacity of LCA. This increased capacity allows for more information to be stored. However, the difficulties begin with the lack of strict regulations on how to process this stored data.

The other challenge of BIM and LCA integration is that lack of comparable studies in the literature [11, 12] that makes the processes difficult to take measures and to find valid and right solutions.

5   Conclusion

This research study identified the benefits and challenges of BIM and LCA integration for the AEC industry by conducting a comprehensive literature review. Totally, twenty-five types of benefits and six types of challenges for the integrated use of BIM and LCA were identified. The results of this study may contribute to increasing the use of the BIM and LCA integration in the AEC industry that in turn allows decreasing negative environmental impacts of buildings through their life-cycle.

This research study shows that the integrated use of BIM and LCA may provide professionals in the AEC industry more accurate and faster results throughout reducing the labour force spent and achieving project objectives in less time. This chapter points out that studies on BIM-based LCA need to be intensified and that deficiencies in the sector should be eliminated. In order to eliminate the challenges of BIM and LCA integration, the use of this sustainability-oriented technological instrument should be encouraged and its use should be expanded.

One of the future directions of this study would prioritize the identified benefits and challenges of BIM and LCA integration based on the subject matter experts' with the aim of adding value to the decision making processes of the building design and construction. The other future direction of this study could be the preparation of the guideline to facilitate the use of this integration. Standardization of LCA software may increase the feasibility of the integration for the AEC industry. Another future research would focus on providing valuable solutions for the interoperability problem. If this issue can be solved in an effective manner, applications of BIM-based LCA will be increased in the AEC industry that in turn provide mitigation of negative impacts of the built environment on the natural environment.

References

1. Lizhen, H., Guri, K., Fred, J., Yongping, L., Xiaoling, Z.: Carbon emission of global construction sector. Renew. Sustain. Energy Rev. **81**, 1906–1916 (2017). https://doi.org/10.1016/j.rser.2017.06.001
2. Buildings and Climate Change Summary for Decision Makers, UNEP SBCI Sustainable Buildings and Climate Initiative (2009). https://europa.eu/capacity4dev/unep/document/buildings-and-climate-change-summary-decision-makers
3. Levine, M., et al.: Residential and commercial buildings. In: Metz, B., Davidson, O.R., Bosch, P.R., Dave, R., Meyer, L.A. (eds.) Climate Change 2007: Mitigation, Contribution of Working Group III to the Fourth Assessment Report of the Intergovernmental Panel on Climate Change. Cambridge University Press, Cambridge (2007)
4. Basbagill, J., Flager, F., Lepech, M., Fischer, M.: Application of life-cycle assessment to early stage building design for reduced embodied environmental impacts. Build. Environ. **60**, 81–92 (2013)
5. Azhar, S.: Building Information Modeling (BIM): trends, benefits, risks, and challenges for the AEC industry. Leadersh. Manag. Eng. **11**, 241–252 (2011). https://doi.org/10.1061/(ASCE)LM.1943-5630.0000127
6. Na, L., Korman, T.: Implementation of Building Information Modeling (BIM) in modular construction: benefits and challenges, pp. 1136–1145 (2010). https://doi.org/10.1061/41109(373)114
7. Meex, E., Hollberg, A., Knapen, E., Hildebrand, L., Verbeeck, G.: Requirements for applying LCA-based environmental impact assessment tools in the early stages of building design. Build. Environ. **133**, 228–236 (2018)
8. Nizam, R.S., Zhang, C., Tian, L.: A BIM based tool for assessing embodied energy for buildings. Energy Build. **170**, 1–14 (2018)
9. Endong, W., Zhigang, S., Barryman, C.: A building LCA case study using autodesk ecotect and BIM Model. In: 47th ASC Annual International Conference Proceedings, Papers in Construction Management, 6. University of Nebraska – Lincoln (2011)
10. Bueno, C., Fabricio, M.M.: Comparative analysis between a complete LCA study and results from a BIM-LCA plug-in. Autom. Constr. **90**, 188–200 (2018)
11. Ortiz, O., Castells, F., Sonnemann, G.: Sustainability in the construction industry: a review of recent developments based on LCA. Constr. Build. Mater. **23**(1), 28–39 (2009)
12. Anand, C.K., Amor, B.: Recent developments, future challenges and new research directions in LCA of buildings: a critical review. Renew. Sustain. Energy Rev. **67**, 408–416 (2017)
13. Eleftheriadis, S., Duffour, P., Mumovic, D.: BIM-embedded life cycle carbon assessment of RC buildings using optimised structural design alternatives. Energy Build. **173**, 587–600 (2018)
14. Shafiq, N., Nurrudin, M.F., Gardezi, S.S.S., Kamaruzzaman, A.B.: Carbon footprint assessment of a typical low rise office building in Malaysia using Building Information Modelling (BIM). Int. J. Sustain. Build. Technol. Urban Dev. **6**(3), 157–172 (2015)

15. Diaz, J., Anton, L.A.: Sustainable construction approach through integration of LCA and BIM tools. Comput. Civil Build. Eng. **2014**, 283–290 (2014)
16. Azhar, S., Carlton, W.A., Olsen, D., Ahmad, I.: Building information modeling for sustainable design and LEED® rating analysis. Autom. Constr. **20**(2), 217–224 (2011)
17. Kriegel, E., Nies, B.: Green BIM: Successful Sustainable Design with Building Information Modeling. Wiley Publishing, Indianapolis (2008). ISBN 978-0-470-23960-5
18. Rezaei, F., Bulle, C., Lesage, P.: Integrating building information modeling and life cycle assessment in the early and detailed building design stages. Build. Environ. **153**, 158–167 (2019). https://doi.org/10.1016/j.buildenv.2019.01.034
19. Abeysundara, Y., Babel, S., Gheewala, S.: A matrix in life cycle perspective for selecting sustainable materials for buildings in Sri Lanka. Build. Environ. **44**, 997–1004 (2009). https://doi.org/10.1016/j.buildenv.2008.07.005
20. Dupuis, M., April, A., Lesage, P., Forgues, D.: Method to enable LCA analysis through each level of development of a BIM model. Procedia Eng. **196**, 857–863 (2017)
21. Ajayi, S.O., Oyedele, L.O., Ceranic, B., Gallanagh, M., Kadiri, K.O.: Life cycle environmental performance of material specification: a BIM-enhanced comparative assessment. Int. J. Sustain. Build. Technol. Urban Dev. **6**(1), 14–24 (2015). https://doi.org/10.1080/2093761X.2015.1006708

A Case Study on the Beacon Technology Implementation in an Underground Station

Gizem Atalay and Umit Isikdag$^{(\boxtimes)}$

Department of Informatics, Mimar Sinan Fine Arts University, Istanbul, Turkey
gzmm.atalay@gmail.com, umit.isikdag@msgsu.edu.tr

Abstract. Beacon Technology is one of the wireless network technologies that work with Bluetooth Low Energy Technology (BLE). This technology was chosen to enable tracking of people and acquisition information in a high capacity underground station. The case study explained in this chapter initiated with the aim of designing an underground station that meets the transportation demands of the growing population by utilizing the facilities brought by Beacon technology to human life. With the help of the Beacon technology, along with the tracking of people, temperature control can be done by utilizing the temperature sensor inside the Beacon. In this chapter, a Beacon deployment that has been implemented for temperature control, staff and passenger tracking in an underground station in Istanbul have been explained in detail. The information acquired from the Beacons would contribute to the design of new underground stations and will facilitate the design decisions made for mitigating the risks in an emergency situation.

Keywords: Underground · Underground station · Bluetooth 4.0 · Beacon

1 Introduction

Istanbul is one of the most important cities in Turkey in terms of history, trade, finance and the economy. According to the Turkey Statistical Institute, in Istanbul, the population was 4 million in 1980 but it reached 15 million inhabitants in 2017 [1]. In addition, there are 3 million 571 thousand registered vehicles in Istanbul in 2018, and these vehicles cover an area of 68 million 343 thousand square meters. The city has a road network of 30,000 km and 2.5 million vehicles join the traffic every day [2]. Considering the energy and time losses caused by traffic congestion, it is necessary to reduce the use of vehicles and to direct people to public transportation platforms in order to solve the traffic problem throughout Istanbul. Therefore, the case study explained in this chapter initiated with the aim of designing an underground station that meets the transportation demands of the growing population by utilizing the facilities brought by Beacon technology to human life. Using low energy consumption BLE (Bluetooth Low Energy) signals, the Beacons can communicate with many smart devices, access location information. Enhanced versions of the Beacons are equipped with sensors that can detect motion, sound, light, humidity, temperature, and so on. In order to design a high capacity underground station, 3 solutions have been proposed in this design for tracking passengers, staff and for conducting temperature control on the XYZ Station* of Istanbul Underground.

© Springer Nature Switzerland AG 2020
S. Ofluoglu et al. (Eds.): EBF 2019, CCIS 1188, pp. 170–181, 2020.
https://doi.org/10.1007/978-3-030-42852-5_14

2 Beacon Technology

Beacons are electronic transmitters with low energy and low-cost wireless notification equipped with Bluetooth 4.0 or BLE technology [3]. A Beacon can be operated with two types of modes. In the first mode, Beacon is placed in a fixed place or on a moving object, then the smartphone or tablet that is connected to the smartphone enters the Beacon domain (coverage area) is tracked. In the second mode, Beacons are placed in a fixed place or on a moving object, and they transfer the data they collected to a wireless network such as a Wi-Fi and output via the cloud. In these two modes, Beacon's proximity feature comes to the fore [4].

2.1 Bluetooth Technology

Bluetooth LE (Low Energy) technology has been developed by SIG (Special Interest Group) formed by Ericsson, IBM, Intel, Nokia and Toshiba [5]. In fact, Bluetooth technology is not a new technology. It was first created by Ericson in 1994 to connect mobile phones and other mobile devices wirelessly and communicate [4]. However, Bluetooth 1.0 has a very low data throughput rate of 1 Mbps, which has caused mismatches between devices. In Bluetooth 2.0, which was developed in 2004, the data transfer rate was increased to 3 Mbps and the mapping problem between mobile devices was eliminated. In 2007, version Bluetooth 2.1 was launched with Safe Simple Pairing (SSP). In this way, the match is filtered to make the transfers more reliable. In 2009, the data transfer rate was increased to 24 Mbps and technology was developed with HS (High Speed) and Bluetooth 3.0 was developed. However, Bluetooth 3.0 consumes more power compared to Bluetooth 2.0 and versions (2.1 and 2.2). In 2010, Bluetooth 4.0 was developed with the Low Energy (BLE) feature designed for low data transfer in short periods. This has reduced the power consumption of devices connected to smart objects and has been shown to operate up to 3 years depending on the preferred battery type (Bluetooth SIG, 2018), [6]. Table 1 provides a comparison of the Bluethooth versions.

Table 1. Comparison of Bluetooth 1.0, 2.0, 3.0 and 4.0 [6, 7].

Bluetooth	1,0	2,0	3,0	4,0
Year	1994	2004	2009	2010
Transfer rate	1 Mbps	3 Mbps	24 Mbps	24 Mbps
Domain	10 m	10 m	10–100 m	10–100 m
Basic Ratio (BR)	X	X	X	X
Enhanced Data Rate (EDR)	–	X	X	X
High Speed (HS)	–	–	X	X
Enhanced security	–	X	X	X
Low energy	–	–	–	X

A Beacon provides internet connection via Bluetooth BLE technology and since SIG has not issued an official standard, every company that develops its own Beacon and establishes its own standard. The first Beacon with the standard was developed by Apple in 2013 under the name of iBeacon. IBeacon has a single data package consisting of the UUID (Universal Unique Identify), Major, Minor and TX Power. The UUID is 16 bytes long and is used to identify the public network. Major is 2 bytes long and detects the presence of the user, such as the presence sensor. Minor is 2 bytes long and helps to establish a proximity relationship with the user's closer Beacon. TX Power is 1 byte in length and measures the distance from the user [8].

In 2015, Eddystone was developed, which is another Beacon with the official standard, supported by Google, Android and IOS. Eddystone has three different package structure which is UID, URL and TLM. [5]. A UID is an ID that identifies the Beacon. It is 16 bytes long, with 10 bytes of general namespace and 6 bytes of 12 characters. The URL is Google's physical web. When smart devices enter the Beacon domain (coverage area) with the URL package, the URL contained in it opens and can be viewed by the user without any application requirements. TLM includes data obtained from sensors such as humidity, loudness, temperature, presence and light in the Beacon as preferred to be used with the UID package [9]. In the basic protocol, iBeacon and Eddystone declare users' locations, In advanced versions, they can have sensors that detect motion, sound, light, humidity, temperature.

2.2   Usage Areas of Beacon Technology

A Beacon can be operated with two approaches. In the first approach, the Beacon is placed in a fixed place or on a moving object, then the smartphone or tablet is connected to the application and the smart devices entering Beacon's domain (coverage area) are contacted and tracked. In the second one, the Beacons are placed in a fixed place or on a moving object, they transfer the data they collected to a wireless network such as Wi-Fi and output via the cloud. In these two modes, Beacon's proximity feature comes to the fore. One of the most common application areas working with these systems is retail sales. For example, when walking in front of a store, the store's ads(i.e. discounts) or products can be reported to smartphones [10]. Another area of application is the museums and the Louvre Museum in Paris is an example of this practice. Thanks to the application installed on the smart device, Mona Lisa and Leonardo Da Vinci's biography pages can be displayed while passing by the Mona Lisa [11]. Shota et al. (2015) developed a system of student attendance using Beacon technology. In this way, the period in which the student participates in the class can be recorded. Another area of application for Beacon technology is healthcare. This technology enables the physician to locate the patient in an emergency [12, 13]. Another study with beacons is the smart office management system. With the help of the Beacons placed in the office and a mobile application, the power saving mode works according to the employees entering and leaving the office. Thus, the energy consumption of monitors and illuminations is changed automatically when employees enter and leave the office [13].

3   Station Architecture

Underground stations are composed of circulation areas that allow pedestrians to reach from the entrance to the platform. However, there are also equipment and office areas required for operation and maintenance of that station. Station circulation areas and spaces required for operation and maintenance are developed in accordance with the decisions taken regarding the standards, regulations and meetings. However, meetings, standards and regulations in the design process are not always sufficient to move to the next stage. In the design process, project costs may be increased due to lack of coordination and cost expenditures.

It is a matter of debate how well the underground stations are designed. As of 2014, Building Information Modeling (BIM) specification was added to the tender documents of Istanbul Underground Metropolitan Municipality Rail System. In the space solutions of the pre-2014 underground projects, due to lack of coordination, unnecessary spaces were existing in the stations. For instance, the dead areas in the floor layout, the non-functional designed spaces, and the unpredictable shaft dimensions have led to designs occupying more space than needed.

In 2014, with the addition of Building Information Modeling (BIM) Specification to the DEF Underground Line Project[*], a new process has started in the underground projects of the municipality. Definitions are established by specifying the targets related to the use of BIM. It was ensured that all disciplines were part of the coordination. Thus, the next step in the station design with BIM was focused on avoiding undefined areas in the floor layout as much as possible.

The ABC Underground Line which was started to be constructed in 2016, the design process was carried out with minimum space requirements determined by operation and disciplines. Although the spaces are kept at optimum, station designs are not composed of passenger areas. There are many spaces that need to be added for normal and emergency response scenarios. Therefore, station structures are designed to be much larger than known. The organization of these spaces is optimized by BIM. However, in order for a station to have a long-lasting life, the station must be able to meet the transportation demands of the increasing population and should have an high performance.

ABC Underground Line is a 13.8 km long underground railway with 11 stations. XYZ Station is the 5th station of the railway. This station consists of 3 floors including the platform, the ticket hall and the technical floor and the in-station circulation of the passengers was the basis of the station design. The passenger enters the station, takes the ticket, passes the turnstile, goes down to the train, waits for the train, rides with the train, gets off the train and leaves the station. However, the situation for the staff is very different. Staff is responsible for passenger safety, turnstile passes, equipment control, station normal and emergency scenarios. Therefore, the spaces used by passengers and staff in station design were separated.

4 Advantages of Beacon Implementation at XYZ Station

Beacon technology has been preferred during the design of an high-performance station to make the station be a long-lasting one and to meet the transportation demands of the growing population. In XYZ Station where the design process was started with BIM software, there is a lot of workflows in many spaces and the workflow control at this station is planned to be carried out with SCADA (Central Control and Data Collection). In this case the workflow control would be performed with BIM software that enables facility management, the workflow and all information would be combined with the final BIM to protect the information infrastructure. Beacons can also be managed from a distance and various sensors can be placed in the Beacon to provide humidity, pressure, light, sound, speed and so on.

4.1 Staff Tracking

Staff working at the station cannot easily follow and track the information about each other's positions directly. The staff communicates with each other via the radio and expresses the location information via the handheld-radio connection orally. The location information of the person closest to the space to be intervened is defined depending on the station control supervisor's knowledge of the station layout and the ability to establish the relationship between the spaces. At this stage, as a result of lack of information, the risk of making mistakes also increases. An information infrastructure can be set up to tracking of staff at the station and the response time to potential problems can be shortened.

The purpose of staff tracking,

- Calling the relevant staff to the scene without delay in the event of an emergency
- Knowing where the staff are in the day and follow-up of staff activity
- Knowing the position of the staff is to eliminate the margin of error.

4.2 Passenger Tracking

In the preliminary and final project stages of underground projects, Normal and Emergency Account Reports are generated to help design decisions. In order to be able to calculate some key values in these reports, the estimated number of passengers in indoor spaces is needed. The outputs in these reports are used to analyze the maximum requirements of stair and escalator widths, turnstile numbers and passenger areas. In the emergency scenario, the outputs are used to analyze the platform and station evacuation times and the minimum space requirements for evacuation. According to the NFPA 130, which is an accepted standard for emergency response, the platform must be discharged within 4 min and the station within 6 min from the incident. In cases where the station and the platform cannot be evacuated within these periods, the evacuation times are reduced by declaring a safe area with a fire curtain. Therefore, the number of passengers is an important fact. However, when preparing these two reports, the number of travellers in most situations can not be predicted accurately and in practice, these numbers are estimated approximately [14]. In this case, the risk of making mistakes in the design of the underground station is increasing. False designs which can be made as a result of incorrect calculation of safe spaces and evacuation times put people's lives at risk. In this context, passenger numbers can be determined as a result of direct tracking to make more accurate decisions for future designs.

As a result of direct tracking of passenger movements,

- The evacuation times of the station and platform will be calculated more accurately and the risks in the emergency situation will be lowered.
- Station designs will be optimized by calculating the maximum widths of stairs, turnstile counts and passenger spaces more accurately.
- Determining where the passengers are predominant, undefined areas will be explored, and the station designs will be optimized.

4.3   Station Ventilation

It is important to ventilate the station in order to create an environment suitable for passengers, staff and equipment during the operation phase. There are Tunnel Ventilation Fan Rooms and Tunnel Ventilation Shaft Rooms in order to check the tunnel ambient conditions at both ends of the platform in case of an emergency at XYZ Station. In the normal case scenario, station ventilation shaft rooms and station ventilation fan room are positioned on the technical floor in order to provide a more spacious environment for the passengers and to better expel the dirty air. Apart from normal and emergency scenarios, air conditioning systems are installed in the spaces where staff are frequently located. Although the environment is suitable for passengers, staff and equipment in underground designs, these environments cannot be controlled. Inability to control ventilation also increases energy consumption. However, to design a high-performance station, the ventilation system must be checked frequently. In the basic protocol, Beacon only reports the location of users, but advanced versions shave sensors for motion, sound, light, humidity, temperature etc. Thanks to the temperature sensor that can be placed inside the beacon, the ventilation system will be controlled in real-time depending on the ambient temperature.

4.4   Implementation of the Beacon Infrastructure

The implementation consists of several layers, including network, detection and application layer. In a Beacon implementation, users do not need to carry any hardware to utilize this technology. In fact, they need to install a mobile application developed for Beacon technology and each user will create his own profile to be able to access this application. Thanks to these profiles, staff and passengers will be distinguished. In addition, the temperature sensor that can be placed inside the Beacons will be controlled. All data will be kept by the server in the station control room. The following elaborates on these three layers of the architecture.

4.4.1   Network Layer

The smart tablet/phone needs an internet connection to initiate the application. This internet connection will be established with Wi-Fi. In this way, Beacon will also benefit from Wi-Fi's ability to provide a wide range of services. Wi-Fi system will be installed in XYZ Station control room (SOR) located on the floor of the ticket hall and this system will also be implemented on the other floors. The station control room (SOR) is a space where the station is monitored and managed. In this room, monitoring and control of the cameras belonging to the station can be recorded to Network Video Recorder. At the same time, this space has information exchange with the main command centre. In the station design, SOR room should be placed in a way to provide visibility with turnstile groups in accordance with the decisions of the related disciplines. In addition, this room, located on the XYZ Station, is located in the middle of the ticket hall floor. Due to its central location, the Wi-Fi network will be installed and distributed in this location.

4.4.2 Detection Layer

Beacon provides internet connection via Bluetooth BLE technology and provides data over the cloud by transferring data to a wireless network such as Wi-Fi. Wi-Fi requires a modem for connection even though it provides a wireless connection. For this purpose, a modem has been installed in the station control room. The indoor area of Wi-Fi's domain is 70 m according to the IEEE.11n standard. The length of XYZ Station, the ticket hall and the technical floor are 52 m and the width is 22 m. The length of the platform floor is approximately 90 m and its width is 33 m. These values are within the domain of Wi-Fi. Thus it is sufficient to provide one Wi-Fi connection to each floor.

Devices with Beacon technology can emit low radio signals and communicate with a Bluetooth-powered smartphone or phone near itself. Beacon placement in an enclosed space should be done at 50 m intervals. With the values of the length and width of the floors in XYZ Station; it is enough to place 1 Beacon on the ticket hall and the technical floor and 2 Beacons on the platform floor. However, if smart devices enter the domain (coverage area) of more than one Beacon, a close relationship is established between the Beacons and a list is created. This list informs the user which Beacon is closer. Thus, more accurate results can be obtained. For this reason, the impact areas of the Beacons have been located as intersecting with each other. The location of some Beacons is given in Fig. 1, and Figs. 4, 5 and 6 provides more detail on the installation.

4.4.3 Application Layer

The ID data obtained from Beacon signals are matched with the previously defined passenger or staff profile in the application software [11, 13]. Figure 2 shows the basic profile information that a Staff must create. The staff provides the application with the necessary information for the profile, such as his/her department, the ID number, and speciality. In this way, the user's type is registered as a staff and the risk of making mistakes is eliminated. Staff have pass permits according to their expertise within the station. With the help of the system established by the beacons, the control of the staffs' pass permits is accomplished on the server-side. For example, an electrical engineer cannot enter a cleaning room, or an unauthorized staff can not enter the server room.

Fig. 1. Placement of Beacons

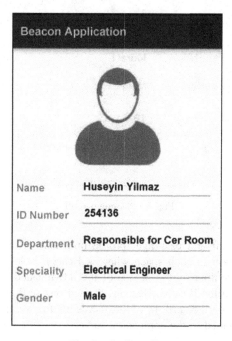

Fig. 2. Staff profile

Figure 3, depicts the profile information that a passenger needs to create. The passenger fills in the necessary information like the user name, gender, year of birth, e-mail via the application. Thus, the user's type is determined as a passenger. In the emergency and normal situation reports prepared during the design phase of the underground stations, the number of trips per/day for a passenger is estimated and taken into account. Thanks to the system installed with beacons, the number of trips becomes clearer and the risk of making planning mistakes is eliminated. In addition, the gender and age information that the passenger must fill in the profile will also help to analyze the passengers. For example, statistical information such as the average age of passengers at the XYZ Station or the number of male and female passengers at the XYZ Station can be derived.

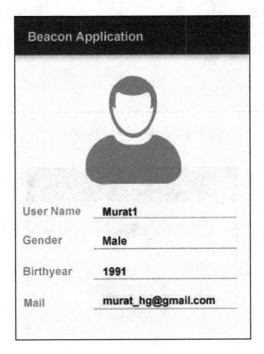

Fig. 3. Passenger profile

Apart from the staff and passenger profile information, the server also gets the temperature information in each space where a Beacon is located. The temperature information is not acquired by the device of the downloaded application but by the temperature sensors in the Beacon. Beacons located on the floors receive the temperature information from the airflow of the vents in the ventilation ducts and this information is transmitted to the application server.

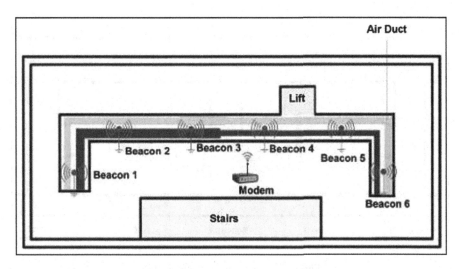

Fig. 4. Deployments in technical floor

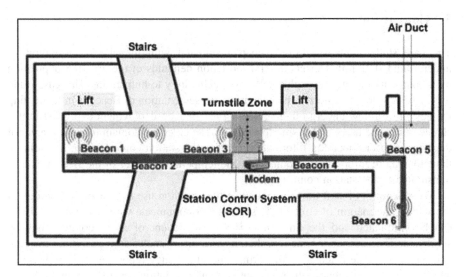

Fig. 5. Deployments in ticket hall

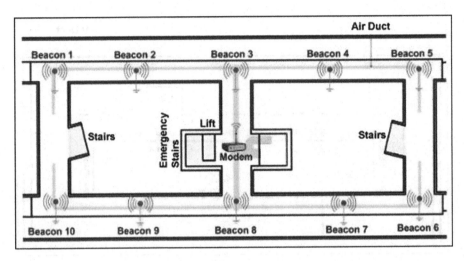

Fig. 6. Deployments in platform floor

5   Conclusions

The case study explained in this chapter initiated with the aim of designing an underground station that meets the transportation demands of the growing population by utilizing the facilities brought by Beacon technology to human life. This case study was also focused on exploring the benefits of implementation of Beacons in facilitating the design of a new underground station. In the Beacon deployment explained in this chapter, once the users with a smartphone or tablet enter the domain (coverage area) of the Beacon, users' location information reaches the station control room. In addition, the temperature information acquired via the temperature sensor in the Beacon is also transmitted to the station control room.

By utilization of staff tracking, which is the common use of Beacon technology in the station, the margin of error of the staff who communicate with each other verbally can be eliminated and the time of arrival in the event of an emergency may be shortened. The secondary benefit is that, as a result of analysis on passenger tracking data, more accurate calculation of normal and emergency reports would be possible, and the risks of emergency situations can be reduced, station designs can be optimized and unidentified areas can be discovered. Finally, with the control of the temperature information and the controlled air-conditioning of the environment, the indoor air quality would be more suitable for the passenger, staff and equipment and the consumption of energy in the event of a change in temperature would prevented.

The system has been developed to provide unilateral information flow in terms of security attacks. No system information is transmitted to the user. However, the user may be exposed to some security attacks from the moment they turn on their Bluetooth. For example, a user may send an anonymous message or virus to another user, or a user may copy all information without the other user's permission. To avoid such situations, packets from the other party using a strong pin code should not be accepted. In addition, Bluetooth security attacks can be prevented with rapidly developing technology nowadays.

*Note: The original name of the underground station and the underground lines has been changed due to confidentiality reasons. XYZ Station, ABC and DEF Underground Lines are placeholder names.

References

1. Haber7 News Item (2017). http://www.haber7.com/kitap/haber/879650-istanbul-nufusunun-tarihi-gelisimi
2. Yeni Akit News Item (2018). https://www.yeniakit.com.tr/haber/istanbul-carnumber
3. Stein, N., Urbanski, S.: Beacon technology with IoT and big data. In: Geng, H. (ed.) Internet of Things and Data Analytics Handbook (2016)
4. Chan, C.Y.: Bluetooth technology. Indian Institute of Technology, Madras, Software Engineering Project Report (2004)
5. Bisdikian, C.: An overview of the Bluetooth wireless technology. IEEE Commun. Mag. **39**, 86–94 (2001)
6. Bluetooth SIG, Core Specification version 4.0. http://www.bluetooth.org/. Accessed 2018
7. Sauter, M.: Bluetooth and Bluetooth. In: Sauter, M. (eds) From GSM to LTE, Advanced Pro and 5G (2017)
8. Jurkovi, L., Hrivíková, T., Hlavatý, I.: E-learning in augmented reality utilizing iBeacon technology, vol. 1, pp. 170–179 (2013)
9. Google beacon eddystone (2018). https://developers.google.com/beacons/
10. Mircoli, M., Mitolo, S., Burzacca, P., Polzonetti, A.: "iBeacon" technology that will make possible Internet of Things. In: International Conference on Software Intelligence Technologies and Applications & International Conference on Frontiers of Internet of Things, pp. 159–165 (2014)
11. He, Z.: A proposal of interaction system between visitor and collection in museum hall by iBeacon. In: 2015 10th International Conference on Computer Science & Education (ICCSE), pp. 427–430 (2015)
12. Lin, X.Y., Ho, T.W., Fang, C.C., Yen, Z.S., Yang, B.J., Lai, F.: A mobile indoor positioning system based on iBeacon technology. In: Proceedings of the Annual International Conference of the IEEE Engineering in Medicine and Biology Society, EMBS, November 2015, pp. 4970–4973 (2015)
13. Kim, E., et al.: An iPhone application for providing ibeacon-based services to students. Int. J. Open Inf. Technol. **3**(3), 57–72 (2014)
14. Eren, T., Gencer, M.: Ankara metrosu M1 (Kızılay-Batıkent) hattı hareket saatlerinin çizelgelenmesi. Acad. Plat. J. Eng. Sci. **4**(2), 25–36 (2016). https://doi.org/10.21541/apjes.27756. https://dergipark.org.tr/en/download/article-file/224121

BIM and Contribution to IFC-Bridge Development: Application on Raymond Barre Bridge

Mojtaba Eslahi[1(✉)], Rani El Meouche[1(✉)], Omar Doukari[2],
and Anne Ruas[3]

[1] Institut de Recherche en Constructibilité (IRC), ESTP Paris,
28 Avenue du Président Wilson, 94230 Cachan, France
{meslahi, relmeouche}@estp-paris.eu
[2] École d'Ingénieurs CESI, 93 Boulevard de la Seine, 92000 Nanterre, France
[3] LISIS/IFSTTAR, Université de Marne-la-Vallée, 5 Boulevard Descartes,
77420 Champs-sur-Marne, France

Abstract. BIM (Building Information Modeling) is a new concept in construction industry and becomes popular worldwide in recent years. BIM is widely used by individuals, businesses and government agencies. It is applied in all phases of construction lifecycle from planning and designing to constructing and maintaining. It contains different structure types of buildings and infrastructures including water, refuse, electricity, gas, communication utilities, roads, railways, bridges, ports and tunnels. The application of BIM in the building industry is relatively widespread while the development of BIM method in the domain of infrastructure is yet in infancy. In this research, we would like to study the compatibility of BIM in modeling the bridge by using Autodesk Revit.

In this chapter, two data exchanging open standards that are mostly used in BIM, in the field of bridge modeling, including IFC (Industry Foundation Classes) and CityGML (Geography Markup Language) are reviewed. A parametric 3D bridge model is established with Autodesk Revit in order to carry out an experiment on bridge information modeling. The Raymond Barre Bridge in Lyon, France is used as case study.

We have divided the process of modeling the bridge to two steps. The first step is structuring the bridge elements, which means to generate the different parts of the bridge including the foundations, deck parts, diaphragms and bowstring; and the next step is to assemble the deck parts and placement of bridge elements. In the modeling process, a large number of customer families are created to represent the missing bridge entities that could result in the information loss in IFC file.

We show that the current IFC is not well developed for bridges and it is needed to define specific entities dedicated to the bridge domain. We also refer to the other research in this domain and their suggestions for extending IFC for bridges such as bridge data dictionary, information delivery manual, missing concepts and new entities for IFC-bridge. The results identify the urgency to improve IFC for infrastructure domain, especially for the IFC-Bridge.

Keywords: BIM (Building Information Modeling) · IFC (Industry Foundation Classes) · IFC-Bridge · CityGML

© Springer Nature Switzerland AG 2020
S. Ofluoglu et al. (Eds.): EBF 2019, CCIS 1188, pp. 182–194, 2020.
https://doi.org/10.1007/978-3-030-42852-5_15

1   Introduction

BIM is a process for representing the physical and functional characteristics of a multi-dimensional model of a construction [1]. The notion of BIM could go back to 1974 of Eastman [2] and the term of building model appeared in the article by Ruffle [3] and Aish [4]. The term of Building Information Model was used later, in an article of van Nederveen and Tolman in 1992 [5], but it was not used popularly until 10 years later in 2002 by Autodesk.

BIM is a new concept of production management with important characteristics including visualization, coordination, simulation, optimization and documentation. In BIM software, the objects can be defined as parameters and their relations to other objects. In the phase of design, BIM defines the construction or building components as combination objects with the information of their geometry, attributes and relations. These attributes and parameters can be used to provide the cash flow, ordering and tracking material and human resources planning. Nowadays, BIM represents a digital model including the three primary spatial dimensions (i.e. width, height and depth) plus the time (4D) [6], cost (5D) [7], energy analysis and sustainability (6D) and maintenance, operations and facilities management (7D).

Using BIM makes it possible to coordinate among the stockholders, take the information of the model from the designers including the surveyors, building architects, landscape architect, civil and structural engineers, electrical and mechanical engineers and share it to the main contractor, subcontractors and the operators. Therefore, it causes to decrease the losses of information that occurred when a new team takes over the project.

BIM for Infrastructure. BIM is used in different kinds of constructions like the buildings, road networks, tunnels and bridges. Most countries that have been involved in BIM for building section have engaged in an extension of BIM to infrastructure [8]. For example, the UK is one of the most advanced countries in BIM projects including infrastructure BIM for which specialists believe they are only 3 years behind the building section. Since 2011, the UK Government (Government Construction Strategy directive - GCS2011) has decided to adopt all building and infrastructure projects in accordance with BIM level 2. This directive has been extended to all industry in spring 2016 [8, 9].

In the United States and EU countries, 20% of the linear infrastructure projects were BIM projects in 2015. This increased to 52% in 2017 and is estimated to exceed 61% in 2019 [8]. Figure one illustrates the level of using BIM in some countries in both building and infrastructure sectors [8] (see Fig. 1).

	Significant level of engagement in BIM	Moderate level of engagement in BIM	Low level of engagement in BIM

Building	USA, Canada, United Kingdom, Australia, New Zealand and Scandinavia	Germany, France, Italy, Belgium, Netherlands, Luxembourg and Japan	South Korea Brazil, China, Qatar and other countries
Infrastructure	USA, Canada, United Kingdom, Australia, New Zealand and Scandinavia	Germany, France, Italy, Belgium, Netherlands, Luxembourg and Japan	South Korea Brazil, China, Qatar and other countries
	These countries continue and extend the BIM approach	These countries have adopted the BIM approach or started to extend it	These countries have started thinking about BIM

Fig. 1. Comparison of different countries on the level of BIM usage (Cerema [8], source: Autodesk)

BIM has been successfully implemented and widely used in the construction sector, but the use of BIM for infrastructure is still much less and needs to be organized. In the infrastructure field, the working methods are different and the design elements are less suited to treat as object-oriented data (e.g. an axis in plan or a cross-section are not recognized as IFC exchangeable objects, these are designed as surfaces and not as separated 3D objects) [8]. These come from the low efficiency of BIM software in the domain of infrastructure.

Several types of research have been done in this field to overcome these lacks. In France, the national project MINnD tries to bring together most of the public and private actors related to infrastructures to do research on the standards of data exchange. This project revolves around several elements, which disseminate current practices, experiments, methodological recommendations and evaluation, in order to create the version of IFC that could adapt better to the field of infrastructures especially for bridges [10]. In this chapter, we discuss using BIM to model a bridge and the standards of sharing information and BIM data among different software applications.

IFC. It is a neutral and open data format of an international standard (ISO 19739) that is developed by buildingSMART in order to facilitate interoperability exchange in the fields of architecture, engineering and construction (AEC) industry. IFC is an object-based file format with a data model that is commonly used in BIM-based AEC projects to facilitate the software interoperability [11].

IFC works well in building modelling, though it has some lacks in building sectors such as incomplete implementation (e.g. extrusion, Boolean operations) or uses that are not really oriented towards the field of infrastructure (e.g. pre-stressing) [12]. Nowadays, IFC tries to cover also the infrastructures such as bridges, roads, railways, tunnels or earthworks and the changes to introduce the information modelling for these infrastructures are in progress [10].

CityGML. It is an Open Geospatial Consortium (OGC) standard based on the Geography Markup Language, which represents the geometrical, semantical, topological, and visual aspects of a 3D city model [13]. It covers all relevant features in urban areas including buildings and infrastructures. The features are organized into modules such as building, transportation, water bodies, tunnel and bridge. In CityGML the features are represented in five discrete Levels-of-Detail (LoDs) from zero to four. Each LoD reflects specific application requirements. Each feature can be simultaneously represented in different LoDs. However, data integration and interoperability are facilitated when the features are in the same LoD.

In CityGML an object of the class Bridge represents a bridge. The bridge model indicates the thematic, spatial, and visual aspects of bridges and construction elements in four levels of detail where the semantic and geometric details increase from LoD1 to LoD4. The attributes class of a bridge demonstrates the construction type of the bridge (e.g. being an arch or a suspension bridge) while the attribute function represents the utilization of the bridge independently of the construction (e.g. railway bridge, roadway bridge, pedestrian bridge) [14].

IFC vs CityGML. Although our work focuses on IFC and its properties in bridge modelling, as evaluation, in this section we will give a comparison of IFC and CityGML. In 2008, Isikdag and Zlatanova indicated that the IFC models contain all necessary information to generate CityGML models in different LoDs [15]. They have defined some rules to make a transformation framework between CityGML and IFC models for geometric transformation and semantic matching. In 2011, Hijatzi et al., made a web-based tool that integrated IFC data into a 3D GIS environment. It could support the navigation and visualization functionalities and some analysis operations such as routing and network analyses [16].

Even though IFC and CityGML are two data exchange standards that are used in the BIM domain, they have some semantic and geometrical differences as follows [14]:

- CityGML can be used in all relevant urban elements such as the buildings and infrastructures, while IFC is still more used for modelling the buildings.
- In CityGML, the building elements are defined as what is observed, like the walls for every single room. IFC defines the construction elements such as walls identified for a whole building.
- As spatial properties definition, CityGML uses boundary representation and focuses on buildings usage and observation. IFC additionally applies the Constructive Solid Geometries (CSG) and sweep geometries.
- In IFC, the objects are defined with one LoD. In CityGML they are represented in different LoDs.

So far, we have reviewed briefly the BIM for infrastructure, especially bridges and the two open data exchange standards that are used in BIM. Next, the Raymond Barre Bridge as a case study will be described. In Sect. 3, the methodology and the modelling process will be explained in detail. The interoperability of the bridge model will be discussed in Sect. 4. The chapter will conclude in Sect. 5.

2   Case Study

The work consists of developing a parametric 3D model of the Raymond Barre Bridge in Lyon using Autodesk Revit.

The bridge is located in the new zone of Confluence, spanning the river of Rhône. It is 260 m long and 17.50 m wide. This bridge consists of three spans; a central span of 150 m framed by two others of 72 m and 38 m.

The cross-sectional profile of the bridge is not symmetrical. It consists of three lines including tramway path, pedestrians and cyclist path. The bridge is a two-girder bridge containing two caissons between which are placed the tramway tracks. The deck parts are not simple and have a raised part in the centre. The cyclist path, as well as the pedestrian area, are located in a cantilevered upstream part of the Rhône. The metal frame of this specific bridge consists of two large arches. Each of these two arches of 150 m is inclined at 10° to the vertical with an opening to the sky (see Fig. 2).

Fig. 2. Raymond Barre bridge (source: Bouygues construction)

3   Methodology and Modeling

Figure 3(a), shows the IFC building breakdown structure [11] and the Fig. 3(b) illustrates the process for the basic framework of IFC-based bridge information modelling [17]. In the IFC-bridge breakdown, the bridge component data can be equivalent to the IfcProduct in IfcBuilding.

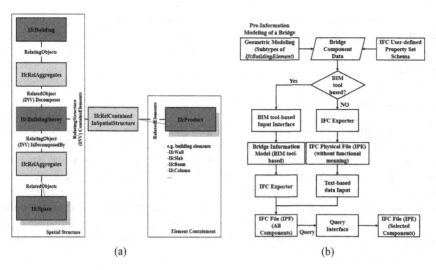

Fig. 3. a: IFC building breakdown structure [11] b: basic framework for IFC-based bridge modelling process [17]

In this study, we have modelled a real bridge on Revit in order to verify the interoperability of the information generated in the model based on the current IFC. Afterwards, the IFC file was exported and then imported again to Revit. We have found that in this process the procedural geometry of the original complex objects has been lost and the exported IFC could not be used appropriately even by the same software which indicates the inability of the current IFC in bridge modelling (see Fig. 4).

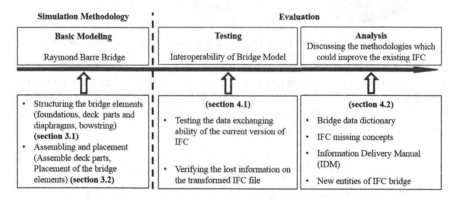

Fig. 4. The method procedure

We have divided the process of modelling the bridge into two steps. The first step is structuring the bridge elements and it means to generate the different parts of the bridge including the foundations, the bridge deck parts, diaphragms and bowstring. The next step is to assemble the deck parts and the placement of bridge elements means to place each component of the bridge in the right location and direction according to the bridge layout. In the modelling process, a large number of customer families are created to represent the missing entities of the bridge to overcome the lacks of modelling a bridge in Revit.

3.1 Generating the Bridge Elements

Revit serves initially for buildings, consisting of the elements such as walls, doors and windows. For example, there is "beam" element in Revit, but the default beam family in Revit is too simple, so it is necessary to create hosted families for the Raymond Barre bridge components. To start modelling the bridge, we have divided the Raymond Barre bridge to three parts i.e. foundations, deck (with railings) and diaphragm, and bowstring. The foundations contain two same abutments each at one end of the bridge, as well as one round foundation and one irregular foundation under the span of the bridge. The deck part consists of beams and railings and the bowstring part is made up of tie rods, brackets and screws.

Generation of Foundations. The Raymond Barre Bridge has four foundations. One round foundation, a polyhedral foundation under the middle bridge span and two triangular prism foundations at the ends of the bridge. Metric Structural Foundation family template fits the foundation elements of Raymond Barre bridge well (see Fig. 5).

Fig. 5. Round, Polyhedral and Triangular prism foundations modelled in Revit

Generating the Deck and Diaphragm Parts. The deck part has a complex cross-section since this bridge is built for the tram, walkers as well as cyclists. The bridge deck parts are divided into three beam members and railways where each kind of component is made separately (see Fig. 6).

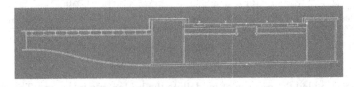

Fig. 6. Deck part of Raymond Barre Bridge

The Raymond Barre Bridge has two diaphragms. The first one is under the pedestrian and the other is under tramway (see Fig. 7). Considering the attributes of the diaphragm, the metric generic model family template is chosen for its generation. There is no default constraint for these types of templates.

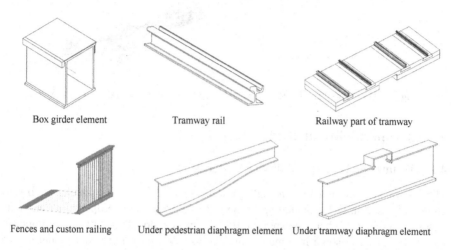

<table>
<tr><td>Box girder element</td><td>Tramway rail</td><td>Railway part of tramway</td></tr>
<tr><td>Fences and custom railing</td><td>Under pedestrian diaphragm element</td><td>Under tramway diaphragm element</td></tr>
</table>

Fig. 7. Deck part of Raymond Barre Bridge in Revit

Generation of Bowstring Part. Two symmetrical bowstring arches, tied rods, brackets and screws constitute the bowstring part of Raymond Barre Bridge. The bowstring part was required to be parametric and it would be necessary to be able to vary the off-plane inclination of the arcs, the height of the arcs, the thicknesses of gussets and screeds, the axle diameter for the gusset/clevis system and the diameter and the number of tie rods.

3.2   Assembling and Placement

This section primarily expounds the procedure of the second step of modelling the Raymond Barre Bridge in a Revit project, including the process of assembling deck parts and the placement of each bridge element group. To make the process of modelling more convenient, the two diaphragms were assembled together in a new metric generic model family template. Then the new family type was loaded to the bridge model and placed along the reference planes. Afterwards, the foundations were loaded and placed to their location.

The deck family and the rail track were applied to the curvilinear model line. The custom families of bowstring arch, tie rod, bracket and screw were uploaded into the bridge project. A bowstring arch was established in its position according to bridge horizontal layout that was joined to the bearing on the round foundation. In the vertical layout section view, an instance of a tie rod family was created between the two brackets. The position of tie rod was slightly adjusted in 3D view and then joined to the brackets (see Fig. 8).

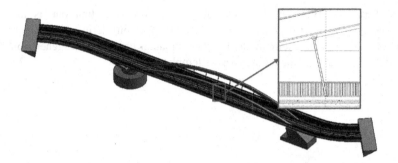

Fig. 8. 3D view of modelled bridge and the placement of tie rod in section view

4 Interoperability of Bridge Model

4.1 Testing the Interoperability of Bridge Model

The interoperability of BIM (modelling) software is always a big challenge. IFC is commonly used in BIM (modelling) projects to facilitate the interoperability and data exchange, however, when we export an IFC file from a modelling software to import it into other software, some information may be lost. We have tested our model in two different ways to know the limitations of the model as well as the constraints of the IFC and to examine whether the existing IFC format can be used to exchange information in bridge modelling.

In the first case, the Raymond Barre bridge model that is built in Revit is exported as a DWG file (.dwg file extension) and then imported into Rhinoceros software (see Fig. 9). In this case, the model is represented well in Rhino, however, some objects are no longer parametric and they lose some semantic information.

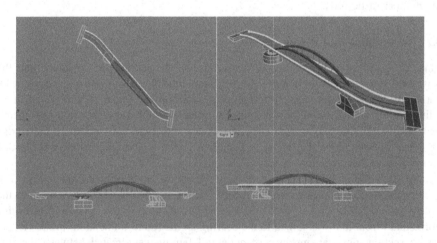

Fig. 9. Exporting the DWG file from Revit and open it in Rhino

In the second case, we have exported the developed model as an IFC file and then imported again to Revit in order to test the interoperability of our parametric model and to evaluate the constraints of the current version of IFC in modelling a bridge. It turned out that a large amount of information has been lost. The transformed IFC file displayed only several foundations, two railings, brackets and tie rods. The information of curvilinear bridge deck, the diaphragms and the bowstring arch were lost in IFC file. Figure 10 illustrates how the transformed IFC file displayed in Revit. Therefore, the IFC file of bridge model is poorly implemented in Revit, which leads to the discussion about the development of IFC for the bridge.

Fig. 10. Large information loss of IFC file

Several methodologies are proposed in order to improve existing IFC and to overcome its problems. The researchers try to create the specific IFC for the bridges, by developing specific entities for the bridge domain, defining the IFC missing concepts and finding a methodology to reduce the loss of information in the process of data exchange, that are discussed in next section.

4.2   Methodologies for Improving Existing IFC

The existing constraints of modelling a parametric bridge show that the current IFC was not well implemented by software vendors and make it necessary to have a specific extension of IFC for the bridges. This is why the IFC-bridge researchers put forward a methodology to improve the existing IFC classes, by highlighting some paramount missing concepts, and to develop specific entities dedicated to the bridge domain. In France, there is a project called MINnD (*Modélisation des INformations INteropérables pour les INfrastructures Durables* - Modeling of interoperable information for sustainable infrastructures) national project where the working team has done an in-depth study on IFC-bridge [10]. They have categorized two types of deficiency in current IFC contain incomplete implementation concerning the existing IFC and the needs to develop the new entities concerning the domain of infrastructure and their environment. They show that the extension of IFC-Bridge is necessary to be done in order to share the common civil engineering features, geometry and alignment. Their research on IFC-bridge demonstrate the needs to define some parameters such as bridge data dictionary, IFC missing concepts, information delivery manual and the new entities of IFC-bridge standard.

Bridge Data Dictionary. A data dictionary aims to describe the constituent elements of bridges, which cover all types of bridges. It can comprise a library of objects together with their attributes and the relationships between the objects as well as their properties. In a project, a data dictionary facilitates the information exchanges between the actors. The data dictionary can ensure interoperability between the software packages. In addition, the project information will be more sustainable using standardized terms. The bridge data dictionary could be integrated to the buildingSMART Data Dictionary (bSDD). The IFC-infrastructure is divided into different domains e.g. alignment, rail, road, bridge and tunnel. For each of them a data dictionary is needed to be developed where, as our knowledge, some of them are in course of developing. A bridge project is not isolated in general and it is connected to other infrastructures such as road, rail or tunnels. Therefore, the bridge data dictionary has to be exhaustive but yet exclusive to have the potential to connect with other components of a project in a BIM system [18].

IFC Missing Concepts. The missing concepts of IFC can be divided into procedural geometry, coordinate systems and analytical representation [12].

Procedural geometry means the abilities to define geometry within a descriptive approach (e.g. extrusions along a 3D curve). This could not be realized in current BIM software. An object in Revit is made of boundary representation (B-Rep), where it is considered a round plate represented as multi-faceted prism before zooming in. In addition, the poor geometric information output of IFC has been confirmed by this model example. As we have seen, the procedural geometry of the original complex objects has been lost and the exported IFC could not be used appropriately by the other software packages and even by the same software, which was one of the problems faced.

Benning [12] holds the point that there are three kinds of coordinate systems important for a BIM project. The first one is the local reference system, which describes the location and position according to an object nearby that is dedicated to project with the very limited spread of less than around 100 m. The next one is surveying system that is a global system, defining the location of elements with several attributes such as latitude and longitude that is often used on long linear or very large surface projects. The last coordinate system is a linear system mainly used for a linear project and making it more convenient to locate target components. Nevertheless, among these three types of coordinate systems, only the local reference system is implemented in the current IFC and have to be defined for the infrastructure domain.

Structural analysis is a complicated domain to tackle for improving IFC infrastructure. Benning [12] points out that the method of load information storage will lead to confusion because the load is applied to the bars of the structural model and the input information would be mixed with the analytical model.

Information Delivery Manual (IDM). IDM should fully cover the domain in a holistic manner in line with the most advanced professional practices. It allows defining the expectation and demands of each actor of the value chain and information exchange between them during the lifecycle of a project in usual words. This process describes the input and the output attributes of each object processed by each actor [10]. The MINnD project looked at the components of the bridge from three views:

- The operational approach that corresponds to the cause of necessity of a bridge that tries to answer why the bridge is necessary: IFC is not appropriate and need to be complemented by other categories to cover operational views.
- The functional approach is concerning the usage of the bridge: IFC is able to describe the functions of the structures, but are still too poor or rarely completed to cover the various models.
- The organic approach concerning the components of the bridge: The IFC is well adapted to the organic description of the structures but must be supplemented to cover the needs of the professionals.

New Entities of IFC-Bridge. Benning et al. [10] made a list of new structural components as IFC entities e.g. pier, pylon, abutment, expansion joint, deck and bearing pad. However, some outstanding bridges such as suspension bridges, cable-stayed bridges and moveable bridges have other new entities to be described. There are also some concepts that exist in the current IFC but they are not appropriate for bridges. The concept of reinforcement for the concrete structures is more dedicated to precast elements and is not sufficient to address the bridge expectations. The pre-stressing system is described in the existing IFC but it is not developed enough and it does not cover the post-tensioned system.

5 Conclusion

BIM has been popularized in the building domain in recent years, whereas the use of the BIM concept for infrastructure is less developed, compared with building domain. In our research, we have reviewed the BIM for infrastructure, especially bridges. We discussed and compared the two open data exchange standards used in BIM including IFC and CityGML. To conduct an experiment on IFC infrastructure, a parametric bridge information model was established with Revit in this work. The study mainly covers the procedures of modelling and structuring the information of Raymond Barre Bridge. In the process of structuring the bridge members, a large number of families were created to represent the missing entities of the bridge. Our result identifies the urgency to improve IFC for bridge modelling. In the version 2017 of Revit there is a plug-in, named Civil Structure 2017. However, this plug-in is a fast tool to build bridge easily but it is not able to establish bridges with complex deck profile. This appeals to the developments of IFC-bridge again.

There is no topography data around the Raymond Barre Bridge, provided in the project. Therefore, the final model is just an independent bridge and it is needed to be inserted in the complete environment. Furthermore, the bridge model just accomplishes a 3D model, without exploiting research on the issues of scheduling (4D) and cost (5D) of the bridge. The further experiment of time and cost could be conducted in future.

To accelerate the delivery of first IFC-bridge entities in late 2018, an international expert group is working on the validation of new IFC-bridge entities. Funding for following and developing these new entities has been raised internationally, which verifies the significance of IFC-bridge and the interest from the international community. Consequently, more efforts will be put into the bridge domain and it is hoped to widely use BIM method for infrastructure in the near future.

In this research, we have concentrated more on IFC application in a BIM system. For the future work, we would like to test the application of CityGML in a BIM system for the same study area to have a more clear idea about their differences and their advantages in using in the infrastructure projects.

References

1. National Building Information Model Standard Project Committee (2019). https://www.nationalbimstandard.org
2. Eastman, C.: An outline of the building description system, Research Report No. 50 (1974)
3. Ruffle, S.: Architectural design exposed: from computer-aided drawing to computer-aided design. Environ. Plan. **13**(4), 385–389 (1986)
4. Aish, R.: Building modelling the key to integrated construction CAD. In: CIB 5th International Symposium, on the Use of Computers for Environmental Engineering Related to Buildings (1986)
5. Van Nederveen, G.A., Tolman, F.P.: Modelling multiple views on buildings. Autom. Constr. **1**(3), 215–224 (1992)
6. Jacobi, J.: 4D BIM or Simulation-Based Modeling. structuremag.org (2012)
7. Ashrae: Introduction to BIM, 4D and 5D. cadsoft-consult.com (2012)
8. Cerema: Construction project planning department, BIM for Infrastructure, Status and Problems (2017)
9. UK BIM Alliance: BIM in the UK: Past, Present & Future (2016)
10. Benning, P., et al.: IFC-Bridge – UC3, Projet National MINnD (2016)
11. BuildingSMART: International home of openBIM, Infrastructure. BuildingSmart Tech (2017). http://www.buildingsmart-tech.org/infrastructure/projects
12. Benning, P.: Contribution to IFC-Bridge Development: Missing Concepts and New Entities. EduBIM (2017)
13. Cox, S., Lake, R., Portele, C., Whiteside, A.: Geography Markup Language GML, 3.1. OGC Doc. No. 03–105r1 (2003)
14. Gröger, G., Plümer, L.: CityGML – interoperable semantic 3D city models. ISPRS J. Photogramm. Remote. Sens. **71**, 12–33 (2012)
15. Isikdag, U., Zlatanova, S.: Towards defining a framework for automatic generation of buildings in CityGML using BIM. In: Lee, J., Zlatanova, S. (eds.) 3D Geo-information Scienc-es, pp. 79–96. Springer, Berlin (2008). https://doi.org/10.1007/978-3-540-87395-2_6
16. Hijatzi, I., Ehlers, M., Zlatanova, S., Becker, T., Berleo, L.V.: Initial investigations for modeling interior utilities within 3D geo context: transforming IFC-interior utility to CityGML/UtilityNetworkADE. In: Kolbe, T., König, G., Nagel, C. (eds.) 5th International 3D GeoInfo Conference, pp. 95–113. Springer, Germany (2010). https://doi.org/10.1007/978-3-642-12670-3_6
17. Park, S.I., Park, J., Kim, B.G., Lee, S.H.: Improving applicability for information model of an IFC-based steel bridge in the design phase using functional meanings of bridge components. Appl. Sci. **8**, 2531 (2018)
18. Cauvin, B., Benning, P.: Contribution to a Data Dictionary for Infrastructures: The Bridge Field; Edu-BIM (2017)

Handling Massive Data Size Issue in Buildings Footprints Extraction from High-Resolution Satellite Images

Sohaib K. M. Abujayyab[1](✉) and Ismail Rakip Karas[2](✉)

[1] Department of Geography, Karabuk University,
Demir Celik Campus, 78050 Karabuk, Turkey
sjayyab@karabuk.edu.tr
[2] Department of Computer Engineering, Karabuk University,
Demir Celik Campus, 78050 Karabuk, Turkey
ismail.karas@karabuk.edu.tr

Abstract. Building information modelling BIM is relying on plenty of geospatial information such as buildings footprints. Collecting and updating BIM information is a considerable challenge. Recently, buildings footprints automatically extracted from high-resolution satellite images utilizing machine learning algorithms. Constructing required training datasets for machine learning algorithms and testing data is computationally intensive. When the analysis performs in large geographic areas, researchers are struggling from out of memory problems. The requirement of developing improved, fit memory computation methods for accomplishing this computation is urgent. This paper targeting to handling massive data size issue in buildings footprints extraction from high-resolution satellite images. This article established a method to process the spatial raster data based on the chunks computing. Chunk-based decomposition decomposes raster array into several tiny cubes. Cubes supposed to be small enough to fit into available memory and prevent memory overflow. The algorithm of the method developed using Python programming language. Spatial data and developed tool were prepared and processed in ArcGIS software. Matlab software utilized for machine learning. Neural networks implemented for extracting the buildings' footprints. To demonstrate the performance of our approach, high-resolution Orthoimage located in Tucson, Arizona state in American United States was utilized as a case study. Original image was taken by UltraCamEagle sensor and contained (11888 columns, 11866 rows, cell size 0.5 foot, 564,252,032 pixels in 4 bands). The case image contained (1409 columns, 1346 rows, and 7586056 pixels in 4 bands). The full image is impossible to be handled in the traditional central processing unit CPU. The image divided to 36 chunks using 1000 rows and 1000 columns. Full analysis spent 35 min using Intel Core i7 processor. The output performance accuracy of the neural network is 98.3% for testing dataset. Consequences demonstrate that the chunk computing can solve the memory overflow in personal computers during buildings footprints extraction process, especially in case of processing large files of high-resolution images. The developed method is suitable to be implemented in an affordable lightweight desktop environment. In addition, building footprints extracted effetely and memory overflow problem bypassed. Furthermore, the developed method proved the high quality extracted buildings footprints that can be integrated with BIM applications.

© Springer Nature Switzerland AG 2020
S. Ofluoglu et al. (Eds.): EBF 2019, CCIS 1188, pp. 195–210, 2020.
https://doi.org/10.1007/978-3-030-42852-5_16

Keywords: Buildings Information Modelling · Buildings footprints extraction · Massive data size · High resolution satellite images · Neural networks

1 Introduction

Building Information Modelling (BIM) is a numerical formalization process of functional and materialistic attributes of buildings [1]. Building Information Modelling is a mutual information resource relevant to the established buildings, of which provide the trustworthy life-cycle foundation for decisions making [2–4]. Building Information Modelling is a smart 3D digital system provide the data, tools and insight for several professionals in construction and architecture to proficiently propose, design, create, and directing buildings and its infrastructure [4].

Apparently, the key stage in BIM system is collecting and storing digital information of every aspect of the existing buildings. Digital information about the buildings helps decision-makers to optimize their actions. Optimized actions can be affected by the design until construction and managing stage during buildings life-cycle [5]. In addition, updating the information issue is a challenging process in a BIM system. Updating the information is time-consuming, financially costly and time challenging. High-resolution satellite images (HRSI) became a great solution for collecting and updating BIM spatial data. Application areas of HRSI have been substantially increased due to the availability of sub-meter spatial resolution of space shot for example, QUICKBIRD, WorldView and IKONOS [6–8]. By processing HRSI, information can be extracted automatically from the images such as the borders of the building, buildings highest point, buildings footprints and roof type by using machine learning algorithms. Buildings footprints define as a zone in location, this zone utilizes by the construction of the building. The Buildings footprints can be determined through the perimeter of the construction. landscapes, Parking lots, and other non-buildings services are excluded from the footprints of buildings [9–11]. Formerly, buildings footprints detection and mapping from high-resolution satellite data has been a dynamic research area in the remote sensing and photogrammetric societies [12, 13].

Automatic extraction of buildings footprints from HRSI has varied difficulties [14]. One of the main challenges is handling the massive data size issue in HRSI. The issue arising from the truth that machine learning algorithms need a specific data structure to apply the analysis. This data structure of machine learning algorithms is input and target sets. Input data set consist of the parameters of each sample. The samples in buildings footprints extraction application area represent the pixel, while parameters represent the bands of the satellite images. So, the process of reshaping the raster spatial data to be suitable for machine learning algorithms data structure is time-consuming. In addition, reshaping the spatial data and establishing the data set required massive random memory, especially if the geographical area is big, and analysis area have a giant number of rows and columns due to HRSI. In addition, the growth in raster datasets resolution led to dramatic increase in the volume of data [15]. Presently, the volume of data reach gigabytes with billions of samples in the remote sensing projects and still growing. In contrast, the processors computing capacity and memory volume increased unevenly for a steady increase in data size. Legacy algorithms and equipment were appropriate for handling minor raster data size. Massive information size issue caused plenty of problems for the specialists such as out of core computation or out of memory [16]. HRSI need huge memory to process and store the data. This problem totally stops the specialists from performing the analysis or limits their analysis only in tiny geographical areas with simple data extraction methods. In some cases, massive data size issue leads to crash the systems, especially if they are using only serial processing or sequential processing in classical personal computers PC's.

However, massive data size issue requires to manage the memory carefully to avoid any crash during the Geoprocessing [17]. Several methods were proposed in the past to handle this issue such as parallel processing, multitasking, distributed systems, supercomputing, cloud computing and using graphics processing unit (GPU). But some of these methods are not suitable for machine learning algorithms. In case of working with GIS environments such as ArcGIS, these methods are available for the built-in functions, while it is not available for the developed functions or other processing environments. Additionally, in case of the need to migrate the data to other environments, for instance, to Matlab software, these methods are not available. In some cases, the main problem is not how long the processing is taking time, but the problem that the system can crash or stop the processing. The system stops the processing due to that the size of data needs random memory more than the available memory in the device.

Thus, the main aim of this article is to tackle massive data size issue in building footprints extraction from HRSI. This chapter presents a technique to process spatial raster data according to chunks computing for sequential processing. Then, the developed method implemented and tested based on case study data. HRSI with massive data size were processed using this tool. The tool was developed using Python programing language. While the machine learning algorithm implemented using Matlab software. HRSI were processed in ArcGIS.

2 Methods

2.1 Developed Method

The developed method designed using Python programing language. The code considered that spatial raster data will be processed in ArcGIS and Matlab. Previously, HRSI which faced the out of memory problem were completely loaded to the computer memory [18]. The developed method relay on dividing the raster array to several tiny cubes, which called chunks (Fig. 1(A)) [17]. Cubes supposed to be small enough to fit into available memory. When satellite images dissociated fittingly, every image cube will be processed individually by a processor. At this stage, raster data are loaded into the memory and computation performed based on sequential processing (cubes by cubes). Thus, reducing the memory usage during the Geo-computation and avoiding the crashing of the analysis.

Small cubes data structure is very suitable for heavy computation of machine learning algorithms data structure. First dimension of the cube represents the number of columns, second dimension represent numbers of rows and third dimension represent the bands of satellite image. Since the HRSI is multispectral images and having limited number of bands (between 3 to 12), the method dividing only the first dimension and storing full third dimension. Cubes of raster data can easily reshape to the suitable and required machine learning datasets. Every cube will represent one separated dataset and will be migrated to Matlab and be tested individually. By this process, the model shortens the image processes through reading the pixel values directly from raster structure. Formerly, methods were transforming satellite images to tabular data sets based on the sampling approach. Sampling approach was transforming satellite images to points, then was reading the numerical number of cells and saved it in the associated attribute table of grid points. After that, the attribute table transferred to Matlab software and machine learning algorithms. Aforementioned data processing was extremely time-consuming compared with the developed method in this article. Instead of reading the sample points one by one, this method read a small zone (cube) from the image, then, applying classification process, then, write the output on the disk, and release the memory before repeating the process using the next zone (cube).

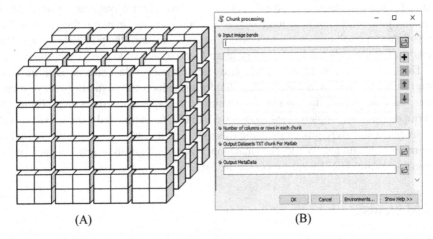

(A)   (B)

Fig. 1. (A) HRSI 3D array divided to chunks. Figure showing storing a three dimensional chunk architecture. Chunk volume (cube) represented by (longitude) * (latitude) * (band). (B) Developed tool in ArcToolbox using Python for chunk processing.

In addition, the chunks data structure is suitable for parallel computing and can be easily configured. Furthermore, the analyzer of HRSI can know and control number of chunks based on their devices available memory. This method is simple and more acceptable for remote sensing society. The method code developed to be suitable for ArcGIS-Arc toolbox environment. One toolbox developed to apply the method for raster data. The tool illustrated in (Fig. 1(B)). The first input of the tool is the HRSI's. The user needs to add the images band by band. The input design to accept raster layers, which accept bands from the hard drive directly without the need to add the data to ArcMap-(table of content). Adding the data to ArcMap-(table of content) is memory consuming. The second input is chunk size. The third input is the output workspace for the TXT datasets. Finally, the fourth input/output is the location of each chunk metadata. Metadata file help to stitched chunks back together via mosaicking it to one meaningful output image.

Chunks size parameter must be defined carefully. Defining chunks size is based on the experiments. If chunks size is too small, queueing up operations will be extremely slow, because each chunk has storage cost. Conversely, if chunks size is too big, benefits of chunks computation may be wasted, because of the possibility that chunk array will not fit into the available memory. Thus, selecting suitable chunks size will avoid any risk for the system. In order to explain the developed method, Python code of the method is described in Algorithm 1.

Algorithm 1. *Python code of chunks method*	
1	`# importing the required Python libraries`
2	`import arcpy, numpy as np, os`
3	`# Reading the input raster`
4	`inputRasters = arcpy.GetParameterAsText(0)`
5	`#defining size of chunk`
6	`chunkssize= arcpy.GetParameterAsText(1)`
7	`#defining out the Workspace`
8	`OutputMetaData = arcpy.GetParameterAsText(2)`
9	`Output= arcpy.GetParameterAsText(3)`
10	`# Loop over raster data chunks`
11	`for x in range(0, inputRasters.width, chunkssize):     # Loop over image columns`
12	`  for y in range(0, inputRasters.height, chunkssize):  # Loop over image rows`
13	`    for in_raster in inputRasters:                     # Loop over input bands`
14	`      IR = arcpy.Raster(in_raster)                     # Reading the input raster`
15	`      # Getting chunk dimensions`
16	`      mx = IR.extent.XMin + x * IR.meanCellWidth # defining minim X coordinate`
17	`      my = IR.extent.YMin + y * IR.meanCellHeight # defining minim Y coordinate`
18	`      lx = min([x + chunkssize, IR.width])        # defining maximum X coordinate`
19	`      ly = min([y + chunkssize, IR.height])       # defining maximum Y coordinate`
20	`      # Extract chunk data`
21	`      Chunk = arcpy.RasterToNumPyArray(IR, arcpy.Point(mx, my), lx-x, ly-y)`
22	`      V = np.ravel(Chunk)`
23	`      RL1.append(V)`
24	`      NewNpArray = np.array(RL1)`
25	`            RL = np.transpose(NewNpArray)`
26	`  raster += 1`
27	`      BlockChank = os.path.basename(in_raster)`
28	`      BlockChank2 = str(BlockChank) + "_" + str(raster)`
29	`      Output3 = str(Output) + str(BlockChank2) + ".txt"`
30	`      np.savetxt(Output3, RL, delimiter=" ", fmt="%s") # Storing the dataset of chunk`
31	`      Arrayshape = Chunk.shape`
31	`      COLUC = Arrayshape[0]`
33	`      R = Arrayshape[1]`
34	`      MCW = IR.meanCellWidth`
35	`      MCH = IR.meanCellHeight`
36	`      Meta = str(MCW) + " " + str(MCH) + " " + str(mx) + " " + str(my) + " " + str(R)`
	`            + " " + str(COLUC)`
	`      MetaData.append(Meta)`
	`np.savetxt(OutputMetaData, MetaData, delimiter=" ", fmt="%s") # Storing Metadata`

2.2   Case Implementation

During recent decades, satellites that providing HRSI have been considerably increased. An example of widespread HRSI satellites are Geoeye-1 (0.41M), Ikonos (0.82M), Pleiades-1A (0.5), Quickbaird (0.61M), Spot-6 (1.5M), WorldView 1–2 (0.46M) and WorldView 3 (0.31M) [6–8]. However, the aforementioned HRSI have commercial-based distribution policy. The required payment amount is out of authors financial budget. Thus, the HRSI is substituted with High-Resolution Orthoimagery (HRO) (Aerial Photography) for this case. An Orthoimage is a Raster data structure that has been geometrically adjusted (orthorectified) to eliminate distortion caused by sensor tilt and variation in topography. The HRO image comprising the same issue of massive data. Thus these images utilized during the experiments to examine the developed tools.

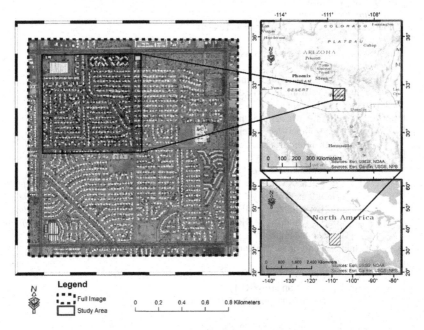

Fig. 2. HRO image as a case study for buildings footprints extraction using chunks processing. The image located in Tucson, Arizona state in United States.

In this analysis, an example Orthoimage acquired from the U.S. Geological Survey (USGS) earth explorer website and donated by Sanborn Map Company. The image located in Tucson, Arizona state in United States. The location map of the case study illustrated in (Fig. 2). Aerial imagery acquired by the department of agriculture in the United States during agricultural growing periods in 2015. The image acquired by UltraCamEagle sensor, which was developed by Microsoft/Vexcel. UltraCamEagle sensor provides a high-resolution image with 4 channels that represent read R, green G, blue B and near-infrared NIR electromagnetic energy [19]. The 4 bands of HRO image illustrated in Fig. 3. The image is containing 11888 columns, and 11866 rows with spatial resolution 0.5 Foot.

To prepare the neural network dataset from this image with 141,063,008 pixels in one band and 564,252,032 in four bands, the process requires high hardware capability. In addition, it is impossible to handle HRSI image for neural networks in central processing unit (CPU). This image needs an advanced processor and big memory to be completely processed as one set. In a case the analyzer needs to perform augmentation process and increase the number of input images, the difficulties and problems will increase. Another step applied to the image was Clipping the image. Clipping process to 1 area to make small buildings footprints readable. The new imageconsisted of 1409 columns, 1346 rows (1896514 pixels in one band and 7586056 pixels in 4 bands).

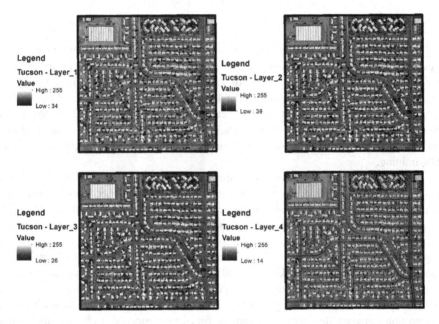

Fig. 3. The Clipped 4 Bands of HRO image (Read R, Green G, Blue B and Near InfraRed NIR). The image consisting 7586056 pixels in 4 bands.

Based on the several experiments in the available memory and CPU, and based on the numbers of rows, columns, as well as the number of bands, the size of the chunks, were defined (1000 columns and 1000 rows). Thus, the complete chunk dataset is was consisting of 62500 pixels. Through applying Algorithm 1, the multi-band raster image was converted to a three-dimensional NumPy array. Then, full NumPy array was automatically divided into data chunks. The chunks data blocks were resized to neural networks testing dataset structure and stored as TXT files. Lastly, datasets were imported in Matlab environment for NN testing. The TXT file format provides high flexibility to utilize the datasets in diverse ML software's.

Table 1. Example part of training dataset of sample points

	Input (explanatory parameters)				Target (Buildings footprints)
	Band 1	Band 2	Band 3	Band 4	
Training set 70%	1020	1640	1266	1252	1
	993	1622	1266	1271	1
	479	790	670	747	0
	1053	1721	1339	1344	1
	1170	1791	1352	1235	1
Validation set 15%	503	857	765	824	0
	416	618	479	504	0
Testing set 15%	1221	1933	1476	1380	1
	456	723	587	635	0

In order to extract buildings footprints through NN, developing a training sample is essential. Sample points of training dataset consisting of 392 points and 4 input bands for the input layer were prepared. An example dataset extracted from the image illustrated in Table 1. The table shows the 4 explanatory parameters data (4 Bands) and their target values. The target values were manually prepared based on the visual interpretation, while explanatory parameters data were automatically extracted based on training sample point processing. The output training dataset imported in Matlab for NN training.

Neural networks are a collection of functions, trying to simulate the work of biological cell for patterns recognition. The human brain consists of 86 billion nerve cells, which called as neurons. Neurons are associated with further cells through Axons. The inspired idea from human biological cell structure and behaviour led to the development of the artificial neural network neurons, weighting process, connections, hidden layers and output structure [20]. Neurons inputs generate electric impulses that rapidly moved over the neural networks. The artificial neuron can receive input variables and execute mathematical processing on the data. The processes outcome transfers to next hidden layer. Outcomes of every neuron is called its transferred output. In addition, the connection between the input and transfer function associated with weights. Neural networks apply training by updating weights values. Neural networks can understand sensory data through a kind of machine perception, clustering or labeling raw inputs. The recognized patterns are numerical and stored in vectors data as parameters. Thus, reshaping data for NN applications is fundamental.

In this study, an Artificial Neural Network was applied for building footprints extraction from HRSI. Neural network was applied in Matlab software. Feedforward neural network architecture utilized in this study as shown in Fig. 4. The training dataset imported and trained using varied Hyperparameters. These parameters are; the size of the hidden layer, transfer functions and training algorithms. Size of hidden layer investigated from 1 to 50 neurons, while the transfer function 'purelin', 'tansig', and 'logsig' investigated in the first hidden layer. Additionally, 'trainscg', 'trainbr', and 'trainlm'. Usually, % 'trainscg' uses less memory. Suitable in low memory situations. 'trainlm' is the fastest. 'trainbr' takes longtime but may be better for challenging problems. The search process to train the networks based on the different parameters to find the optimal performance accuracy. The training and optimizing process based on Hyperparameters described in Algorithm 2.

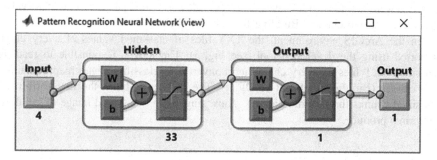

Fig. 4. Feedforward neural network architecture

Algorithm 2. Matlab code of NN model with three Hyperparameters	
1	load input, target
2	Ta={'trainscg' 'trainbr' 'trainlm'}; %Training As
3	T_Fs ={'purelin' 'tansig' 'logsig'}; %transfer As
4	St = 1; % Start of Hidden Layer Size
5	En = 50; % Max of Hidden Layer Size
6	for jalgo=1:length(Ta)
7	for jtrans=1:length(T_Fs)
8	for j= St: En
9	%Generating NN
10	net = patternnet(j);
11	%Selectin training algorithm
12	net.trainFcn = Ta{jalgo};
13	%Selectin training transfer algorithm
14	net.layers{1}.transferFcn = T_Fs{jtrans};
15	%hidden Layer Size
16	net.layers{1}.size = j;
17	%training the network
18	[net,tr] = train(net,input,target);
19	%testing the network
20	y = net(input(:,tr.testInd));
21	t = target(:,tr.testInd);
22	[c(jalgo,jtrans,j)] = confusion(t,y);
23	end
24	end
25	end
26	Accuracy=(1-c)*100;

Finally, the extraction process of buildings footprints implemented based on chunks datasets one by one. The optimal NN parameters and structure were used to test the dataset of each chunk datasets. Algorithm 3 describes the testing steps of chunks datasets and extraction of the footprints of the buildings. The outputs from the neural network were stored as TXT files. The TXT files containing lists of classified values that represent two classes (Building footprint or Other).

In the ArcGIS environment, the TXT files of classified values of every chunk imported using the developed tool (see Fig. 5). The tool is responsible to read the classified TXT files of every chunk and convert it to classified raster map containing two classes (Building footprint or Other). The tool recombines the image from the classified chunks through mosaicking. Thus, single-band classified image of buildings footprints produce.

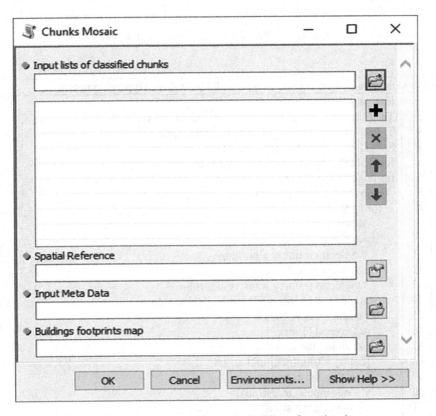

Fig. 5. ArcGIS tool to recombines the buildings footprints image

Algorithm 3. Matlab code of optimal NN for buildings footprints extraction from chunks datasets	
1	%Access to chunks datasets
2	[file,path] = uigetfile('*.txt*','MultiSelect','on');
3	[m,n] = size(file);
4	for i=1:n %Iterating over the chunks datasets
5	PathOfPointsChunks = fullfile(path,file(i));
6	%Read chunks datasets
7	input2=dlmread(char(PathOfPointsChunks));
8	input2=input2';
9	% Buildings footprints extraction using the develop network
10	Y=net(input2);
11	% Store the classified output of each chunks
12	Y=Y';
13	filename=['Output'+convertCharsToStrings(file(i))];
14	fopen(filename,'wt');
15	dlmwrite(filename,Y, 'delimiter', ' ', 'newline', 'pc')
16	end

3   Results

Data of case study successfully tested using the developed method and tools. In this analysis, the tool divided the study area to 36 chunks based on (250 * 250 pixels). Average storage size of chunks files is 1 MB, which was easily processed by CPU. Full analysis spent 1 h. The tool directly divided the image, read pixel values and reshaped every chunk array. Then arrays stored in TXT files and migrated to Matlab. In Matlab software, chunks arrays were tested one by one through looping over the chunks files. The testing process was applied to automatically extract building footprints from HRSI. Extraction process implemented using neural networks as one of the machine learning algorithms. NN highly recommended for satellite image processing and mapping.

The neural network used 4 input bands for the input layer. The optimal NN model achieved by using (33 neurons and 'tansig' transfer function in the first hidden-layer, and 'trainlm' training function). The optimal trained network reaches to optimal accuracy after 67 iterations. Confusion matrix metric utilized to measure performance accuracy. The achieved performance accuracy is 99.3% for the training dataset, while the accuracy of the testing dataset is 98.3%. Figure 6 illustrate the percentage of true and false positive and negative percentages as well as the overall accuracy for training and testing datasets.

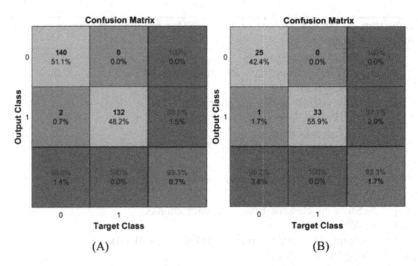

Fig. 6. Confusion matrix metric and performance accuracy of (A) training and (B) testing datasets.

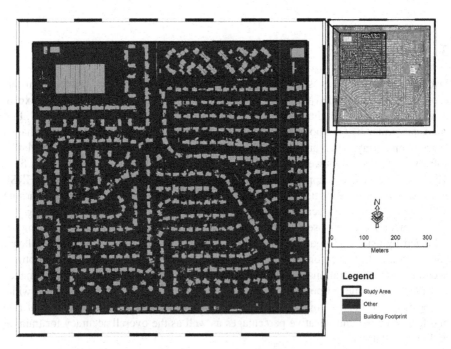

Fig. 7. Output of the neural network model based on chunk processing. The map illustrating the extracted buildings footprints after solving vast data size issue. Map show tow categories (Building footprint or Other)

The full image was smoothly processed through looping over the 36 chunks. Then, chunks datasets effectively moved to ArcGIS and recombined in one full image. The output files from Matlab that consisting the list of classified values stored in TXT format. Then, the TXT files imported in the developed tools to resize the classified lists to chunks and Mosaic them in one full classified image with two classes (Building footprint or Other). The output extracted buildings footprints raster map illustrated in Fig. 7. Additionally, several post-processing steps were applied to improve the final output such as filtering the noise pixels, clean the boundaries, and filling the gaps as well as all the polygon that having an area less than 20 m^2 eliminated, then the raster map converted to a vector map. The vector map contained 575 buildings footprints. Three sections from the study area illustrated in Fig. 8 using the big map scale. The figure illustrates the original image and the extracted building. The figure shows the high quality of building footprints extraction.

Based on the former processing stages, the image of the case study processed without facing the out of memory problem. Additionally, the developed method was capable to process any size of image. By enhancing the functionality of HRSI processing using Python chunks computing, the benefits are marked in the area building footprints extraction. The main benefit is to get memory usage reduced. The method was effectively implemented in the application area of buildings footprints extraction [21–23], and highly recommended for further application.

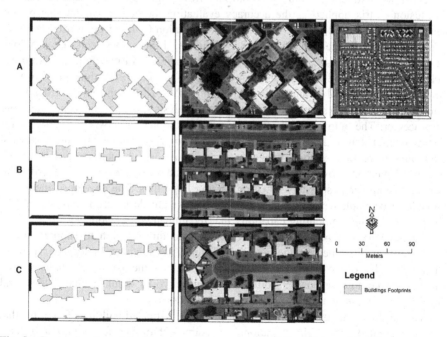

Fig. 8. Comparing the original image and the extracted building. Extracted buildings footprints are useful in BIM applications.

4 Conclusion

Automatic extraction of buildings footprints from high-resolution satellite images utilizing machine learning algorithms is computationally more intensive than traditional raster Geoprocessing. Working with full images for a big geographic area is challenging for the central processing unit (CPU), due to out of memory problems. In addition, the cost of migrating big data and repeating the processing to extract the datasets, and testing buildings footprints datasets using machine learning algorithms required high memory usage. High usage of memory leads to stop the analysis or even to crash the analysis systems. Thus, the need for developing a methodology to solve high memory usage in spatial data is essential.

This article established a method to process the spatial raster data based on the chunks computing. Chunk computing breaks down raster array to several tiny cubes. Cubes must be small enough to fit into offered memory and prevent memory crash. Instead of reading and processing full high-resolution satellite images, this method read a small portion from the image, apply ML Geo-computation, write the output on the disk, and release the memory before repeating the process with the next portion. The implementation was established using Python programming language and Matlab. Spatial information and established toolbox processed and prepared in an ArcGIS environment. Matlab environment was used for machine learning. Neural networks was executed for extracting buildings footprints from high-resolution satellite images. Confusion matrix applied as the accuracy evaluation metric. To validate the performance of the proposed method, massive high-resolution Orthoimage utilized in a case study. Obtained image contained (11888 columns, 11866 rows, cell size 0.5 foot, 564,252,032 pixels in 4 bands). The case image contained (1409 columns, 1346 rows, cell size 0.5 foot, 7586056 pixels in 4 bands). In a normal situation, this image is impossible to be totally handled in a common CPU. The image is divided into 36 chunks using 1000 rows and 1000 columns. Full analysis spent 35 min using Intel Core i7 processor. The output performance accuracy of the neural network was 98.3% for testing dataset. Outcomes proved that buildings footprints can be smoothly extracted from high-resolution satellite images, and avoiding out of memory problem. The employed method shows that Chunk computing can solve the memory overflow in personal computers, especially when processing large files. The developed method is suitable to be implemented in an affordable lightweight desktop environment, rather than, needing high computing capability that recommended previously.

Future work can be including an expanding to this research to support further processing functions besides the buildings footprints extractions. In addition, increase the functionality of the method to automatically calculate the optimal chunk size based on different computing power. Additionally, future works should include global and focal raster computation besides local raster operations.

The developed method provides medium quality extracted buildings footprints that can be integrated with BIM applications. An example, buildings footprints can be used in the regular detection of illegal housing developments or comparing extracted buildings polygons with Cadastral maps. In addition, it can be used in medium accuracy mapping for fast information updating. The buildings footprints can be used in unusual circumstances for example during the floods or to find the remained buildings, thus comparing with the database of buildings. Finally, footprints can be used in the initial information survey in developing areas that do not contain buildings data.

Acknowledgment. This study has been supported by 2221 – Fellowship Program of TUBITAK (The Scientific and Technological Research Council of Turkey). We are indebted for their supports.

References

1. Kreiner, H., Passer, A., Wallbaum, H.: A new systemic approach to improve the sustainability performance of office buildings in the early design stage. Energy Build. **109**, 385–396 (2015). https://doi.org/10.1016/j.enbuild.2015.09.040
2. Cavalliere, C., Dell'Osso, G.R., Pierucci, A., Iannone, F.: Life cycle assessment data structure for building information modelling. J. Clean. Prod. **199**, 193–204 (2018). https://doi.org/10.1016/j.jclepro.2018.07.149
3. Muller, M.F., Esmanioto, F., Huber, N., Loures, E.R., Canciglieri, O.: A systematic literature review of interoperability in the green Building Information Modeling lifecycle. J. Clean. Prod. **223**, 397–412 (2019). https://doi.org/10.1016/j.jclepro.2019.03.114
4. Yin, X., Liu, H., Chen, Y., Al-Hussein, M.: Building information modelling for off-site construction: review and future directions. Autom. Constr. **101**, 72–91 (2019). https://doi.org/10.1016/j.autcon.2019.01.010
5. Wikipedia: Building information modeling. Wikipedia (2019). https://en.wikipedia.org/wiki/Building_information_modeling (accessed May 13, 2019)
6. Japanese Earth observing satellite, Advanced Land Observing Satellite - Phased Array type L-band Synthetic Aperture Radar (2019). https://www.eorc.jaxa.jp/ALOS/en/about/about_index.htm. Accessed 9 Apr 2019
7. Alaska Satellite Facility's: ALOS Dataset Information (2011). https://vertex.daac.asf.alaska.edu/. Accessed 11 Apr 2019
8. Nefeslioglu, H.A., San, B.T., Gokceoglu, C., Duman, T.Y.: An assessment on the use of Terra ASTER L3A data in landslide susceptibility mapping. Int. J. Appl. Earth Obs. Geoinf. **14**, 40–60 (2012). https://doi.org/10.1016/j.jag.2011.08.005
9. Park, Y., Guldmann, J.-M.: Creating 3D city models with building footprints and LIDAR point cloud classification: a machine learning approach. Comput. Environ. Urban Syst. **75**, 76–89 (2019). https://doi.org/10.1016/j.compenvurbsys.2019.01.004
10. Sinha, R., Lennartsson, M., Frostell, B.: Environmental footprint assessment of building structures: a comparative study. Build. Environ. **104**, 162–171 (2016). https://doi.org/10.1016/j.buildenv.2016.05.012
11. Green Build: Building footprint, Green, Build (2019). https://leeduser.buildinggreen.com/forum/building-footprint-6. Accessed 13 May 2019
12. Tournaire, O., Brédif, M., Boldo, D., Durupt, M.: An efficient stochastic approach for building footprint extraction from digital elevation models. ISPRS J. Photogramm. Remote Sens. **65**, 317–327 (2010). https://doi.org/10.1016/j.isprsjprs.2010.02.002
13. Huang, J., Zhang, X., Xin, Q., Sun, Y., Zhang, P.: Automatic building extraction from high-resolution aerial images and LiDAR data using gated residual refinement network. ISPRS J. Photogramm. Remote Sens. **151**, 91–105 (2019). https://doi.org/10.1016/j.isprsjprs.2019.02.019

14. Gavankar, N.L., Ghosh, S.K.: Automatic building footprint extraction from high-resolution satellite image using mathematical morphology. Eur. J. Remote Sens. **51**, 182–193 (2018). https://doi.org/10.1080/22797254.2017.1416676

15. Hamzeh, M., Abbaspour, R.A., Davalou, R.: Raster-based outranking method: a new approach for municipal solid waste landfill (MSW) siting. Environ. Sci. Pollut. Res. **22**, 12511–12524 (2015). https://doi.org/10.1007/s11356-015-4485-8

16. Li, D., Wang, S., Li, D.: Spat. Data Min. (2015). https://doi.org/10.1007/978-3-662-48538-5

17. Li, J., Finn, M.P., Blanco Castano, M.: A lightweight CUDA-based parallel map reprojection method for raster datasets of continental to global extent. ISPRS Int. J. Geo-Inf. **6**, 92 (2017). https://doi.org/10.3390/ijgi6040092

18. Norman, M., Mohd Shafri, H.Z., Idrees, M.O., Mansor, S., Yusuf, B.: Spatio-statistical optimization of image segmentation process for building footprint extraction using very high-resolution WorldView 3 satellite data. Geocarto Int. 1–24 (2019). https://doi.org/10.1080/10106049.2019.1573853

19. Gruber, M., Ponticelli, M., Ladstädter, R., Wiechert, A.: UltraCam Eagle, details and insight. Int. Arch. Photogramm. Remote Sens. Spat. Inf. Sci. **39** (2012)

20. Al-Mahallawi, K., Mania, J., Hani, A., Shahrour, I.: Using of neural networks for the prediction of nitrate groundwater contamination in rural and agricultural areas. Environ. Earth Sci. **65**, 917–928 (2012)

21. Vallet, B., Pierrot-Deseilligny, M., Boldo, D., Brédif, M.: Building footprint database improvement for 3D reconstruction: a split and merge approach and its evaluation. ISPRS J. Photogramm. Remote Sens. **66**, 732–742 (2011). https://doi.org/10.1016/j.isprsjprs.2011.06.005

22. Brédif, M., Tournaire, O., Vallet, B., Champion, N.: Extracting polygonal building footprints from digital surface models: a fully-automatic global optimization framework. ISPRS J. Photogramm. Remote Sens. **77**, 57–65 (2013). https://doi.org/10.1016/j.isprsjprs.2012.11.007

23. Alshehhi, R., Marpu, P.R., Woon, W.L., Mura, M.D.: Simultaneous extraction of roads and buildings in remote sensing imagery with convolutional neural networks. ISPRS J. Photogramm. Remote Sens. **130**, 139–149 (2017). https://doi.org/10.1016/j.isprsjprs.2017.05.002

Author Index

Printed in the United States
By Bookmasters